FRIEDRICH
SCHILLER

FRIEDRICH SCHILLER

Crime, Aesthetics,
and the Poetics of Punishment

Gail K. Hart

Newark: University of Delaware Press

© 2005 by Rosemont Publishing & Printing Corp.

All rights reserved. Authorization to photocopy items for internal or personal use, or the internal or personal use of specific clients, is granted by the copyright owner, provided that a base fee of $10.00, plus eight cents per page, per copy is paid directly to the Copyright Clearance Center, 222 Rosewood Drive, Danvers, Massachusetts 01923. [0-87413-895-7/05 $10.00 + 8¢ pp, pc.]

Other than as indicated in the foregoing, this book may not be reproduced, in whole or in part, in any form (except as permitted by Sections 107 and 108 of the U.S. Copyright Law, and except for brief quotes appearing in reviews in the public press).

Associated University Presses
2010 Eastpark Boulevard
Cranbury, NJ 08512

The paper used in this publication meets the requirements of the American National Standard for Permanence of Paper for Printed Library Materials Z39.48-1984.

Library of Congress Cataloging-in-Publication Data

Hart, Gail Kathleen.
  Friedrich Schiller : crime, aesthetics, and the poetics of punishment / Gail K. Hart.
     p. cm.
  Includes bibliographical references and index.
  ISBN 0-87413-895-7 (alk. paper)
  1. Schiller, Friedrich, 1759–1805—Philosophy. 2. Punishment—Philosophy. 3. Punishment in literature. I. Title.
PT2467.Z5H37   2005
831'.6—dc22
                                                    2004021639

PRINTED IN THE UNITED STATES OF AMERICA

Contents:

Preface	7
1. Admiration for Aberrants and Schiller's School Days	11
2. What Does the Dramatic Stage Actually Do? Exposure, Demonstration and *Wirkung* in the *Schaubühne* Essay and the Execution of Maria Stuart	24
3. "Die Schande nimmt ab mit der wachsenden Sünde": Early Schiller and the Charisma of the Criminal	54
4. Schiller and the Prison in and around *Spiel des Schicksals*	72
5. Murderous Fathers: *Wilhelm Tell* and the Decriminalization of Murder	93
6. Schiller's Heart, Joan's Crimes, and Johanna's Glory: Rescuing the Feminine from History	119
7. Schillerian Intertextuality in the Twentieth Century: Lost Honor, Aesthetic Education, and Free Will	135
Notes	165
Bibliography	176
Index	181

Preface

THIS BOOK HAS ITS ORIGINS IN SEVERAL SEMINARS ON LITERATURE and punishment that I taught during the 1990s. The courses followed different aspects of the topic, examined different groups of texts, and were presented to different audiences, specifically undergraduate honors students and later graduate students at UC Irvine and advanced students of *Germanistik* at the Georg-August-Universität in Göttingen. Some of the undergraduates, among them Sarvenaz Fouladi, Erik Habecker, and Greg Kemble, made me think much harder about the execution of Schiller's Maria Stuart, an exercise that led me to incorporate more of Schiller's work in the next seminar, where the graduate students, including Diane Ewing, Camilla Moskowitz, and Christina Swanson helped me appreciate the nuances of Schiller's response to the state's punishing apparatus. My Göttingen *Hauptseminar* was called "Schiller der Killer," and, with the exception of *A Clockwork Orange*, all the primary texts we read were Schiller's. In that group, I was privileged to hear about current German views and images of an author so many of my students had been forced to read in high school—a bracing experience. All in all, one learns a great deal from teaching.

One also learns a great deal from colleagues, especially from those who are so generous as to read one's prose repeatedly from early stages through to later, more refined versions. Thomas P. Saine read early, middle, and later drafts of the whole book, as did my dear friend, Stephanie Hammer, whose *Schiller's Wound* (Wayne State University Press, 2001) is a model of original and adventurous thinking about a classical poet whose work has become mired in standard interpretations or coercive high school curricula. She helped me over a number of stumbling blocks and through various narrow passes as I have tried to follow her example in offering an alternative Schiller who is nonetheless recognizable to scholars and to other readers of his work. One of the finest Schiller scholars alive, Lesley Sharpe herself, offered to read the whole manuscript during an e-mail correspondence on minor professional matters. This was an occasion of intense *Freude* for me since my reverence for her work is deep and longstanding. I have benefited tremendously from her comments and her notes on the manuscript. Ruth Kluger helps me with everything and in the case of this project, she read sections, discussed arguments, suggested texts and bibliography, and encouraged me to finish and publish. She also housed me, fed me, refilled my wine glass, and inspired me with her unique brand of brave and independent thought. As if that were not enough, she introduced me to Gesa Dane, who answered all of my questions, read parts of the manuscript, gave me great ideas, and let me read her own excellent work on law and literature. Hi Gesa.

Jill Kowalik was my friend and discussion partner for over fifteen years and she also read and commented on my work. Despite the cancer that was literally killing her for the last fourteen years of our friendship, she was an encouraging and uplifting critic with an exciting mind and zero tolerance for muddled thinking. I have dedicated this book to her because she was an exemplary colleague, a brilliant critic, a tireless political and environmental activist, and an extraordinary human being and because I miss her very much.

Regina Sonnenberg and her staff in Lesesaal 1 of the Göttingen university library gave me work space and access to the fine collections of the library and its affiliates. They were also helpful and efficient—the nicest librarians I have ever met. The sun does not shine much in Göttingen, but the climate is very friendly in its libraries. I am also grateful to the readers for the University of Delaware Press, for their careful work and suggestions. Finally, I thank my friends, especially Glenn and Ursula Levine, who indulged my *Spieltrieb* by letting me play with their wild children.

Translations of the German quotations in the text are my own. An earlier version of chapter 5 appeared in *Goethe Yearbook* 12 (2004), and I thank the Goethe Society of North America for permission to republish it here. The material on *Maria Stuart* in chapter 2 appeared as an article in *Seminar* (35.2:1999) and I am grateful to that publication for permission to reprint. Finally, the discussion of Schubart and his time in the dark hole formed the basis for my Presidential Address at the annual meeting of the Pacific Ancient and Modern Language Association in 2000, and I acknowledge *Pacific Coast Philology*, which published my luncheon talk (36.2001), for allowing me to use that material in chapter 4.

FRIEDRICH SCHILLER

1
Admiration for Aberrants and Schiller's School Days

THIS STUDY IS CONCERNED WITH SCHILLER'S LITERARY REFLECTIONS on punishment, especially retributive varieties, including incarceration and the death penalty. Such a focus evokes questions of current practice, and this is both desirable because it repositions and reactivates valuable knowledge, and unavoidable since arguments for and against retributive justice have changed or evolved very little since Schiller's time. I will not address current events or specific political issues in subsequent chapters—and they will receive only brief mention here—but I do hope that this consideration of Schiller's negotiations with punishment in drama and narrative prose will also connect to extra literary thinking about penal matters and control within democratic society. If art/literature is an imitation of nature/social life, it is also an interpretation of it and such interpretive activity yields provocative contexts for reflection on established practice.

Schiller frequently addresses penal tactics, incarceration, and execution in his work, but with an ambivalence or outright distaste that is unusual for his time or ours. Almost no one runs for political office in the United States without taking a clear stand on capital punishment, that is without expressing either strong support for or opposition to it. The highest elected office, for example, has generally required a supporter: "(for now at least) a candidate for president must support the death penalty."[1] Yet, even with the recent increase in the frequency of executions, an elected official is unlikely ever to find herself or himself called upon to participate in legislating or executing or having anything to do with a death sentence—unlike minister Goethe, who in addition to being an active poet, also voted for the preservation of the death penalty for infanticides, a legislative gesture that had swift and direct consequences for a child murderess, whose case was pending in Sachscn-Weimar.² Most of the U.S. death penalty discussion is far more abstract and remote from its object and this lack of a firm connection between theory and practice raises for me the larger question of what it means to punish, either judicially or aesthetically/poetically. Or, more precisely, what are the politics and poetics of punishment? This book will investigate only the latter, but with an eye to parallel structures and the interrelatedness of judicial punishment and the literature that seeks to understand and improve on it, as well as to the literary qualities of our narratives of "true" crime and retribution.³

If, as abolitionists convincingly claim, the U.S. death penalty serves no practical purpose, such as restitution, deterrence, or cost-cutting, it seems obvious that the existence of capital punishment statutes, at this writing in thirty-eight states, the federal government, and the military, serves a larger social need for the relief to be gained by retribution, revenge, and especially symmetry. As Richard Evans notes:

> Fundamentally, the most powerful and persistent motive for execution has always been retribution, the belief that death can be the only adequate expiation for certain crimes, the feeling that lesser punishments are insufficient, the conviction that those who commit the most serious offenses must pay for them by suffering the ultimate penalty, death.⁴

The balance, ordering or reordering, and regularity achieved by adequately punishing an offender in such a staged "ritual of retribution"⁵ are, I will claim, not unrelated to the instinct for harmony that governs eighteenth-century notions of beauty, and it is this affinity, between the pursuit of symmetry in social penal discourse and the symmetry that pleases or satisfies the aesthetic spectator that brings me to Schiller and his lifelong work with beauty, freedom, *and* criminality. It is not my purpose to argue this analogy as a central thesis, but rather to present it, by way of introduction, as an underlying web of potential ideals and ideologies that may explain in a very general way how a particular body of work, with all its homage to beauty and symmetry, came to encompass such anomalous extremes. Schiller's "doubleness," his ability to declare a position and simultaneously to retract it—or his inability to exclude one possibility while embracing the other—is especially prominent in questions of criminality and punishment. Here, symmetry, be it the retributive or rehabilitative forces that restore social equilibrium or the deterrent forces that leave it intact, is, in many ways, an ideal that instigates a reluctant departure or deviation from itself. This is not an instance of the alternative aesthetics described by Carsten Zelle in *Angenehmes Grauen,* where the pleasures of the unpleasant, of fear or strong negative affect come to the fore, but rather a refusal of symmetry in service of other ideals.[6]

"*Hat er aber gemordet, so muss er sterben*"[7] (If he has murdered, then he must die). Thus did Kant articulate a sentiment that appears to govern penal law even in the U.S. and many parts of the world today. Kant, in his support of the death penalty, wrote that if one were to dissolve civil society, one would first have to execute all of the murderers because they deserve it and it would be immoral not to do so. *If* he has murdered, *then* he must die. The project of this study will be to follow the ways in which Schiller drives a wedge between these two clauses, that is, how certain of his dramas and narratives rupture the iron symmetry of cause and effect expressed in Kant's penal dictum. Schiller, though he repeatedly addresses crime and criminality, does not punish, that is, he does not depict scenarios where credible offenders meet with the appropriate penalties. Much to the contrary, within the didactic form of the theatrical play he repeatedly fails to drop the other shoe or to balance the traditional scales of justice. So this study will ask, among other things, *if* he has murdered, . . . *then what*? And, to broaden the question, *if* he or she has robbed, burned, waged war against the victor, plotted to kill a monarch, shot an evil governor in a narrow pass, killed a forest ranger, or run afoul of the powerful. . . . *then what*? How does Schiller compensate or substitute for the conventional symmetry he disrupts by thematizing crime without punishment? Part of the answer will be the idea of prevention, the ways in which theater can edify, educate, and thus obviate those actions that provoke punishment. This notion of prevention also involves the matter of control and even coercion, forces that are generally bound up in almost any attempt at education, aesthetic or otherwise. The limits of this control are nowhere specified and, whereas most have perceived Schiller as a benevolent educational and dramatic theorist, others read him as aspiring to coercion.[8]

Hat er aber gemordet, so muss er sterben. To begin with, we have a typical case of a Kantian certitude—this one never directly addressed by Schiller—yielding, in this discussion, to some form of Schillerian *Spieltrieb* [instinct for play], as in Schiller's "overcoming" of the Kantian tendency to oppose duty and inclination with his theory of the *schöne Seele* [beautiful soul]. Interestingly, Kant also found loopholes or granted exceptions to the death sentence for infanticides and duelists, in the first case according to the logic of "if an unmarried woman has killed her illegitimate infant, then let us consider her less culpable, because she acted to protect her honor and the child she has murdered was born outside the law and its protection." Duelists similarly have no other way to protect their honor but to engage the opponent and possibly kill him. They, like the infanticide and her infant, are outside the law. Even the very early Schillerian criminal, Karl Moor, knew (apparently) of such arguments and used them to his advantage by declaring: "Nein ich mag nicht daran denken. Ich soll meinen Leib pressen in eine Schnürbrust, und meinen Willen schnüren in Gesetze" (No, I don't even want to think about it. Should I put my body in a corset and let my will be corseted in law).[9] Karl steps outside the corset of the law that has failed him and becomes a confused and perhaps non-culpable criminal—that is, if his declaration and circumstances suffice to position him outside or beyond the law. Everyone looks for exceptions, but the Schiller texts discussed here have a special fascination beyond being examples of Schiller's famous synthetic third way (out of an equal and opposite reaction to crime in this case). They represent a body of reflection on lawlessness and opposition to law that, via the subversion of punishment, underscores his work on beauty and freedom.

As I have noted elsewhere, Schiller's philosophical and theoretical essays owe much of their rich and potent complexity, as well as their power to frustrate, to a resistance to resolution.[10] Having built a magnificent edifice of terminological abstraction, and accomplished much within, Schiller is often reluctant to install the rhetorical "roof" that might contain and conclude all that has gone before. When he seems to be nearing a conclusion or some sort of closure, he tends to further bifurcate his categories lest something as blunt and inadequate as resolution interrupt his thinking. I believe that the implementation or nonimplementation of punishment in the plays and prose has a similar basis. Punishment in the spirit of Kant's dictum and even in the writings of more liberal eighteenth-century penal theorists, will ideally *resolve* the crime. Crime offends king, society, church, and/or deity and the proper punishment should be an appropriate counter to the infraction, thus restoring social harmony and even returning the offender to God's grace. But as I will argue here, Schiller appears to have viewed punishment as a resolution that oversimplifies the criminal acts that fascinated him, one that somehow canceled the magnificent aberrations that constituted the criminal. It was not a matter of a complementary pairing of the offense and the social response that nullified it, but of the investigation of the antisocial as free and creative. Schiller's admiration for aberrants is clear in the introductory paragraphs to "Verbrecher aus verlorener Ehre," where he writes,

In der ganzen Geschichte des Menschen ist kein Kapitel unterrichtender für Herz und Geist als die Annalen seiner Verirrungen. Bei jedem großen Verbrechen war eine verhältnismäßig große Kraft in Bewegung. Wenn sich das geheime Spiel der Begehrungskraft bei dem matteren Licht gewöhnlicher Affekte versteckt, so wird es im Zustand gewaltsamer Leidenschaft desto hervorspringender, kolossalischer, lauter . . . (VII:562)

[In the entire history of mankind, there is no chapter more edifying for the heart and the mind than the chronicle of man's aberrations. For every great crime, there is a commensurately great power at work. If the secret play of desire lies hidden in the weaker realm of ordinary emotions, it will be all the more conspicuous, colossal, loud . . . under conditions of powerful passion.]

Schiller never formally entered the eighteenth-century debate on punishment and reform, nor did he participate in the contemporary arguments over the utility of punishment. He remained silent on Beccaria's notorious treatise, *Dei delitti e delle pene* [On Crimes and Punishments] (1764), which drew strong criticism from Kant and support from Voltaire and many others for its recommendations against the death penalty. There is no public commentary from Schiller on the process of transformation cited by Foucault,[11] from a penal system that saw its mission as that of inflicting pain and thus punishing and supposedly deterring crime, to one that endeavored to control and reform offenders. Yet Schiller addresses all of these issues both directly and indirectly in his plays and prose, where his observations on the (often averted) collisions between character and punishment have a powerful impact.

As noted above, Schiller the poet avoids punishment, often where it seems logically unavoidable. One particularly glaring example of this subversion of punishment is his Joan of Arc play, *Die Jungfrau von Orleans* [The Maid of Orleans] (1801). Though he felt no need to follow the historical script and indeed intended to make things more dramatic than history allowed—with, among other things, the addition of a love interest—Schiller transgresses seriously when he allows his heroine to die in battle. The historical Joan was convicted after extensive trials, and burned as a heretic and was, as Schiller composed his drama, still no saint. Yet, rather than allow his *Jungfrau* to be contained within the historical definition of her as a heretic and transgressor of gender codes, and to die as a result of church-and-state retributive force, Schiller has her expire heroically on the battlefield, and nowhere does he endorse either the divine or demonic explanation of her accomplishments. The unresolved Joan of Arc thus lives on and Schiller's play, because it portrays Joan in a positive or ambiguously positive light, is often credited with having started the process of her canonization that concluded successfully in 1920 almost five hundred years after her death in 1431. Thus the ultimate reward followed (none too closely) on the ultimate punishment for the historical Joan of Arc and the poet who subverts punishment seems to have had a hand in this reward.

Joan is not alone in being the beneficiary of Schiller's mercy. The fictional Moor brothers do not end well, but they succumb to a kind of intrapunition that excludes the state as penal authority. Franz kills himself to ward off impending punishment and Karl, though he seems to be headed for genuine legal retribution, initiates the process himself, thus becoming the agent of whatever follows. It is significant that, in the space of the play, nothing follows for the man who has committed or participated in multiple murders and caused incalculable damage to property. Wilhelm Tell gets away with murder, and there are numerous other instances of thwarted legal punishment in Schiller's work. As Schiller's contemporary and acquaintance, Hölderlin, has written, somewhat playfully:

> Strafe ist das *Leiden* rechtmäßigen Widerstands und die Folge böser Handlungen. Böse Handlungen sind aber solche, worauf Strafe folgt. Und Strafe folgt da, wo böse Handlungen sind.[12]

> [Punishment is the infliction of just deserts and the consequence of criminal actions. Criminal actions are those that result in punishment. And punishment results where criminal actions are committed.]

The absence of punishment certainly diminishes the appearance of crime and, as we will see, Wilhelm Tell in particular profits from the interruption of the "Hat er aber gemordet, so muss er sterben" sequence. I would not go so far as to assert, with Hölderlin's circularity, that crime unpunished is not crime, but crime without punishment is, at the very least, relativized crime and this study will examine this diminishing of official malefaction in its repeated occurrences.

The Karlsschule

It is very likely that Schiller's interest in crime without punishment began in his own experiences, as an absolutist subject, of punishment without crime. His years as a pupil in the Hohen Karlsschule have often been described in the vocabulary of penal confinement[13] and even more specifically in the terminology of Foucault's studies of the modern prison,[14] inasmuch as the Karlsschule was a highly organized disciplinary mechanism with impeccable surveillance of its inmates by teachers, guards, and, importantly, by each other. Foucault cites Frederick II of Prussia as an early innovator in the practice of disciplining bodies and reducing them to efficient mechanical status:

> A body is docile that may be subjected, used, transformed and improved. The celebrated automata, on the other hand, were not only a way of illustrating an organism, they were also political puppets, small-scale models of power: Frederick II, the meticulous king of

small machines, well-trained regiments and long exercises, was obsessed with them. (Foucault, 136)

Karl Eugen, Duke of Württemberg, who spent his youth at Frederick's court learning how to be an effective ruler, brought a similar obsession with the mechanics of order and obedience to the foundation of his school. Timetables determined the order and duration of all activities and cadets were classified and divided into various groups according to strict standards of measurement. Movements were uniform and the tempo was prescribed throughout the day. After his visit to the school Friedrich Nicolai wrote the following description of a regulated meal:

> Sehr seltsam sah es aus, daß die Schüler mit Rechtsum und Linksum Front gegen den Tisch machten, daß aufs Kommando zum Beten mit klatschendem Laut alle Hände sich zum Gebete falteten, daß nach geendetem Gebete und entfalteten Händen jeder nach dem Tempo seinen Stuhl ergriff und ihn mit so schnellem und egalem Geräusche rückte und sich daraufsetzte, als wenn ein Bataillon das Gewehr abfeuert, ja ich glaube fast, sie fuhren auch nach dem Tempo mit dem ersten Löffel in die Suppe.[15]

> [It made a very odd impression when the cadets marched with left-right, left-right and stood at attention before the table; and that when the order was given to pray all hands came to praying position with a single clapping sound; and that after the prayer and the unfolding of hands, each grasped his chair in time with the others and pulled it out and sat upon it with quick, identical sounds, as if a battalion had fired its guns in unison. Yes, I almost think that they dipped their spoons into the soup in unison.]

Nicolai's observations, and his amazement at the level of bodily discipline that may even extend to synchronized soup consumption, indicate the success of the external aspects of the program. Cadets lived and breathed, ate and slept within the corset of law and regulation, such that they appeared to Nicolai, in their cage of discipline, to be machines.

In 1774, Karl Eugen attempted to increase the observation and regulation of the inner regions of his externally disciplined pupils as he introduced a policy of requiring the older cadets to write reports on their fellow *Karlsschüler* and on themselves. These documents were to assess the young men's level of reli-

1: ADMIRATION FOR ABERRANTS AND SCHILLER'S SCHOOL DAYS

gious conviction and devotion, as well as their attitudes toward the duke, their teachers and fellow pupils. Cleanliness was also to be evaluated (VIII:1137) and Schiller found himself lacking in this respect:

> Ebenso habe ich Reinlichkeit am Körper bisher nicht so beobachtet, als es meine Schuldigkeit gewesen. Aber verzeihen Sie mir Durchleuchtigster Herzog, diese Fehler, denken Sie an die Gnade zurück, die meine Eltern und ich selbst aus Ihrer Hand empfangen. (VIII:25)

> [Also, I have not observed personal cleanliness to the extent of my duty. But forgive me most exalted Duke these errors; think back to the favor my parents and I have received from your hands.]

Such self-exposure—though it may have been calculated to distract from other, more serious deviations—was nonetheless a violation of one's own privacy and this was the rule at Karl's school.

The goal of such regular surveillance, with its probing of thought and religious practices, was to instill and install an internalized self-surveillance system that would lead to lifelong productive obedience to the duke and service to the state. Within the Karlsschule, where he remained from 1773 to 1780, Schiller followed a strict regimen, rising, washing, dressing, eating, studying, presenting himself for review, and retiring according to a schedule set by school administrators and approved by the duke. Pupils who committed infractions, from failure to comply with regulations to bed-wetting, had small pieces of paper describing the offenses pinned to their coats and these notes were read by Karl Eugen as he reviewed his cadets. Thus the duke could actually "see" their lapses in behavior as if he could look into their minds and hearts and find the areas of resistance to his program. The panoptical principle, espoused by Jeremy Bentham for the sake of penal control and reform, had its counterpart in these optical inspections by the apparently omniscient duke. With the institution of the reporting system, all who resided at the Karlsschule became participants in the duke's system of surveillance and functioned as extensions of the eye of Karl, which is large and bulging in portraits.

Schiller was selected for incarceration and surveillance by his duke at a time when he aspired to study theology, a discipline that was not available at the Karlsschule. Johann Kaspar Schiller politely declined the duke's offer more than once on his son's behalf, but when the duke insisted, it became clear that they had no choice but to send the boy to Karl Eugen to study law and further to be *Karl Eugen's* son, inasmuch as the duke, a man with no legitimate children, referred to his cadets as his sons and they were required to call him father. Thus was Schiller removed from his home and his parents, diverted from his chosen profession, and "planted" in a carceral institution whose purpose it was to "form" ("Jünglinge für die Zukunft zu bilden" [to form/educate youths for the future])[16] rather than reform—since, after all, no crime preceded this penal servitude.

As in more conventional prisons, a network of resistance and subversion existed in the Karlsschule. There was clandestine distribution of stimulants such as coffee and tobacco (Lahnstein, 70) and a review of the infamous reports reveals the development of a rhetoric of clichés, reassurances, and references to minor failings that subverted the surveillance to an extent, allowing, tactfully, for some semblance of privacy and concealment of private thoughts—though this was not always the case. Partly because of these small acts of solidarity and camaraderie, Schiller, the innocent man in the "joint," was able, despite surveillance, to write an entire play *about criminals*. *Die Räuber* [The Robbers] owes its existence to late-night writing sessions by candlelight, both in the dormitories and the infirmary, where, apparently no one squealed. Schiller had to conceal *Die Räuber* under the pages of his medical dissertation, because the writing of imaginative literature was, during the time appropriated for sleep and study within the walls of the Karlsschule, a crime. Schiller's writing was further criminalized when, as a regiment's physician in 1782, he was caught having gone A.W.O.L for a performance of his play. In this case, the duke forbade him to write literature at all and it was this final act of tyranny that caused Schiller to break out of what had become the slightly larger prison of Württemberg, where absolutist caprice could define crime.

Thus, while receiving one of the finest educations available—for Karl had engaged superior teachers and constructed an exemplary curriculum—Schiller also learned about a level of institutional confinement that was virtually identical with that of the modern penal institution. Within this system, crime was anything the duke said it was, and offenses against his order were criminalized and punished within the institution. As Hölderlin suggested, crime can be defined by punishment, and Schiller ultimately fled not so much, one senses, to avoid punishment but most likely to prevent forced cessation of the crime. Interestingly, the duke who had previously threatened Schiller with incarceration in one of his official prisons, had a sealed warrant prepared for the purpose of stopping that crime. Had Schiller been discovered working on any form of imaginative writing, he would have been carried off to the grim dungeons at the fort Hohenasperg[17] and most certainly deprived of pen and paper, as C. F. D. Schubart had been when Karl Eugen criminalized his critical journalism. Schiller was a criminal. He wrote against the express prohibition of his duke and he fled Württemberg unlawfully. So it was as criminal and fugitive, one who had already done time at the school, that Schiller began his dramatic career.

This book will not follow the strict chronology of Schiller's works in the hope of illustrating a development from one position on punishment to another (more mature) one, largely because the fundamental aesthetic engagement with penal law and penal practices seems to me not to have changed significantly over time. Clearly, Schiller developed as a stylist, as a dramatist, and perhaps as a philosopher from his early years to his early death, but that development is not my topic and I will be making a number of temporal leaps. Chapter 1, for example, reads the late play *Maria Stuart* against the very early essay, "Was kann eine gute stehende Schaubühne eigentlich wirken?" (What Can a Good, Established Dramatic Stage Actually Achieve?). Maria's execution and the manner of its foreshadowing and (non)presentation reflect the judicial principles of *Schaubühne*. Another unusual feature of chapter 1 is that it takes the *Schaubühne* essay seriously as a document representing Schiller's ideas on the effects of drama on an audience, ideas he worked with throughout his life. The essay, which is widely read, is often downplayed as young Schiller, or pre-Schiller, or not-Schiller, because it incorporates a number of contemporary positions on the value of theater and served Schiller's immediate purpose of gaining and extending patronage as a representative of this valuable theater. Still, the positions Schiller takes in *Schaubühne*, especially those regarding the dramatist's power over an audience, continue to affect his practice throughout his life and I believe that understanding *Schaubühne* is fundamental to understanding Schiller. Chapter 2 describes the taxonomy of crime that inhabits the plays, the aesthetic value of various brands of criminal activity and the question of punishment for these transgressions. *Fiesko,* an early drama, actually presents a hierarchy of criminal activity that shows the "greatness" of the perpetrator increasing with the severity of the crime. The valuations of *Fiesko* are also present to a lesser extent in *Die Räuber.* The third chapter, on the prose narrative *Spiel des Schicksals,* moves from execution and the ranking of crime to the unaesthetic experience of incarceration and the interventions the jailer makes in the prisoner's "personal narrative" or self. Chapter 4 addresses murder, namely the one that Wilhelm Tell so conspicuously gets away with, and follows this discussion with an examination of "Verbrecher aus verlorener Ehre" (Criminal from Lost Honor) and Christian Wolf's very different experience of murder. Chapter Five considers the question of gender crimes or gender transgressions in the historical sources for *Die Jungfrau von Orleans* and follows Schiller's amelioration of these violations along with the elimination of the punishment mentioned above. A final chapter examines several contemporary pieces and their affinities with Schiller's work on crime and punishment, namely Heinrich Böll's *Die verlorene Ehre der Katharina Blum* (*The Lost Honor of Katharina Blum*), Anthony Burgess's novel *A Clockwork Orange,* and Stanley Kubrick's extraordinary film version of that novel. A short summary concludes the volume.

To return briefly from the end foreshadowed to the beginning of this investigation and to emphasize a point made above, the *Schaubühne* essay, more than any other piece, provides a foundation for my work on these matters because it is here that Schiller outlines a program of *Wirkung* that replaces the symmetry of retributive punishment or harsh deterrent penal measures. Though it precedes Schiller's intensive engagement with Kant, beginning in 1791, or perhaps *because* it precedes this period of deep reflection on and appropriation and transformation of Kant's critical philosophy, the essay presents the palpable principles of a program that culminates in the richer, but far less palpable, project of aesthetic education and the aesthetic state. The energetic immediacy of *Schaubühne* and the other early dramatic essays provides access to Schiller's practical (insofar as one can use that term in this context) thinking on the stage and its purpose that is not available in the more abstract regions of his aesthetic theorizing—during which period Schiller all but abandoned dramatic writing and devoted himself to more panoramic examinations of humanity and what it means to be human.

2

What Does the Dramatic Stage Actually Do? Exposure, Demonstration, and *Wirkung* in the *Schaubühne* Essay and the Execution of Maria Stuart

ON JUNE 26, 1784, SCHILLER MADE A PRESENTATION TO THE KURPFÄL-zische Deutsche Gesellschaft, in which he defended the theater and asserted its value as a moral force in contemporary society. The working title of the lecture was "Vom Wirken der Schaubühne auf das Volk" [On the Effects of the Dramatic Stage on the People], and it subsequently appeared in the *Rheinische Thalia* (1785) as "Was kann eine gute stehende Schaubühne eigentlich wirken?" and then again, with very slight alterations, in the fourth volume of Schiller's *Kleine prosaische Schriften* (1802) as "Die Schaubühne als eine moralische Anstalt betrachtet" [The Dramatic Stage as a Moral Institution] (VIII:1247). Already the collection of titles indicates a deep concern with the effects of theater on an audience and not merely in terms of their entertainment or aesthetic judgment. Schiller's piece was about *Wirkung* and I will use the German word here because it suggests not only an effect but also the process of *having an effect* and it is this dynamic process that will be the explicit and implicit theme of significant sections of this study. Already in 1784, Schiller had arrived at a fairly detailed theory of reception, based on his assumptions about audience psychology and he had also outlined the ways in which a dramatist could access and address minds and hearts for the sake of the greater social good. To echo the final title of the essay, Schiller regarded the stage as a moral institution—with considerable normative power.

In a study of punishment and penal tactics in Schiller's drama and prose, the importance of *Wirkung* and Schiller's position on the efficacy of art are central. Schiller the aesthetician began his ruminations on art and efficacy in the early dramatic essays that regard the stage as a conduit for ideas and images that will improve spectators, educating them to morality and a more inclusive humanity. In later works, especially *Über die ästhetische Erziehung des Menschen in einer Reihe von Briefen* (1795) [On the Aesthetic Education of Man in a Series of Letters], the idea of the direct utility of art yields to a more autonomous and ludic role in human life that carries similar benefits for the beholder, but without entering so directly into his or her practical affairs. The more indirect route of aesthetic education is not necessarily free of coercive force, inasmuch as education is generally applied or imposed from without, nor is it necessarily dissimilar to hegemony since it is intended to assume a directive function within. In the aesthetic letters, the stimulus (art/beauty) works on the recipient by inducing a state of free play of the senses that represents humanity at its highest level. The paradox of induced freedom has troubled a number of critics and we will discuss this vexing matter presently. But for now we return to the fugitive Schiller.

Schiller's flight from Württemberg, a criminal act if viewed from within the duchy, was also a secession, a declaration of independence from the state he broke with. Schiller crossed a border, left a corrupt and oppressive state, and established a position outside the Law of Karl and within a new order—though he did not do this without significant regrets, as his letters to the duke indicate. The new order, the counter-realm to the rigidly structured principality he left, was located in his dramatic practice, and the claims he made for the power of the stage in *Schaubühne*. For Schiller, the theater was not only a moral institution, but also a state unto itself[1] and it had distinct advantages over the traditional political unit.

In an earlier essay that is generally linked to *Schaubühne*, "Über das gegenwärtige teutsche Theater" [On the Contemporary German Theater] (1782), Schiller complained that the German stage was morally ineffective. He did not doubt its possibilities, however. In 1782, he considered the theater to be fully equipped to educate spectators and thus improve society, but he found that the German theater was missing its mark:

> eine solche Anstalt, möchte man erwarten, sollte die reinern Begriffe von Glückseligkeit und Elend um so nachdrücklicher in die

> Seele prägen, als die sinnliche Anschauung lebendiger ist, denn nur Tradition und Sentenzen. *Sollte,* sage ich;—und was *sollten* die Waren nicht, wenn man den Verkäufer höret? (VIII:168)

> [Such an institution, one would expect, should imprint the purer concepts of happiness and misery much more firmly on the soul, because sensual illustration is far more lively than mere tradition and maxims. *Should,* I say;—and what shouldn't the product be capable of, if one listens to the salesman?]

The reference to the *Verkäufer* is telling. At this point, Schiller had not yet become the salesman who speaks in *Schaubühne* though he seems, self-consciously, to anticipate that role and rhetorically *Schaubühne* reads very much like a sales pitch—though the seller is sincere. In the 1782 piece, however, product development is deemed to be incomplete and the consumers are partially liable. Schiller concludes that spectators are not applying the lessons of the theater to themselves, but merely recognizing their neighbors in the errant dramatic figures and cautionary plots. Though spectators and (French) dramatists bear some responsibility, Schiller ultimately blames the actors for the misfiring of moral messages. How well, for example, can a debauched actress play the part of a seduced innocent? (VIII:174) This rhetorical question implies a theory of acting that would call for a very close brand of typecasting, and Schiller underscores his assertions with the suggestion that amateurs might do a better job than professionals (VIII:174), apparently looking for a deep sincerity of portrayal that issues from personality and experience. Beyond character flaws and the accidents of casting, the essay identifies numerous other lapses in thespian artistry that tend to diminish audience perception of the beneficial aspects of the spectacles.

Despite the author's preoccupation with actors, the concerns and convictions that emerge in *Schaubühne* are adequately prefigured in "Über das gegenwärtige teutsche Theater," indicating a consistency of thought and expectation over the brief period between the pieces—that persists in a more subtle and mature form in my reading of the practice. The major difference between the two texts is that in the first case, the stage is, in practical terms, not doing its job, whereas in the latter essay—actually a lecture, that is a text written for oral/dramatic presentation—the stage is, in the abstract, highly effective. In both cases, the mission of the dramatic stage is that of presenting vivid and convincing examples of proper and improper behavior that will influence (enthralled) spectators to improve themselves and embrace humanity. It is all about *Wirkung* and the power behind this efficacy, though purely rhetorical, is nonetheless considerable and the tropes that represent this power tend toward the intimation of external intervention in spectators' lives and this brings us to the question of coercion within an oeuvre that for the most part eschews punishment. From the perspective of a didactic dramatic tradition and an ethical aesthetic, the potential advantages of the effort or intention to influence spectators and re-form them more or less justifies any potential violation or invasion of privacy. But Schiller's language seems to suggest a very strong and specific kind of influence that, though it stops short of mind control, does not rule out access to the regions where such control is exercised.

In a discussion of Schiller's transformation of Kant's categories of the sublime,[2] Paul de Man declared him to be a "practical" thinker, one who empiricizes and therefore ideologizes Kant, and remains—even after his engagement with Kant—a dramatist concerned with filling his theater. This is a daring—and perceptive—qualification within a tradition that finds its polarities in Goethe's attachment to experience and the material vs. Schiller's abstract leanings. Though Schiller is the abstract, theoretical-minded member of that pairing, de Man finds him retreating from abstractions, deserting and even misusing the philosophy he devoted so much effort to understanding and appropriating. Schiller began reading Kant in 1791, starting with *Kritik der Urteilskraft* [The Critique of Judgment], and German literary and intellectual historians have generally drawn a distinction between pre- and post-Kantian Schiller, between the still practical-minded theatrical and literary practitioner and the more philosophical thinker who stopped writing for the theater for a long period of time in order to devote himself to Kantian abstractions. Of course there are continuities, but also palpable differences in Schiller's methods and his objects over time and over Kant. Practical *Wirkung* yields to Beauty's liberating aura and practical psychology to categories and abstract typologies. I consider the Schiller of *Schaubühne* (seven years before he read Kant), who labels the stage "eine Schule der praktischen Weisheit" [a school of practical wisdom] (VIII:194), to be a theoretician of the practical—and this entails some awkwardness—one who is and will remain obsessed with *Wirkung*. Though he may have been "practical" in his later operations on Kant, I regard the early Schiller as the practical prescriptive aesthetician who then developed these inclinations in a more purely theoretical direction. The later theoretical essays, the treatises on aesthetics and philosophy, retain this drive toward effect and having an effect, though that process is more remote and the effect itself is far more abstractly nuanced. Yet, even after this development or maturation, Schiller's concern with control persists and this has engendered some serious reflection by scholars who recognize the category of the aesthetic as a potentially normative tool. Though the later essays are not within the scope of this study, I want to sketch the issue of coercion and control below as it arises in the early essays and in the later post-Kantian ones because it is a necessary corollary to my focus on *Wirkung*.

Schiller makes a very bold statement about *Wirkung* in *Schaubühne* that indicates that the stage has the power to imprint its images on human minds, determine the nature of the impressions transmitted, and cause these images to remain with the spectator, thus continuing to influence that individual:

> Es ist nicht Übertreibung wenn man behauptet, dass diese auf der Schaubühne aufgestellten Gemälde mit der Moral des gemeinen Manns endlich in eins zusammen fliessen, und in einzelnen Fällen *seine Empfindung bestimmen*.... Diese Eindrücke sind unauslöschlich, und bei der leisesten Berührung steht das ganze abschröckende Kunstgemälde im Herzen des Menschen wie aus dem Grabe auf. (VIII:191, italics mine)

> [It is no exaggeration to assert that those images that are transmitted by the stage eventually become one with the morality of the common man and in certain cases *determine his sensations*.... These impressions are indelible and the slightest stimulus can recall the whole cautionary aesthetic image to the hearts of men as if it had returned from the grave.]

This is strong stuff as excerpted here, but it is nearly as strong in its full context, namely that of a somewhat histrionic treatise on the merits of the dramatic stage, where distinct claims are made for the power of the theater, but rarely so precise and definite as "seine Empfindung bestimmen." Did Schiller get carried away by his rhetoric? This certainly happened at times and it happened with some frequency, but in the case of the theatrical project of penetrating spectatorial hearts and minds and determining a beneficial effect, there are similar remarks in other commentaries of the time that tend to support the sincerity of the speaker.

As young Schiller formulated his theory of drama and its effects on an audience, he made frequent reference to the secret regions of the human heart, mind, and soul and speculated on the ways in which the dramatist might access these spaces. He writes of "die Vorteile der dramatischen Methode, die Seele gleichsam bei ihren geheimsten Operationen zu ertappen" [the advantages of the dramatic method for catching the soul at its most secret operations] (II:15; *Die Räuber*, "Vorrede"); and glories in his ability, "des Zuschauers Seele am Zügel [zu] führe[n], und nach meinem Gefallen einem Ball gleich dem Himmel oder der Hölle zu[zu]werfen" [to lead the spectator's soul on a bridle and according to my pleasure to throw it to heaven or to hell as if it were a ball] (II:558; *Fiesko*, "Erinnerung an das Publikum" [Memento to the Audience]). There are more such references in the *Räuber* apparatus and in *Schaubühne* itself, but these should suffice to illustrate that at this point in his career, to put it bluntly, *Schiller saw the theater as a "practical" means for entering into the minds of his audience and "repairing" deficits therein for the greater good of humanity and the nation.* These are not modest ambitions, and the language that conveys them suggests that more than the usual theatrical sway is at stake.

The critical discussion of Schiller and coercion seems to be concentrated on the later work, especially on aesthetic education and the "violence" that de Man and others have perceived at its roots,[3] though Adorno already sees signs of a fascistic fascination with power in the early plays with their usurper figures. He concludes that, "Im innersten Gehäuse des Humanismus, als dessen eigene Seele, tobt gefangen der Wüterich, der als Fascist die Welt zum Gefängnis macht" [At the deepest core of humanism, in its very soul raves the imprisoned brute who as fascist makes a prison of the world].[4] Adorno exaggerates in his "unmasking" of the classical bourgeois dramatist, but his hyperbole testifies to the existence of a stimulus, of *something* in the rhetoric, to which he can overreact. That certain something is, I believe, a deep engagement with coercive control, on the one hand as a means to an end, on the other as a device to be transcended. Both de Man (RR; AI) and Terry Eagleton[5] have remarked the weight of Schiller's influence on contemporary thinking and teaching about art and the aesthetic, understood as a kind of hegemonic control that has determined our humanistic assumptions about art and its role in human life. De Man declared in a lecture that "we are all Schillerians" (AI:7) in "whatever writing we do, whatever way we have of talking about art, whatever way we have of teaching, whatever justification we give ourselves for teaching, whatever the standards and values by means of which we teach" (AI:142).[6] Eagleton sees Schiller's category of the aesthetic as a double-edged phenomenon that "provides some of the vital constituents of a new theory of bourgeois hegemony; but it also protests with magnificent passion against the spiritual devastation which that emergent social order is wreaking" (Eagleton, 118), thus implicating Schiller in both oppression and resistance in a manner perfectly congruent with the poet's doubleness. Constantin Behler's analysis, which subsumes de Man and Eagleton, provides some valuable summary and insights for a shorthand consideration of late Schiller as coercive or hegemonic. Behler notes with reference to Foucault and in dialogue with de Man's assertion that Schiller's categories are "still the taken-for-granted premises of our pedagogical, historical, and political ideologies" (RR, 266) that:

> Schiller's aesthetic humanism and humanist aesthetics is not simply a dream, utopia, or imaginative production, because his discourse did succeed in rendering its objects—aesthetic artifacts, human beings, society, history—as programmable, i.e., as accessible to a knowledge that could be strategically deployed to shape and transform them.[7]

Behler's assertion of programmability could easily have been grounded in the earlier work, though it reflects reactions to the later program of aesthetic education that Schiller promoted in *Die Horen* and that survived in university teaching and more general bourgeois thinking about art.

From Foucauldian technologies of power and the process of fascistic social shaping, we can look back to the *Schaubühne* essay and see what may have been the "shape" of things to come, namely the use of *Wirkung* as a (perhaps) not-yet-contaminated strategy of control. In a long section called "The Hidden Violence of Bildung," Behler examines Schiller's reflection on his declared poetic intention of having an effect, influencing, guiding, directing the reader or spectator and his conviction that the experience of art engenders a *free* play of the senses or that beauty is actually *freedom* in the realm of appearances. In this case, Behler references the important 1794 essay on poetry "Über Matthissons Gedichte" [On Matthisson's Poetry] where Schiller actually faces the paradox of induced freedom and seeks in typical fashion to overcome it:

> So ergeben sich daraus zweierlei Foderungen, denen kein Dichter, der diesen Namen verdienen will, sich entziehen kann. Er muss fürs erste unsre Einbildungskraft frei spielen und *selbst handeln* lassen, und zweitens muss er nichts desto weniger seiner Wirkung *gewiss* sein, und eine *bestimmte* Empfindung erzeugen. . . . Wie hebt der Dichter nun diesen Widerspruch? (VIII:1018)

> [Thus there are two obligations that no poet worthy of the name can ignore. First of all, he must let our imagination play freely and *act on its own* and secondly he must nonetheless be certain of the effect he intends and induce a *specific* reaction. . . . How can the poet resolve this contradiction?]

Though Behler sees a solution in Schiller's response to his rhetorical question, I believe that Schiller dodges the question by reformulating the paradox in a way that ignores the tension between inner and outer determination and enlisting "nature" as an impenetrable "a priori" that does not admit of definition:

> Dadurch, dass er unserer Einbildungskraft keinen anderen Gang vorschreibt, als den sie in ihrer vollen Freiheit und nach ihren eigenen Gesetzen nehmen müsste, dass er seinen Zweck durch Natur erreicht und die äussere Notwendigkeit in eine innere verwandelt. Es findet sich alsdann . . . dass die höchste Freiheit gerade nur durch die höchste Bestimmtheit möglich ist. (VIII:1018–19)

> [In that he prescribes for our imagination no other path than that which it would have to take in full freedom and according to its own laws; in that he accomplishes his purpose through nature and transforms the outer necessity into an inner one. Thus the greatest freedom is only possible by means of the highest level of determination.]

In 1794, ten years after *Schaubühne* was delivered and three years after he began his studies of Kant, Schiller formulates, but does not relieve, the contradiction inherent in induced freedom, a matter that goes uncommented in the early theatrical essays, though some energies are expended there in expressing respect for individual humanity. Ultimately, this is a dilemma that all but the crassest of didactic writers must face. The will to improve readers or spectators must at some point yield to or deny the ideal of individual self-determination. Examples or nudges may guide the process of self-determination, but the lines that should not be crossed are less than clearly drawn.

The control or coercion behind the ideal of *Wirkung* in the early essays may be relativized by comparison to the model of political power that prevailed in German territories and in Schiller's life to that point. It can also be amplified or demonized by reference to political developments involving control or coercion for the "greater good" of individuals and society in subsequent centuries—Elizabeth Wilkinson and L. A. Willoughby have famously cited Josef Goebbels's Schillerian reference to the statesman as artist who shapes society.[8] *Wirkung* is both benevolent and sinister, but for the purposes of this study, I want to evoke this larger context for the discussion of *Wirkung* as control or influence, while scrutinizing its immediate role in the drama and prose pieces I have selected. The question of control will be most prominent in the final section on *A Clockwork Orange* but it has relevance for all chapters and for the apprehension of Schiller's engagement with punishment. Schiller tends not to punish and he also criticizes particular methods of punishment, but he does seek to have some of the effects punishment intends, namely deterrence and reform. One side of *Wirkung* is its substitutability for punishment and this trend begins in *Schaubühne* and with this in mind, we now return to this seminal early essay for a review of its presentation of the stage as a state unto itself.

Schaubühne was, as noted, delivered at a gathering of the Kurpfälzische Deutsche Gesellschaft and it marked Schiller's entry into that group, whose purpose was to promote German culture and the German language in the face of French influence, which was especially prominent in the theater. Membership in the society also meant citizenship in the Palatinate, so that the stateless author, the fugitive from Württemberg, was relegitimized as a citizen of another state even as he outlined his views of the theater as a parallel government with a unique type of *Wirkung*.

Schiller, experienced *Karlsschüler*, absolutist subject, and budding dramatist, had very definite expectations of his theatrical domain that he viewed as a counter-position to the absolutist state, inasmuch as the theater was a realm where politics and morality were not estranged from one another (VIII:1251). The theater observed higher and more complex standards of law, yet, as we have seen, *this* state was not without its control mechanisms. *Wirkung* is, in Schiller's usage, linked to control and though the theater's methods of dealing with human vice or human weakness are more enlightened than those of the duke, there is nonetheless an effort to enter the hearts and minds of spectator-subjects and to effect the desired change and improvement within. Those desirable changes or improvements are not minutely specified as was the regime of the Karlsschule. It is rather a matter of educating spectators and readers to morality, linking them more meaningfully to a tolerant community of humanity.

Given this purpose, Schiller's theater also has a judiciary. While portraying the stage as the site of public education and personal edification, he also identifies it as an alternative judicial system, one that is ultimately more effective than contemporary courts:

Die Gerichtsbarkeit der Bühne fängt an, wo das Gebiet der weltlichen Gesetze sich endigt. Wenn die Gerechtigkeit für Gold verblindet, und im Solde der Laster schwelgt, wenn die Frevel der Mächtigen ihrer Ohnmacht spotten, und Menschenfurcht den Arm der Obrigkeit bindet, übernimmt die Schaubühne Schwert und Waage, und reißt die Laster vor einen schrecklichen Richterstuhl. (VIII:190)[9]

[The jurisdiction of the stage begins where the reach of worldly laws ends. If justice be blinded by gold and indulge in the service of vice, if the crimes of the powerful seem to mock its weakness, and human fear seems to stay the arm of the authorities, then the stage takes over sword and scales and drags these vices before a fearsome judge's bench.]

In this account of the stage usurping the courts' authority, that which appears at first to be mere judicial metaphor is reified considerably as Schiller proceeds to develop a theory of theatrical justice, reform and retribution, enforced by "heilsame Schauer" [therapeutic shudders][10] (VIII:191) that overcome the spectators as they recognize vice and foolishness. It is in this shudder of recognition that the stage stakes its claim to *Wirkung*. Effective drama engenders a visceral reaction to the perceived resemblance of one's own moral tendencies to those of a non-exemplary figure. Schiller the dramatist is, according to Schiller the essayist, not only in spectators' heads and hearts, but also in their guts.

Like worldly courts, Schiller's stage also has a penal function and here it is important to distinguish between (lack of) punishment within the plays and narratives (not at issue at the moment) and the punishment that the dramatic stage may mete out. In addition to engendering the spectator's discomfort, the stage "punishes" the transgressions it illuminates and here too it has an advantage over the conventional state and its judiciary:

> So gewiß sichtbare Darstellung mächtiger wirkt, als toder Buchstabe und kalte Erzählung, so gewiß wirkt die Schaubühne tiefer und dauernder als Moral und Gesetze. Aber hier *unterstützt* sie die weltliche Gerechtigkeit nur—ihr ist noch ein weiteres Feld geöffnet. Tausend Laster, die jene ungestraft duldet, straft sie; tausend Tugenden, wovon jene schweigt, werden von der Bühne empfohlen. (VIII:191, Schiller's emphasis)

> [Just as visible depiction has a greater effect than dead letters and cold narration, so does the stage have a deeper and more lasting effect than morality and laws. But here the stage merely *supports* worldly justice—in reality it has a much greater sphere of influence. A thousand vices that morality and laws tolerate without punishment are punished by the stage; a thousand virtues that they pass over silently are recommended by the stage.]

This passage echoes the earlier essay that privileges sensual illustration over tradition and maxims in its hierarchical positioning of visual representation over dead letters and cold narration, and claims for the theatrical imitation of life a special power to root out those failings that law cannot address and to recommend virtuous alternatives. Yet this is not a civic project that can be measured in terms of crime statistics. As Schiller notes:

ich selbst bin der Meinung, daß vielleicht Molieres Harpagon noch kein Wucherer besserte, daß der Selbstmörder Beverlei noch wenige seiner Brüder von der abscheulichen Spielsucht zurückzog, daß Karl Moors unglückliche Räubergeschichte die Landstrassen nicht viel sicherer machen wird. (VIII:194)

[It is my personal opinion that Moliere's Harpagon has probably not improved any usurer, that the suicide Beverley has rescued very few of his brothers from the terrible will to gamble, that Karl Moor's unfortunate robber story will not make the highways any safer.]

It is less a matter of direct and immediate crime-fighting, than of spreading an awareness of human vice and inducing spectators to rigorously examine their own practices and to change those practices, this change being both the basic assumption and goal of theatrical practice as it proceeds from *Schaubühne*. The method applied induces not only a private, individual awareness, but also a more public and communal seen-ness, a sense of being observed by the community as part of the community. In his resounding and inspirational conclusion, Schiller declares it a triumph for nature,

wenn Menschen aus allen Kreisen und Zonen und Ständen, abgeworfen jede Fessel der Künstelei und der Mode herausgerissen aus jedem Drange des Schicksals, durch *eine* allwebende Sympathie verbrüdert, in *Ein* Geschlecht ihrem himmlischen Ursprung sich nähern. Jeder einzelne genießt die Entzückungen aller, die verstärkt und verschönert aus hundert Augen auf ihn zurück fallen, und seine Brust gibt jetzt nur *Einer* Empfindung Raum—es ist diese: ein *Mensch* zu sein. (200)[11]

[when people from all regions and classes, having cast off the chains of artifice and fashion, removed from the demands of fate, become brothers by virtue of one unifying affect, and approach their heavenly source as *one* race. Each individual feels the rapture of all, which, strengthened and beautified by hundreds of eyes, falls back on him, and his breast is filled with only one sensation, that of being *human*.]

Alle Menschen werden Brüder [all people become brothers]—and this includes a populist version of Big Brother, who is watching with hundreds of eyes from within the community. The appropriately dramatic finale to Schiller's essay describes a communal realization of humanity that is both an exchange and intensification of theatrical pleasure, expressed in terms of observation, namely the power of the focused gaze of a hundred eyes that falls on the individual within this (benevolently?) controlled environment. The gaze or the observation is reciprocal and there is no counterpart to the isolated panoptical Eye of Karl that, strengthened by the eyes of his student spies (*Alle Schüler werden Spitzel* [all schoolboys become spies]), rests on each individual *Karlsschüler*. That absolutist power position repels reciprocity whereas the ocular dynamics of the theater encourage it. Yet this does not preclude the application of guidance and control by a more diffusely modern type of power. Power, here, is a moral organizing principle, as opposed to brute absolutist caprice, and it achieves *Wirkung* in the communal visibility of the subject in the theater. Rather than responding to a blunt command, Schiller's ideal spectators respond to a web of community (moral) expectations and norms. This response is facilitated, if not coerced, by the dramatic stage and its maxims. That the man who had recently written *Die Räuber* could write such a treatise on didacticism and even cite *Räuber* in support of it, speaks to the inevitable disparities between theory and practice and to an author's peculiar perception of his own work. There can be little doubt that viewing *Räuber* was a rousing experience, but whether the enthusiastic response was a result of the "therapeutic shudders" referenced in *Schaubühne* or whether a great deal of corrective self-recognition occurred is doubtful and, in any case, beyond recuperation. The point is that Schiller's theory of the theater had a strong practical streak and some very specific notions of audience improvement.

Foucault identifies the roughly eighty years following the grisly public execution of Robert Francois Damiens (whom Schiller also mentions in *Schaubühne*) in 1757 as a time of transition in European penal practices. The spectacle of corporal punishment that was intended to hurt the offender and discourage the spectators from similar crimes yields to more subtle techniques of addressing the criminal urge:

> The fact remains that a few decades saw the disappearance of the tortured, dismembered, amputated body, symbolically branded on face or shoulder, exposed alive or dead to public view. The body as the major target of penal repression disappears. (Foucault, 8)

The focus on the martyred body yields to a relatively new practice:

> If the penalty in its most severe forms no longer addresses itself to the body, on what does it lay hold? The answer of the theoreticians—those who, about 1760, opened up a period that is not yet at an end—is simple, almost obvious. It seems to be contained in the question itself: since it is no longer the body, it must be the soul. The expiation that once rained down upon the body must be replaced by a punishment that acts in depth on the heart, the thoughts, the will, the inclinations. (Foucault, 16)

Schiller's regimented education and his dramatic career fall within this period of transition and his theater, a correctional institution as well as a state, strives to partake in those "technologies of the soul," questionable though they may be from certain angles, that replaced brutal repression—just as the dramatist eschews or undermines methods of punishment aimed at the body and embraces a *Wirkung* aimed at the secret chambers of the heart and soul.

Though Schiller's passionate insistence on a shift from dead letters and maxims to living theatrical demonstration as a means of social improvement seems to run counter to Foucault's progression from the grueling public theater of punishment to the "carceral" reeducation of criminals, Schiller invests the theater with the power to achieve those effects that carceral regulation aims at. Foucault writes of the isolation and individualization of the delinquent and Schiller's theater brings its errant visitors together for their rehabilitation—both in theory and in practice, as the famous review of *Die Räuber* attests: "Fremde Menschen fielen einander schluchzend in die Arme!" [Strangers fell sobbing into each other's arms].[12] Yet, like the enlightened penologists of the later eighteenth century, Schiller is fundamentally concerned with access to the inner regions of the spectator-subject and a reading of Schiller's dramatic theory through Foucault's standard account of a revolution in penology further nuances the nature of the *Wirkung* Schiller pursued along aesthetic paths. Schiller sought to reform his immobilized or captive spectators within a carefully calculated program that captured their attention and then illustrated proper and improper modes of behavior.

As noted, Schiller never commented publicly on the important eighteenth-century debates about penal theory. Nowhere in his work, for example, does the word "Beccaria" occur, though Beccaria's protests against the death penalty found significant resonance in contemporary thinking about drama and its deterrent function.[13] Yet here in the pre-Kantian *Schaubühne* essay, there are echoes of Beccaria's (and Bentham's) utilitarian credo, as Schiller identifies the highest goal of the stage (as well as of philosophers and lawgivers) as the "Beförderung allgemeiner Glückseligkeit" [promotion of general happiness] (VIII:186). Seeking to do the greatest good for the greatest number, the stage enforces a code of conduct and punishes infringements via exposure and demonstration. Both of these processes occur on the stage, but the first is directed toward the spectators who are to recognize and shudder and the second ostensibly toward the fictional figures who err and suffer for it. Theoretically, the process of exposure is supported by the application of poetic justice, but is this "demonstration," the just punishment of fictional transgressions, necessary to the exposure? Yes and no. Crime unpunished may be, in Hölderlin's terms, crime relativized, but as we will see repeatedly in Schiller's poetic work, there is a case to be made for letting crime stand uncorrected, that is, letting the spectators reflect on a problem or crime that is not solved or canceled for them by the depiction of its "solution" or punishment. The spectator may presumably profit from seeing wickedness met with an equal measure of retributive force—or she may profit from contemplating the absence of retribution as most of Schiller's dramatic *practice* neglects, sometimes brilliantly, to apply that force. This study is in general concerned with the demonstration aspect, the ways in which figures are punished or not punished, and the ways in which punishment is thus staged and reviewed—the ways in which theater itself usurps the role of civil punishment and suggests alternatives. However, in this segment I want to establish the intentions behind exposure, the method of attack, before moving on to one of the more profound instances of effective demonstration, namely the execution of Maria Stuart.

Schiller, the salesman of *Schaubühne,* ranked successful theatrical spectacle among the highest achievements possible because such spectacles had access to the hearts and minds of spectators, and because the exhibition of virtue and the exposure of vice led to changes of heart and mind that would ultimately promote general welfare and happiness. By addressing the aesthetic sense, a middle faculty between feeling and understanding, "Sinnlichkeit und Verstand," theater trumps religion, which is mainly concerned with the sensuous aspects of its subjects, and it also exceeds the power of law, which is aimed at the understanding. By straddling these realms and operating within this middle faculty, the stage can appeal to understanding, while adding the advantages of religion to that appeal:

> [Religion] setzt ihre Gerichtsbarkeit bis in die verborgensten Winkel des Herzens fort, und verfolgt den Gedanken bis an die innerste Quelle. (VIII:189)

> [Religion extends its jurisdiction into the most hidden corners of the heart and pursues thoughts to their most inner source.]

There is a creepy hint of violation by the thought (and feeling) police in this passage that proposes to annex the advantages of religion to a theory of the stage. Schiller does indeed reject the idea of "Menschen zu drechseln" [to manufacture identical individuals as from a lathe] or the regimented education of the young in "Gewächshäusern" [greenhouses], (VIII:198; a reference to the Karlsschule, which was identified as a military "Pflanzschule"), and this early form of aesthetic education or edification was to be less literally prescriptive. However, he does commit to technologies of the soul and admires the techniques of those who practice the profession he first aspired to when he decided to study theology. The appeal to the heart and the penetration of heart and mind with tonic images of a better self constitute the effectiveness of the well-established theatrical stage.

Nor does Schiller neglect to provide practical examples of such penetration and improvement. As Lady Macbeth and Franz von Moor confront their consciences, their spectators are impressed and influenced for the better. The name of Franz Moor in particular revives the memory of a number of evils that the spectator has seen punished by the terrible advent of the conscience Franz strives to subdue and the despair of his suicide. Thus "Franz Moor" becomes a kind of shorthand reminder of the consequences of behaving in any way like Franz and also contains the revulsion the dramatist intended his audience to feel at the thought of the numerous failings Schiller exposed in this figure. Once again, Schiller the theorist sees a direct and practical link—though not necessarily a simplistic one—between the theatrical display of vice or virtue and human behavior.

This link extends also from the general improvements to be effected by the theater to the hearts of the highest heads of state:

> Menschlichkeit und Duldung fangen an, der herrschende Geist unserer Zeit zu werden; ihre Strahlen sind bis in die Gerichtssäle, und noch weiter—in das Herz unserer Fürsten gedrungen. Wieviel Anteil an diesem göttlichen Werk gehört unseren Bühnen? Sind *sie* es nicht, die den Menschen mit dem Menschen bekannt machten, und das geheime Räderwerk aufdeckten nach welchem er handelt? (VIII:196)

> [Humanity and tolerance are beginning to be the dominant spirit of our time; they radiate into the courts of law and even further—into the hearts of our rulers. How much of this divine work is accomplished by our theaters? Aren't they the vehicles for acquainting people with people, and for uncovering the secret clockwork according to which men behave?]

The project of the stage as alternative to the absolutist state is that of spreading humanity and tolerance to the point where such virtue and enlightenment will penetrate the courts and also the hearts of the princes. The control exerted by the theater's communal affirmation of virtue and rejection of vice does not stop at the palace gate, but rather affects those former centers of power, who will now use that power subject to the steady influence of an enlightened humanity. In other words, the theater may work to shape government and its practices. And this brings me to *Maria Stuart* as one example of the direction this project can take, though not without a considerable leap forward in time.

Roughly twenty years separate Schiller's early theatrical essays from his mature play about the Queen of Scots, but I am considering them in sequence here because I believe that *Maria Stuart*, in its staging of punishment, constitutes a commentary on penal practices. This commentary has its roots in the claims Schiller made in 1784 for the mission of the dramatic stage. *Maria Stuart* has many aspects that have been fruitfully pursued by generations of scholars and the play is not at all known to posterity as a contribution to penology or to penal reform.[14] Nonetheless, I would like to investigate one very specific aspect of *Maria Stuart,* namely its staging of a critical demonstration of the inadequacy of the ultimate civil punishment, namely the spectacle of the death penalty. To write of Mary Stuart at any length is to write of execution. The truncated queen's motto, "in my end is my beginning," was entirely appropriate because her "end," fraught as it was with issues of legality and royal relations, was the most conspicuous part of her life. But before we turn to Schiller's negotiations with the decapitation of Mary Stuart, it will be useful to reflect briefly on the spectacle of execution in general and the purposes it is intended to serve.

The Word Made Flesh

As we know, the *proper* conduct of such a spectacle is a very difficult business and it is more than apparent from historical accounts and contemporary practice that most executions are botched executions. This is not because they fail to achieve their most obvious goal—the production of a dead body—but rather because they so rarely conform to the meticulous scripts or protocols that are supposed to define them. The principal purpose of execution, a process very close to drama in its pageantry, is the depiction, for witnesses, of an *idea* of justice. If it were not for the social will to demonstrate and exhibit this idea that encompasses state sovereignty, moral symmetry, and pedagogical promise, the condemned man or woman could be killed quickly and simply after sentencing—or not killed at all.

So, an execution is a serious symbolic event—with serious nonsymbolic consequences—a spectacle that is intended to reflect community (or monarchical) sentiments about punishment with a high degree of specificity. For example, a certain precise level of brutality—or of "humanity"—must be maintained in the actual application of the instruments of death. Early modern European protocols call for elaborate and exact sequences of torments, loosely based on the principle of *contrapasso,* whereas late twentieth-century U.S. scenarios dictate that the condemned shall not suffer pain.[15] Nevertheless, whether the method is brutal or humane, there will always be problems with the ideal implementation of the procedure because the procedure, as conceived and written, *is* ideal—an ideal of legal punishment—and the implementation very viscerally real. In order to elaborate these botched conjunctions of the ideal, as given in language with the physical "real," I want to mention a few of the problems faced by the organizers, recorders, spectators, and perpetrators of execution.

One of these is control of the condemned. Beyond the intricate rules for the application of the instruments of death, there are also numerous prescriptions and conventions that regulate the actions of the condemned. The opinions or expressed opinions of this central figure have value because he or she is the primary receptor of execution, and his or her statements and behaviors before and during the ordeal are—again ideally—to be confined within certain limits of acceptable, and accepting, behavior. An affirmation from the victim obviously lends legitimacy to the entire procedure and there is a long tradition of euphemistic description that appears to exaggerate the compliance of those executed. Here it is helpful to return to Foucault's reference to the Damiens execution, where it is repeatedly stressed that Damiens, otherwise foul-mouthed, did not curse (3–5). Though the executioners had trouble enacting the entire protocol on him—he did not quarter as easily as expected—he is reported to have done his duty as the condemned and to have played his part correctly. Of course it seems unlikely that a man given to cursing would intentionally refrain from profanity, while undergoing such torment, but the record testifies—either in its emphasis on a particular fact or in its invention of that fact—to a social need for an accepting victim who views his punishment as deserved. With the authority of the victim behind it, the community can rejoice in the justice or symmetry of its practices and the imbalance created by the crime is corrected by the welcome punishment—or so it is written.

That there really were many cooperative victims of executions is highly likely. Conventions of courage before death, and the presence of a minister who, with divine authority, encouraged humble submission, certainly played a role in many of the displays of proper behavior that have been reported—and not all of these reports need be doubted or doubted in their entirety. There were also more practical considerations: often a reduction of sentence (fewer torments) or even a reprieve was announced on the scaffold itself and many of the well-behaved may have been hoping for such beneficence.¹⁶

Another expectation faced by organizers of execution, those *other* dramatists, is that the spectacle shall be conducted so as to edify the citizens whose laws are being enforced, whether this be through public display or concealment—again, according to the requirements of a particular punishing community. Whereas it was always difficult to maintain the solemnity that should attend the ultimate punishment at public executions—which tended to become unedifying folk festivals with booths and refreshments—the indoor execution before a few representative witnesses runs the risk of escaping public notice and becoming an abstraction or a non-event. In both cases, the pedagogical or patriotic intent of the event can be poorly transmitted or falsely received and *Wirkung* subverted.

There are many other considerations in the planning and enacting of capital punishment, but even this briefest of surveys makes it obvious that the multiple requirements and the grave nature of the occasion create numerous opportunities for logistical error, miscalculation, noncooperation, and improper presentation at an execution. However, the real problem with the proper conduct of such an event lies in the nature of the act itself and its forced confrontation of the ideal with the physical real. The point of execution is to "execute" The Law, *as written*, on the human body, an utterly impossible conjunction of text and organism. Kafka addresses this problem brilliantly in "In der Strafkolonie" [In the Penal Colony] (1919), where the myth that powers the remnants of the "old regime" is precisely this ideal of the harmony of literal/legible law and living/dying body. The victims of the amazing apparatus will, during the course of many hours, *feel* the law, namely the commandment they have transgressed, being *written* on their bodies, a writing they *read* in the experience of their physical pain. Sadly, for those who hold such ideals of punishment, a demonstration in the narrative present shows that the machine's "writing" is not only illegible to all, but that it is actually a savage and sloppy impalement. The execution of Kafka's officer is yet another botched execution, but it is set up to question the ideals behind the execution ritual: "kein Zeichen der versprochenen Erlösung war zu entdecken" [no sign of the promised redemption could be discovered].¹⁷ That is, the word was not made flesh. This failed redemption—a failure to *real*-ize the word of the law—is the residue of capital punishment, a practice that has brought the highest legal, moral, and theological ideals to the ritualized killing of a criminal.

Dramatic Composition and Heroic Composure

Mary Stuart, Queen of Scotland, Queen of France, and claimant to the throne of England was a "serial" queen whom the English considered a treasonous pretender and the Scots a murderer. She was beheaded in 1587 in England and her execution, though hastily organized and held indoors, was extremely well documented. It was also badly botched. Not only was the "text," the legal foundation for the judgment that resulted in the death sentence, tainted, but the actual implementation of the sentence was marked by numerous errors. Two moments stand out from among the many accounts of things that went wrong. First of all, the headsman missed her neck with his first blow, but struck the back of her head, failing to kill her. He then struck another blow that almost severed the head and certainly caused or initiated death. But this second swing of the axe left a sinew intact, which the queen's executioner then had to sever with a sawing motion.[18] Thus the deed required three blows, an egregiously shoddy job, especially in light of reports of contemporary public executions, where headsmen were attacked by the crowd if they failed to accomplish their mission with a single blow (van Dülmen, 138). Any headsman would have felt some apprehension before the deed and one can only imagine the pressure on the unhappy executioner of a queen.

The other problem was the grotesque-comical moment when the headsman, according to protocol, held Mary's laboriously severed head aloft to announce that the queen's enemies may perish thus, only to have the head fall to the floor and roll about. Mary had worn a wig or headpiece (accounts vary) and gravity had disengaged the head from its covering, leaving the state's official holding only the covering at this solemn moment (Middendorf, 6).[19] "Thus may perish the Queen's enemies," the text they sought to illustrate with the suspended head of Mary Stuart, became an ironic caption to a frightening scene whose symbolic import escaped the control of its organizers or authors.

Now, I would like to move from this unhappy mixture of ideas and viscera to Schiller's reception of it more than two centuries later. How does Schiller read this scene of gory dismemberment and degraded humanity, which he studied in detail for his play *Maria Stuart*? What does he literally *make* of this event as he writes his historical drama? As one might expect, Schiller, apostle of the human spirit, sometime Kantian, and theoretician of the sublime, fixed on another characteristic of these historical accounts, namely Mary's unwavering courage in the face of insult and execution. By all accounts Mary was calm and dignified throughout her ordeal, weeping briefly when it was made known that she was to be denied the ministrations of a Catholic chaplain and subjected to the admonishments of a Protestant one. She did not acknowledge the justice of her sentence—she maintained that she was neither subject to English law nor guilty according to it—but she also did not resist.

This historical example of regal bearing is reflected and augmented in Schiller's *Maria Stuart* in the overwhelming emphasis on composure or *Fassung*—a strategy that distances his enterprise from the bloody head. This emphasis is so strong that it actually constitutes a competing plot, namely the story of exemplary *Fassung* that frequently supersedes the unfolding of historical events. From Maria's first words, "Fass dich!" [Compose yourself!] (V:15) to the final moment of the play where the stage directions prescribe that Elizabeth *"bezwingt sich und steht mit ruhiger Fassung da"* [masters her emotions and stands there with calm composure] (V:148), readers of *Maria Stuart* are really following a tale of composure—composure being the exercise that suppressed the horror of the queen's execution. Within this story, we find "good" composure, such as that achieved by Maria in her long incarceration—the spiritual benefits of the carceral come into focus[20]—and there is "bad" composure, such as that forced and false composure of political advantage demonstrated by Elizabeth in the stage direction quoted above. Composure is highly dramatized through its loss in the famous scene in the third act where Schiller brings together two formidable queens and has them express surprisingly common and vulgar jealous passions. And finally there is the dramatic suspense built around the issue of composure after the death decree has been dispatched and embodied in the question, "Will the Queen turn away from earthly remedies and accept her terrible fate with composure?"

This latter question is arguably the crux of *Maria Stuart* as drama of the human spirit in conflict with great force or power—the precise circumstances for sublime transcendence.[21] And yet, when this sublime and defining affirmation of humanity occurs, in the solemnly significant moment when Maria Stuart *accepts her fate*, we, the audience, are not present. Only Hanna Kennedy, the nurse, saw this transfiguration, and she only reports her experience in answer to Melvil's question:

> Nahm sie die Todespost mit Fassung auf?
> Man sagt, daß sie nicht vorbereitet war.
> (V:124)

> [Did she receive the news of death with composure?
> They say she was not prepared.]

At Melvil's urging, Hanna launches into a description of what must be the central event of Schiller's play:

> Das war sie nicht. Ganz andre Schrecken warens,
> Die meine Lady ängstigten. Nicht vor dem Tod,
> Vor dem Befreier zitterte Maria.
> —Freiheit war uns verheißen. Diese Nacht
> Versprach uns Mortimer von hier wegzuführen,
> Und zwischen Furcht und Hoffnung, zweifelhaft,
> Ob sie dem kecken Jüngling ihre Ehre
> Und fürstliche Person vertrauen dürfe,
> Erwartete die Königin den Morgen.
> (V:124)

> [She was not prepared. Very different fears
> Troubled My Lady. It was not death,
> But the liberator who caused Maria to tremble.
> —Freedom was promised to us. This very evening
> Mortimer promised to spirit us away,
> And between fear and hope, unsure
> Whether she could entrust her honor
> And her royal person to the impudent youth,
> Did our queen await the morning.]

According to this account, Maria was preoccupied with the problems she would face once the unstable Mortimer had freed her. She, who loved Lord Leicester, would have to deal with Mortimer's indecent advances and protect her honor and her abstract "fürstliche Person" from concrete physical violation. Hanna continues:

> —Da wird ein Auflauf in dem Schloß, ein Pochen
> Schreckt unser Ohr und vieler Hämmer Schlag,
> Wir glauben die Befreier zu vernehmen,
> Die Hoffnung winkt, der süße Trieb des Lebens
> Wacht unwillkürlich, allgewaltig auf—
> Da öffnet sich die Tür—Sir Paulet ists,
> Der uns verkündet—daß—die Zimmerer
> Zu unsern Füßen das Gerüst aufschlagen!
> (V:124–25)

> [Suddenly there is a tumult in the castle, a knocking
> Startles our ear and the sound of many hammers.
> We believe it is the liberator,
> Hope beckons, the sweet will to live
> Awakens spontaneously, powerfully—
> Then the door opens—It is Sir Paulet
> Who announces—that—the carpenters
> Are now building the scaffold beneath our feet.]

Melvil then asks the all-important question, "Wie ertrug Maria diesen fürchterlichen Wechsel?" [How did Maria endure this terrible reversal?], and Hanna, after pausing to renew her *Fassung*, delivers her most important lines:

> (*nach einer Pause, worin sie sich wieder etwas gefaßt hat*)
> Man löst sich nicht allmählich von dem Leben!
> Mit einem Mal, schnell augenblicklich muß
> Der Tausch geschehen zwischen Zeitlichem
> Und Ewigem, und Gott gewährte meiner Lady
> In diesem Augenblick, der Erde Hoffnung
> Zurück zu stoßen mit entschloßner Seele,
> Und glaubenvoll den Himmel zu ergreifen.
> Kein Merkmal bleicher Furcht, kein Wort der Klage
> Entehrte meine Königin—
> (V:125)

> [(*after a pause in which she has composed herself somewhat*)
> One does not part with life gradually
> The exchange of temporal for eternal

Must happen all at once, quickly, in a moment,
And God granted My Lady the strength
In this moment to renounce earthly hopes with a resolute soul
And to reach to Heaven with faith.
No sign of pale fear, no word of lament
Dishonored my queen.]

Thus Schiller secures the dignity of the human spirit—threatened by the bloody head—in Maria's calm acceptance of her impending death. A heroic and redemptive revision of mentality has occurred. Mary overcomes the hatred and ambition she exhibited in her altercation with Elizabeth—reversing the fight scene, with its emphasis on sexual-corporeal behavior—and she triumphs over force and power by *willing* their ends. As Schiller has famously written in "Über das Erhabene" [About the Sublime], "Eine Gewalt, dem Begriffe nach zu vernichten, heißt aber nichts anders, als sich derselben freiwillig unterwerfen" [To annihilate the very concept of a force means nothing other than to freely submit to it] (VIII:823). But Schiller has conspicuously refused to display this climactic moment or even to allow Maria to describe the experience. A useful explanation for this undramatic behavior is provided by a recent essay on Schiller and the sublime, which highlights Schiller's revisions of the Kantian sublime in "Über das Pathetische" [About the Pathetic][22] (de Man's discussion of the same maneuver was linked to an earlier version, "Vom Erhabenen," [On the Sublime] AI:134ff.). Where Kant contended in the third critique that the sublime, much like the deities of certain cultures, is *undarstellbar* [not representable or depictable], Schiller expands the category of *Undarstellbarkeit* [unrepresentability] to ideas in general and he discourses on the impossibility of depicting ideas in a positive or straightforward manner in "Über das Pathetische":

Nun sind aber Ideen im eigentlichen Sinn und positiv nicht darzustellen, weil ihnen nichts in der Anschauung entsprechen kann. Aber negativ und indirekt sind sie allerdings darzustellen, wenn in der Anschauung etwas gegeben wird, wozu wir die Bedingungen in der *Natur* vergebens aufsuchen. Jede Erscheinung, deren letzter Grund aus der Sinnenwelt nicht kann abgeleitet werden, ist die indirekte Darstellung des Übersinnlichen. (VIII:430)

2: WHAT DOES THE DRAMATIC STAGE ACTUALLY DO? 49

[Now, ideas are not susceptible to representation in the actual sense and in positive terms because there is nothing in the visible world that corresponds to them. But they can be represented in negative terms and indirectly if there is in the realm of appearances something for which we cannot find the conditions in nature. Every appearance whose final cause cannot be grounded in the sensual world is the indirect representation of the supersensuous.]

Where composure, real or forced, can be depicted dramatically—as the stage direction prescribing calm composure suggests—the ideation of relinquishing hope, revising one's vision of the future, and courageously facing the worst, which results in composure, is *undarstellbar*, subject only to indirect illustration. We do not see the process of sublime transformation because Schiller, even as dramatic practitioner, observes the prohibition he cited in his essay and refuses to allow the physical real of the stage to represent or even stand in for the moment of spiritual triumph—even though, or perhaps because, this moment is the moral high point of his drama. Ideas and ideals do not become "flesh" on the stage according to conventional codes of representation. Schiller's spectator must hear (or read) and interpret the nurse's report.

Before returning to execution and Mary/Maria Stuart's execution, both of which, the general practice and the particular instance, are straightforward or direct attempts to depict/*darstellen* the written law on the human body, I want to examine a related misapprehension of the physical-corporeal and its noncorrespondence with the ideal or linguistic-figural.

While giving directions for the disposition of her property, Schiller's Maria includes instructions for the disposition of her heart and these instructions blur the line between the figurative use of language, in tropes of affection and longing, and the physical referent of the word used in these tropes, namely the organ that pumps blood:

> Und weil mein Leichnam
> Nicht in geweihter Erde ruhen soll,
> So dulde man, daß dieser treue Diener [Melvil]
> Mein Herz nach Frankreich bringe zu den Meinen.
> —Ach! Es war immer dort! (V:138)
>
> [And since my body
> Shall not rest in consecrated earth,

> Please allow this faithful servant
> To bring my heart to France to my loved ones.
> Ah! It has always been there.]

Schiller's dramatic figure, who is about to undergo a ritual designed to make edifying spectacle of her death, directs that Melvil have the heart removed from her body and that he transport it to France where "it" has always been. But can this "it" unite the physical object and the figural functions of the word for which it stands? To make literal (and extra-literal) flesh of the word (heart) in this particular way is to partake of the slippery relay between thing and idea/word that governs capital punishment. The dramatic figure represents a body with a blood pump and this (theatrical representation of a) physical being proposes that her physical blood pump be joined with the metaphor for her affection, a direct reification or *Darstellung* of figural speech that, if enacted (or literally imagined) would destroy the idea, just as Mary Stuart's rolling head disrupted the spectacle of justice.

Interestingly, Queen Elizabeth, Maria's most powerful enemy, does not make such errors in her negotiations with language, but rather controls signification and bends it to her needs. Her entrapment of Davison, who does and does not do her will with the death warrant, is one example. Another, more compact, instance is her manipulation of the symbolic value of the ring as a sign (linguistic and physical) of a significant bond—here that of betrothal. When pressed by the French diplomats for some more concrete or definite indication of her intention to marry the Duke of Anjou, she presents Bellievre with a ring:

> Hat die Königin doch nichts
> Voraus vor dem gemeinen Bürgerweibe!
> Das gleiche Zeichen weist auf gleiche Pflicht,
> Auf gleiche Dienstbarkeit—Der Ring macht Ehen,
> Und Ringe sinds, die eine Kette machen.
> —Bringt seiner Hoheit dies Geschenk. Es ist
> Noch keine Kette, bindet mich noch nicht,
> Doch kann ein Reif draus werden, der mich bindet. (V:49)

> [Does not a queen
> Have some advantage over a common citizen's wife!
> The same sign indicates the same duties,

The same servitude—The ring makes marriages
And it is rings that form a chain.
—Bring this gift to His Highness. It is
Not yet a chain and it does not bind me,
But it could become a circlet that does bind me.]

The Queen of England makes a semiotic adjustment that alters the character of an ancient token of betrothal and marriage—a token ring that does not betoken what rings betoken, but could do so sometime in the future—and she does so with full awareness of the vulnerability of "fixed" signification before sovereign power. The state and its sovereign can transgress and modify linguistic signification—as did that legendary naked emperor who claimed to be wearing new clothes—but Maria, the now-empty vessel of sovereign power, has no such prerogative. As condemned, she can only submit to Elizabeth's written will. Elizabeth and her subjects will attempt to depict (contrived) ideals of justice on the (composed) body of Maria Stuart.

SCHILLER'S *UNDARSTELLUNG* OF MARIA'S EXECUTION

As the moment arrives for Maria Stuart to face her death, she exits the stage, a model of composure, leaving behind the rapidly de-composing Leicester, who becomes the audience's only link to the scene of her execution. Dorothea von Mücke views this substitution of the increasingly hysterical lord for the calmly heroic queen as a castration-for-decapitation substitution (von Mücke, 228), and thus makes interesting sense of Leicester's softening against his own stated resolve, "Mit einem ehrnen Harnisch angetan / Sei deine Brust, die Stirne sei ein Felsen" [Let your breast be secured by an iron plate, your brow a rock] (V:141).

This replacement of the victim with her former lover is also a very conspicuously overdetermined instance of the "indirect representation of the supersensuous" as it conceals and effaces the scene of execution, offering only a distraught reporter of that scene, *who refuses to look at what he is reporting*:

> Ich kann, ich kann das Schreckliche nicht schauen,
> Kann sie nicht sterben sehen—Horch! Was war das?
> Sie sind schon unten—Unter meinen Füßen

> Bereitet sich das fürchterliche Werk.
> Ich höre Stimmen . . .
> (V:141)
>
> [I can't, can't look at the horror,
> Can't watch her die—Hark! What was that?
> They are already below—Under my feet
> The terrible deed is being prepared.
> I hear voices . . .]

Leicester will relay what he *hears* from below, but inasmuch as Hannah and Maria have recently, from the same position, mistaken the sounds of the scaffold being erected for a rescue attempt by Mortimer and his cohorts, it seems, at the very least, that acoustics are not good in Fotheringay Castle. Furthermore, Leicester's perception is compromised by his hysteria and, ultimately, when he reports elements of the scene that could not possibly be heard, "Sie wird entkleidet. . . . Sie kniet aufs Kissen—legt das Haupt" [She is being undressed, kneeling on the pillow, laying her head] (V:142), it becomes clear that he is either imagining or hallucinating the scene he relays to the audience. If Hannah's report of Maria's transformation qualifies as indirect depiction of an idea, that of the human spirit overwhelming force by willing its ends, then Leicester's evocation of her execution is something else again. Leicester labors at a far greater remove from his object and his own struggle supersedes the event he strives both to perceive and ignore. The indirect depiction in Hannah's crucial speech yields to a qualitatively different—though not unrelated—*Undarstellung* or "undepiction" in Leicester's obfuscating hysteria. What happens "below" is not accessible even to the witness whose fabulations echo in its place. The bloody execution of Mary Stuart, that terrible display of sovereign power's gory failure to inscribe its law onto the "queen's enemy," is refined into an erasure in Schiller's play. All that emerges here is the trace of regal composure that we recognize in its opposite, the ravings of a madman.

Obviously, one cannot expect a naturalistic recreation of such a bloody historical scene in a classical play, but Schiller appears to be addressing complications beyond propriety and the logistics of the dramatic stage. If ideas are undepictable in drama or subject only to indirect depiction, then a state-ordered execution presents a particularly difficult dramatic problem since the procedure understands itself as a drama or pageant depicting the triumph of ideas or ideals of justice over the criminal, upon whose body these ideas and ideals are to be inscribed. The lawgivers labor to realize in their production what the dramatist knows to be futile in his, and the latter opts to conceal the execution. He does not do so in order to "leave it to the imagination" of spectators who know the history—as might be the practice in other plays by other playwrights. On the contrary, as noted above, Leicester's hysterical reporting confounds audience access to the event he believes he is hearing. That event, undepicted and improbably distorted, recedes from viewer consciousness and makes way for a final impression of a composed queen with her head firmly attached. Schiller circumvents the gore, and succeeds in segregating ideas from viscera, even when confronting a legal tradition that merges them.

This strategy of blocking access to the penal pageant, of nullifying the symbolic value of an event that, historically, failed in every respect but that of killing the queen, may well have been part of the project Schiller suggests with *Schaubühne*, namely that of humanizing rulers, of sending *effective* dramatic messages "into the courts of law and, even further, into the hearts of our rulers." It is unknown whether the powerful ever shuddered at the undepiction of Maria Stuart's decapitation, or, as Schiller put it, whether the streets were much safer after Karl's Moor's unfortunate demise, but *Wirkung* cannot be measured in crime statistics or even in degrees of penal reform. There is no reliable record of this type of effect, influence, or control. What does remain is the powerful critique of a practice that seeks to realize ideals by making visceral interventions in living physical bodies.[23] At the very least, Schiller has defended the borders of his theatrical state, where symbolism is at home, and at the very most he has convincingly illustrated the fundamental incompatibility of ideals of justice and symmetry ("If he has murdered, then he must die") and the violence applied in their name.

3
"Die Schande nimmt ab mit der wachsenden Sünde": Early Schiller and the Charisma of the Criminal

THERE IS ONE FIGURE IN SCHILLER'S DRAMATIC WORK WHO IS ACTUally executed in full view of the hypothetical spectators and that is the Moor, Muley Hassan, in the first version of *Die Verschwörung des Fiesko zu Genua* [The Conspiracy of Fiesco in Genua] (1783). *Fiesko*'s Moor, whom I will refer to as Hassan to avoid any confusion with the Moor brothers who are also the subject of this segment, dies by means of a procedure that is almost the exact inverse of Maria Stuart's resonant and undepicted death. In Schiller's classical play, every aspect of Maria Stuart's exit is carefully prepared and complicated arguments for and against her punishment accompany the action, as does the hope for her survival. In *Fiesko*, the much earlier *Sturm und Drang* drama, the questions of whether and why are not as weighty and the deliberations are minimal. Throughout the play, Hassan appears to be marked for an execution that he keeps escaping. He announces in the fourth act, "In Italien wächst mein Strick nicht. Ich muss ihn anderswo suchen" [My gallows do not grow in Italy. I must seek them elsewhere] (II:410). *Galgen* and *Strick* or gallows and noose have already become something of a *leitmotiv* for Hassan, the only stable attributes of a very protean and ultimately incomplete figure—a criminal without psychology—as he moves through the intrigues of the Genoese succession. He manages to avoid his fate through most of the play by means of extraordinary luck and Fiesko's complex understanding of crime and the punishments it merits. After Hassan has attempted to stab him, Fiesko tells him that he has *earned* his execution, "Den Galgen hast du verdient" (II:337), though he does not intend to pay his debt and reinstate the pre-crime symmetry by punishing this offense. So the would-be assassin collects the fee he has not earned and dodges the retribution he deserves and this lopsidedness persists even after his punishment arrives. Hassan's punishment is at best tangential to his major crimes and not at all a corrective to the imbalance of earned and unearned deserts. Maria, on the other hand, believes that she has not earned the punishment she is scheduled to receive, but she accepts it as indirect retribution for the murder of her second husband, Darnley. Hassan will die for crimes other than attempted murder or the treachery he commits by informing Andreas Doria of the revolutionaries' plot. His gallows and his noose do indeed "grow" in Italy, and the checkered career of Hassan, with its steady progress toward the gallows, does in a sense foreshadow the movement of *Maria Stuart* with its penal teleology.

The end of the Hassan subplot arrives suddenly when the figure actually commits a crime for which Fiesko is willing to punish him, the same combination of larceny and arson for which Karl Moor and his band are known, but not punished. In this case, Fiesko invokes the laws of the state as authority for formal punishment: "Deine Verräterei ging dir hin, weil sie mich traf. Auf Mordbrennereien steht der Strick" [Your treachery was tolerated because it was directed against me. But for arson and murder, the punishment is hanging] (II:429). For an *oeuvre* that, as we will see, denies, protests, conceals, and debases punishment as an inadequate answer to the complex human behavior that is classified as crime, what follows is rather startling. In response to Fiesko's command, soldiers haul Hassan off and hang him right onstage: *"ab mit Soldaten, die ihn in einiger Entfernung aufhenken"* [*away with soldiers who hang him at a distance*] (II:430). The event we see is in no way as significant as the event we don't see in *Maria Stuart*. It proceeds without the ritual trappings of Mary Stuart's death and its visibility is compromised by its brevity and the marginality of the victim. With regard to marginality and minority status, the irony is obvious and the findings of the United States Supreme Court in *Furman vs. Georgia* concerning race and class and their effect on the application of capital punishment could also be extended to Schiller's stage/state—though class at least has been a core value of drama historically. Nonetheless, we the spectators have witnessed an execution. Schiller has displayed—just this once—the process by which criminals are deprived of life in retribution for their crimes. Hassan would be a very minor Maria, if one were tempted to develop that comparison, and why his case should result in such a demonstration is not clear, though allowing the audience to witness the event may have been an efficient way to communicate the certainty of his removal in a play rife with false reports and intrigue and in the case of a figure who seems to survive everything. There is certainly no deep reflection on the nature of capital punishment, unless it be Fiesko's distinction between offenses that he can forgive and ones that the state must punish, yet the demonstration occurs and the spectators are its witnesses.

Before looking at the various rankings of criminal magnitude that appear in Schiller's work, I want to mention the one other execution that Schiller has described in print. Despite rather detailed description, it falls closer to the undepicted death of Maria Stuart than to the visible enactment of Hassan's demise. In "Des Grafen Lamoral von Egmont Leben und Tod" [The Life and Death of Count Lamoral of Egmont], a *Thalia* piece from 1789, Schiller provides a brief account of the events leading up to Egmont's death in 1568. Not unlike Leicester, listening and interpreting the sounds of Maria's execution, Schiller the historian gives a slightly incomplete account of the procedure:

> Da biß er die Zähne zusammen, warf seinen Mantel und Nachtrock nieder, kniete auf das Kissen, und schickte sich zum letzten Gebet an. Der Bischof ließ ihn das Krucifix küssen und gab ihm die letzte Oelung, worauf ihm der Graf ein Zeichen gab, ihn zu verlassen. Er zog alsdann eine seidene Mütze über die Augen und erwartete den Streich—Über den Leichnam und das fließende Blut wurde sogleich ein schwarzes Tuch geworfen. (VI:407)

> [He clenched his teeth, threw his coat and gown down, knelt on the pillow and began his final prayer. The bishop let him kiss the crucifix and gave him the last anointment, and then the count gave him the sign to withdraw. He then pulled a silk cap over his eyes and awaited the blow—A black cloth was immediately thrown over the corpse and the flowing blood.]

Within the space of the hyphen, the *Strich* following *Streich* or blow, the *gestrichene Streich* [elided blow] must be assumed or imagined since there is no other logical link to the bleeding corpse that ensues. The blow that caused death, the central moment of the execution is elided and only the result, the visceral echo of that blow confirms its occurrence.[1] If we look at these three examples pulled from various texts and from various times, Hassan's enacted death from 1783, Egmont's graciously elided beheading from 1789 and Maria Stuart's elaborately effaced execution from 1801, we encounter three very different methods of communicating the fact of someone's being put to death. There does appear to be a movement from the obvious to the artful and that movement from crass, ordinary, and racialized victim strung up in plain sight to a member of the nobility expiring in discreet hyphenated silence, to the elaborate undepiction of the execution of royalty shows at the very least an awareness of rank, and a respect for greatness and it is also these qualities that characterize Schiller's apprehension of the possible variety of crimes, to which we now turn.

Not only does Muley Hassan bear the distinction of being the only Schillerian figure to be capitally punished onstage, but he also serves as a spokesperson—one of several—for a hierarchy or taxonomy of crime that figures prominently in early Schiller's reflections on human behavior and the merits of punishment. During his first conversation with Fiesko, Hassan lays out four different "Spitzbubenzünfte" [villains' guilds] in order of increasing merit. I enumerate them in somewhat abbreviated form below:

[1] ... das verächtliche Heer der langen Finger. Ein elend Gewerb, das keinen großen Mann ausbrütet ... und führt—höchstens zum Galgen

[2]. ... Spionen. ... denen die großen ein Ohr leihen, wo sie ihre Allwissenheit holen, die sich wie Blutigel in Seelen einbeißen, das Gift aus dem Herzen schliefen, und an die Behörde speien

[3]. ... Meuter, Giftmischer, und alle, die ihren Mann lange hinhalten, und aus dem Hinterhalt fassen. ... Hier tut die Gerechtigkeit schon etwas übriges, strickt ihre Knöchel aufs Rad, und pflanzt ihre Schlauköpfe auf Spieße

[4]. ... Männer *in Hitze* die ihren Mann zwischen 4 Mauern aufsuchen, durch die Gefahr eine Bahn sich hauen, ihm gerade zu Leib gehen, mit dem ersten Gruß ihm den Großdank für den zweiten ersparen. ... Man nennt sie nur die Extrapost der Hölle. (II:338)

[1. the despicable hordes of the long fingers. A miserable profession that never produced a great man and leads at the very best to the gallows.

2. Spies . . . to whom the great lend an ear and gain their omniscience, who gnaw into the soul like leeches, take poison from the heart and spit it out to the authorities.

3. Mutineers, poisoners, and all of those who bide their time with their victim and ambush him. . . . Here justice supplements their punishment, binds their ankles to the wheel, and plants their clever heads on pikes.

4. Men in a state of passion who seek their victim between four walls, hack their way through the danger, approach him directly, and with the first greeting spare him the trouble of a second. . . . One calls them the special delivery from Hell].

Hassan's quirky catalog contains the two major categories that inhabit Schiller's thinking and also reflect contemporary cultural assessments: the abject thief, identified as the practitioner of a miserable trade that has never produced a great man, and the more exalted murderer, who exhibits passion and daring during the performance of his task. Hassan's account is much more elaborate and somewhat more nuanced than others we will encounter and he even prescribes or describes the punishments adhering to the various graded levels of criminal activity. But this is only one of many statements by Schillerian figures and Schiller himself seeking to establish the ascending magnitude of crimes. This evaluative taxonomy is important for any state or judiciary but I am using "magnitude" in a double sense, both as an indicator of the level of malefaction and as a mark of the greatness of the action itself, regardless of criminal content. The arc of greatness in action intersects that of magnitude of crime and the figure of Hassan, the petty thief and spy who fails to murder, contrasts accordingly with that of Fiesko, whose historical predecessor was described by Rousseau and cited by Schiller as a sublime criminal (II:1150). As Fiesko notes in some of his most famous lines:

> Es ist schimpflich eine Börse zu leeren—es ist frech, eine Million zu veruntreuen, aber es ist namenlos gross eine Krone zu stehlen. Die Schande nimmt ab mit der wachsenden Sünde. (II:381)

[It is disgraceful to empty a purse, it is brazen to embezzle a million, but it is immeasurably great to steal a crown. The shame decreases as the magnitude of the crime increases.]

In yet another recital of these distinctions, Gianettino Doria, corrupt politician, enemy of Fiesko, and rapist of Bertha, comments on the reduced incidence of reprisal for the perpetrator of high-magnitude crimes:

> Alltagsverbrechen bringen das Blut des Beleidigten in Wallung, und alles kann der Mensch. Außerordentliche Frevel machen es vor Schrecken gefrieren, und der Mensch ist nichts. (II:395)
>
> [Everyday crimes make the victim's blood surge, and he can do anything. But extraordinary crimes cause the victim's blood to freeze and he can do nothing.]

Both Fiesko and Gianettino convey additional dimensions of the taxonomy of crime,[2] and collectively they underscore the contrast between the wretched agent of petty crime, who is generally despised, and the awe-inspiring nature of the serious criminal. Schiller's *Fiesko*, with its cluttered romantic and political agendas, is also a dissertation on crime, a reasoned consideration of the types and levels of criminal activity and the punishments that adhere to them. As for Fiesko's just deserts and the possible conclusions one could draw from reflecting on the end of one who plotted to overthrow the government, this is the closest Schiller comes to hypertext composition. The play exists in several published and stage versions and the diligent philologist can choose from a variety of endings: Fiesko may drown; he may be stabbed to death; or he may survive and renounce power (II:1215). Gerhard Kluge even mentions an undocumented version in which Fiesko stabs himself (II:1215). Such is the range of poetic justices for the man who sought to rule Genoa and *Fiesko*, though rich in ideas about crime, seems relatively indifferent to the punishment it does not even bother to conceal.

Man wird meinen Mordbrenner bewundern, ja fast sogar lieben

Die Räuber is a play that took shape as it was being concealed from the panoptical gaze of Karl Eugen, the supreme father, and it exhibits a sustained patricidal impulse, though in terms of actual depiction, this most serious of all crimes is obfuscated through the various *Scheintode* that Old Moor experiences and the rather sudden manner of his actual death in a moment when he does not command the spectators' attention. *Die Räuber* is ultimately the chronicle of a painful and disorienting lack (of a strong father, of heroic models, of order itself),[3] but it features a (compensatory?) Baroque plenitude of narratives and events, of crimes, and dire experiences.[4] The simultaneity of plots and intrigues, of contradictory reports and competing versions of reality in *Räuber* is enabled by Schiller's effacement of the liminal. This gesture ensures that there is almost no in-betweenness in the play, no transitional phases and no recognizable borders between values and states of being and their traditional opposites. There is furthermore no clear sense of where things begin and end. Figures are good and bad, dead and alive, exalted and despised, loved and hated, all in vivid synchronic detail. Not only does the father appear to have died and remained alive, but Franz writes letters creating alternative accounts of events that take on a life of their own. Hermann gives conflicting reports about Karl's living and dying, and we are also told that Roller was killed, only to hear of his dramatic rescue from the gallows. Nor do these tales apply to stable objects. There are doublings and triplings of characters and subplots, such as the Karl–Amalia, Graf von Brand–Amalia, Kosinsky–Amalia repetitions with almost no distinctions among them so that even the action is fluidly dispersed among the actors, such that it often seems not to matter who carried out particular actions or even that they were actually carried out. Similarly with sensations and emotions, Karl especially, but also his father and companions, move from the extremes of one emotion to the extremes of the opposite one without transition—sometimes sincerely and sometimes deceptively. Almost anything is possible within the anti-liminal logic of the play and it is in this drama, with its permeability and free play of extremes and absolutes, incongruities and opposites, that Schiller establishes the figure of the sublime criminal. As he notes in the *Selbstrezension* [auto-review or review of his own play], "Wenigstens dünkt mich dass solche [erhabene Verbrecher] bedürfen notwendig eine eben so grosse Dosis von Geisteskraft, als die erhabene Tugendhafte, und die Empfindung des Abscheus vertrage sich nicht selten mit Anteil und Bewunderung" [At least it seems to me that such figures (sublime criminals) require a dose of spiritual strength equivalent to that of the sublime virtuous figures and that feelings of repulsion cohabit well with interest and admiration] (II:296). Schiller prepares the ground for the introduction of this contradictory type by shredding dichotomies, equalizing opposites, and intervening in established social and theatrical values, so that his audience might react with love or near-love to the figure of a plundering, arsonous, and larcenous murderer.

Actions in *Die Räuber* are also subject to an anti-liminal logic that merges sublimity and criminality. They are good and bad, legal and illegal simultaneously and crime is both easy and difficult to identify, inasmuch as the particular deeds bear the labels of recognizable crimes, but are committed by agents we are encouraged not to identify as criminal. If Hölderlin's standard holds and crimes are those actions that draw punishment, then crime is very rare in this crime tale about robbers. Furthermore, transgressions are always tempered by "greatness" and the magnitude of the deed they represent. This scale of valuation, though valid and controlling is unstable and not at all as transparent as the reversals of crime-benevolence represented by Robin Hood, though he is also part of the play's conceptual apparatus. This is an "Umwertung *einiger* Werte" [transvaluation of *some* values], to adapt Nietzsche's phrase, and the revaluation is relative to circumstances and agent. This results in part from the instability of the prevailing "order," the waning ethos of the state and loss of confidence in its ability to apply and enforce its own laws.[5] *Fiesko* also unfolds against the background of a discredited state, but here the state is at least a palpable entity, whereas *Räuber* offers only the confused times, the vague agencies that oppose the robbers, and the strange father who allows Karl's patrimony to be so easily embezzled. These instabilities and absences authorize an unfocused resistance in the forgivable or unpunishable crimes of the robbers.

Schiller was quite obviously aware of the slipperiness of the value structure of his play, because he did a great deal of "explaining" when it appeared and for several years thereafter, in a series of companion texts. There is an official preface, there is a suppressed preface, and there is the *Selbstrezension*, a long anonymous review of the play in which Schiller dons the mask of a drama critic to record what we might regard as an ideal reception of the piece. These documents form part of the play's primary apparatus and there are in addition numerous passages in unrelated essays that address the values of *Die Räuber* and the figures of Franz and Karl. This is not a play that speaks for itself. It comes to us embedded in explanation and within this mass of authorial commentary, there is repeated reference to the hierarchy of crime and especially to the thief-murderer dichotomy.

But the commentary actually begins within the play. As the robbers close in on Franz Moor and he considers his options for eternity, he tries to make a case for divine mercy based on the following rationale: "Ich bin kein gemeiner Mörder gewesen, mein Herrgott—hab mich nie mit Kleinigkeiten abgegeben, mein Herrgott—" [I have never been an ordinary murderer, Lord God, I have never involved myself with trivial matters, Lord God]. The servant Daniel then notes that "Auch seine Gebete werden zu Sünden" [Even his prayers become sins] (II:150) and thus effectively characterizes Franz's argument as flawed, unlikely to persuade the intended recipient. This argument, however, when applied to Karl *is* intended to be persuasive and it is apparently the foundation of the play that glorifies Karl *because* of a great expansive nature that enables him to lead a band of robbers in the Bohemian woods. As Alan Leidner notes, the audience is situated to *forgive* Karl,[6] that is not to "punish" him for his crimes, as God will not forgive Franz. The argument for the magnitude of crimes committed will not work for the abjected Franz, who is not only not a common murderer, he is not a murderer at all, as the *Selbstrezensent* confirms: "Franz [ist] zu feig einen Mord auszuführen" [Franz is too cowardly to accomplish a murder] (II:295). Franz has after all attempted to kill his father—without success, though he is unaware of this—in order to secure the patrimony he has stolen from Karl. But if read consistently with certain other passages in *Die Räuber* and elsewhere in Schiller's early work, Franz's lack of majesty and his miserable end may just be the result of his success as a thief and his failure as a murderer. His brother Karl, the real patricide and mass murderer, registers incomparably higher on the scale of charisma and admiration and emerges a great man, where the relatively harmless Franz becomes the object of deepest disdain. He remains a thief, someone who steals surreptitiously for his own gain, and does not even measure up to the robbers who, dynamic and courageous, steal openly for themselves and others by means of force.

Schiller's early works, both dramatic and theoretical, betray a preoccupation with "greatness," an amplitude of soul or spirit that expresses itself in actions that we might not ordinarily regard as great. Janz writes of *Fiesko*, "das Thema dieses Historiendramas ist Fiescos Größe, die sich selbst absolut setzende Subjektivität, die sich über der 'Menschlichkeit reissenden Strudel' erhaben weiss" [The theme of this historical drama is Fiesco's greatness, that subjectivity that positions itself as absolute, that knows itself to be elevated above the torrential whirl of humanity].[7] With minor adjustments, such a description would also apply to Karl Moor. Both protagonists appear to have that certain something that raises them above the common herd and in both cases, Schiller does an awkward and incomplete job of establishing this quality, relying on the audience to suspend disbelief to an uncommon degree in order to enjoy watching great men do whatever it is they do. In the case of Fiesko and Karl Moor, what they do is commit crimes and, though they themselves bluster grandiosely and other figures talk up their greatness, their crimes and the nature of these crimes are the actual expression of their personal magnitude.

In both plays and in theoretical commentaries written by Schiller in the 1780s and early 1790s, the occasional attempts to *specify* what kinds of (mis)deeds identify a great man involve, as noted, repetitive reference to the juxtaposition of theft and murder. This trope and the fact of its frequent reprisal as an explanation of the difference between great and common men (or what they do) are crucial to an understanding of young Schiller's awkwardly elusive concept of greatness. As the *Selbstrezensent* writes:

> Unterdessen hatte sich Karl Moor an der Spitze seiner Rotte durch außerordentliche Streiche weit und breit ruchtbar und furchtbar gemacht. Sein Anhang wuchs, seine Güter stiegen, sein Dolch schröckte die kleinere Tyrannen, und autorisierten Beutelschneider, aber sein Beutel war der Notdurft geöffnet, und sein Arm zu ihrem Schütze bereit. Niemals erlaubte er sich spitzbübische Diebery, sein Weg ging gerade, er hätte sich bälder zehn Mordtaten als einen einzigen Diebstahl vergeben. (II:294)

> [In the meantime, Karl Moor had made himself notorious and feared through the extraordinary deeds he performed at the head of his rob-

ber band. His following grew, his wealth increased, his dagger terrified the petty tyrants and their authorized thieves, but his purse was always open to the needy, and his arm ready to protect them. Never did he allow himself a sneaky theft, his path was straight, he would have forgiven himself ten murders before he could have countenanced a single act of theft.]

Given the context, Schiller's anonymous review of his own play, the characterization of Karl is enlightening—as is the urgency with which he is established as non-thief, that is as someone who openly takes the property of others (robber) but would never do so surreptitiously (thief). That he could forgive himself multiple murders, though not a lowly theft, reflects not only the dismal status of thievery, but the dramatic value of serious crime. In the "Unterdrückte Vorrede" [suppressed preface] to the 1781 version, Schiller made the claims that "man wird meinen Mordbrenner bewundern, ja fast sogar lieben" [they will admire my incendiary, indeed they will even love him] and that only the rabble would find an "Apologie des Lasters" [a justification of vice] in his drama (II:163). Even a finding of vice is relative to character. Schiller needs the charisma of crime—somewhat tempered by the repeated imprecations against the times and the implications that law has not served its true purpose—to explore the kinds of great deeds that challenge order and define great men. As Leidner has convincingly argued, it was the communal urge to forgive Karl that accounted for the success of the play—once forgiven, we may assume, mass murder may lose its sting and remain as a most amazing accomplishment. As Schiller notes in "Über das Pathetische," "Der nämliche Gegenstand kann uns in der moralischen Schätzung mißfallen, und in der ästhetischen sehr anziehend für uns sein" [The same subject can offend our moral sensibilities and yet be very attractive to us in an aesthetic context] (VIII:442). Or, as he says of himself in the *Selbstrezension*: "So gewiss ich sein Werk verstehe, muss er starke Dosen in Emeticis eben so lieben als in Aestheticis" [If I understand his play, he must like strong doses of emetics as well as of aesthetics] (II:311).[8]

The aesthetic and emetic aspects of murder and crime are given more thorough treatment in the brief "Gedanken über den Gebrauch des Gemeinen und Niedrigen in der Kunst" [Thoughts on the Use of the Common and the Base in Art], which was published in 1802, but most likely written in the early 1790s (VIII:1369). Here Schiller reprises the theft-murder contrast and makes it much more practically explicit than the overwrought rhetoric of the *Selbstrezension* would allow.

> Stehlen z.B. ist etwas absolut niedriges, und was auch unser Herz zur Entschuldigung eines Diebes vorbringen kann ... so ist ihm ein unauslöschliches Brandmal aufgedrückt, und ästhetisch bleibt er immer ein niedriger Gegenstand. Der Geschmack verzeiht hier noch weniger als die Moral, und sein Richterstuhl ist strenger; weil ein ästhetischer Gegenstand auch für alle Nebenideen verantwortlich ist, die auf seine Veranlassung in uns rege gemacht werden. ... Wird aber dieser Mensch zugleich Mörder, so ist er zwar moralisch noch viel verwerflicher; aber ästhetisch wird er dadurch wieder um einen Grad brauchbarer. (VIII:455–56, Schiller's emphasis)[9]

> To steal, for example, is something *absolutely base,* and in spite of the reasons our heart suggests to excuse a thief, there is an indelible brand on him and he will always be a base object *aesthetically.* Taste pardons far less than morality and its judgment is stricter because an aesthetic object is also responsible for subsidiary ideas that are activated in us at its instigation. ... But if this person is also a *murderer,* then he is morally much more reprehensible, but *aesthetically* he becomes a degree more useful.]

If Franz is a thief (of patrimony) and Karl a murderer (of father, beloved, and enemies), their relative positions on the scale of greatness derive from Schiller's careful consideration of a hierarchy of crimes that serve as the expression of character—though it must be said from another evaluative perspective that Franz is a *great* cowardly villain and a *great* theatrical role.

As noted in the introduction above, the Moor brothers punish themselves. Franz strangles himself with a hat cord and Karl goes off to find that poor man with eleven children who may benefit from the bounty on his head, becoming the agent of his own projected punishment. *Die Räuber* completely undermines the ideal symmetry or economy of crime and punishment by obfuscating crime and excluding the appropriate penal agencies. Even where minor figures are apprehended and held for legal punishment, this punishment is not applied in an adequately retributive or deterrent manner. Roller escapes at the last minute after Karl has already tried to free him by offering to substitute himself for his colleague in the holding cell. This hints at an interchangeability of criminals or permeability of the species when it comes to punishment, such that one could die in place of the other, even though Roller refuses the favor. Spiegelberg, on the other hand, does allow someone to die in his place. He personally accuses a local physician of being Spiegelberg, bringing about the physician's arrest. The man then confesses that he is Spiegelberg and thus perpetrator of the many crimes the latter is accused of, and he is then hanged as Spiegelberg. Thus the real Spiegelberg is able to see "himself" hanged:

> Ich musste nachher eine Prise Tabak in die Nase reiben, als ich am Galgen vorbeispazierte, und den Pseudo-Spiegelberg in seiner Glorie da paradieren sah—und unterdessen, dass Spiegelberg hangt, schleicht sich Spiegelberg ganz sachte aus den Schlingen, und deutet der superklugen Gerechtigkeit hinterrucks Eselsohren, dass's zum Erbarmen ist. (II:70)

> [I had to take a pinch of snuff as I strolled by the gallows and saw Pseudo-Spiegelberg displayed in all his glory—and in the meantime, while Spiegelberg was hanging, Spiegelberg slipped quietly out of the clutches of the law and gestured to omniscient justice with ass's ears, such that it was pitiful.]

The portrait Spiegelberg paints of contemporary justice and its genuine blindness, as well as Karl's ability to substitute himself for a condemned friend at will, make the state's penal apparatus seem utterly comical. The high ideals and ancient judicial traditions that address crime with punishment are subverted and ridiculed by one great man and another despicable one. The interchangeability of a serious criminal in Spiegelberg's case with an upstanding citizen illustrates how poorly focused and easily misled such systems are and how little protection they afford the innocent.

The punishments that are attempted in *Räuber* are either misapplied or unsuccessful and the image of Spiegelberg taunting justice with ass's ears diminishes it considerably. There is also a strong current of indifference to penal law, which is here neither effectively retributive nor a credible deterrent, and therefore not a reliable regulator of society. If Spiegelberg has murdered, then Pseudo-Spiegelberg must die. The "pseudo-" punishment of one of Schiller's most reprehensible figures involves a strong critique of real and aesthetic penal practices. *Die Räuber* does not propose an alternative to the system it criticizes, first and foremost because the play has other goals, but also because it does not recognize punishment, by which I mean the state's penal arsenal (laws, the judiciary, enforcement), as being inherently related to crime or its prevention. Penal practices are the residue of an ancient, corrupted system that runs on its own, often without any connection to its original objectives. Much like the remnants of the old regime in Kafka's *Strafkolonie*, the system exists for its own sake and has long since detached itself from a just and effective regulatory function. Penal sanctions appear to accompany crime and to claim a connection to it, but faith or trust in the system is merely a kind of unrecognized superstition, a belief that the elaborate penal rituals and the human sacrifices involved in these rituals will balance the scales of justice and prevent further evil.

As for the hierarchy of misdeeds, most governments have a clear judicial ranking of the seriousness of crimes and the circumstances accompanying them and this seriousness is generally expressed or measured by the magnitude of the punishment. Schiller's stage, as supported by Schiller's commentary, observes a similar hierarchy of offenses, but here crime as a concept and as an occurrence exists independent of punishment. Punishment is neither used as an index of malefaction nor is it often a consequence that follows on crime ("böse Handlungen sind welche, auf die Strafe folgt"). If it does, it is not the other side of the scale of justice, the corrective that restores social equilibrium. Schiller's intervention in the "if he has murdered, then he must die" equation, is somewhat surprising given the tendency of eighteenth-century drama toward symmetry and balance. Crime unpunished could constitute a creative variation on that symmetry, but only if featured and emphasized as such. Schiller's stage shows an indifference toward punishment at this point, coupled with an admiration of the criminal that precludes the application or depiction of legal sanctions. Most telling is a remark in the "Erinnerung an das Publikum" [Memento to the Audience] that accompanied the 1784 stage version of *Fiesko*. Schiller discusses the differences between his first version in which Verrina kills Fiesko, which he considers a *Lesedrama* [closet drama] and the second, stageable version in which Fiesko triumphs, does not get killed, refuses the crown and becomes Genoa's happiest citizen:

> Vielleicht aber auch, dass ich für den ruhigen Leser, der den verworrensten Faden mit Bedacht auseinanderlöst, mit Fleiss anders dichten wollte, als für den hingerissenen Hörer, der augenblicklich geniessen muss—und reizender ist es nun doch mit einem grossen Manne in die Wette zu laufen, als von einem gestraften Verbrecher sich belehren zu lassen. (II:557)

> [Perhaps also because I wanted to write differently for the calm reader who can unravel the most intricate knots with care, than for the captivated spectator, who must understand things instantly—and it is much more exciting to follow the story of a great man than to be instructed by a punished criminal.]

This is one of Schiller's strongest statements on punishment and the stage. He announces that he considers the figure of the punished criminal to be undramatic and actually at odds with the figure of the great man, as if suffering punishment somehow compromises greatness. He also acknowledges the dullness inherent in the type of edification that results from the depiction of crime and its punishment and renounces this kind of didacticism. Drama feeds on excitement and exalted actions. Just retribution—which the state may not even be capable of—does not qualify as excitement nor does it feed greatness. Great crimes are committed by dynamic, active, courageous great men, and there are no "great punishments" in the state's penal repertoire that could measure up to these great crimes. However, as Schiller noted in *Schaubühne*, where the state's penal arm fails, the dramatic stage compensates to some extent. In the case of the tortured figures of Fiesko and Karl Moor, greatness is its own punishment.

The next of Schiller's dramas after *Räuber* and *Fiesko*, *Kabale und Liebe* (1784), is less concerned with greatness in matters of crime, than with bureaucracy and what might be termed white-collar crime. There are no charismatic criminals in the bourgeois tragedy, but crime is a factor. Wurm, who is the embodiment of evil and one of the worst villains Schiller has ever produced (II:1421) is neither a murderer nor a thief, but a lowly secretary who schemes with Präsident von Walther to enhance the latter's career. Behind their current intrigues is an originary abomination, von Walther's murder of his predecessor and this bloody removal of the precursor is the dark secret that animates the bureaucrat and his master and gives weight to their actions—though they are characterized less by the murder than by their current intrigues. Ferdinand murders Louise, but we are not really supposed to see it this way and, in any case, he blames his father, who blames Wurm, who blames him back.

Kabale und Liebe takes place within a fully established and well-defined state with a stable ruler, who is nonetheless a tyrant. Proceeding from his example, underlings, including von Walther and Wurm, also abuse their positions, as reflected in von Walther's grandiose threat to adapt the judiciary to his own personal ends:

> Die Gerechtigkeit soll meiner Wut ihre Arme borgen. Für diesen Schimpf muss ich schreckliche Genugtuung haben—Ein solches Gesindel sollte meine Plane zerschlagen und ungestraft Vater und Sohn aneinander hetzen?—Ha Verfluchte! Ich will meinen Hass an eurem Untergang sättigen, die ganze Brut, Vater, Mutter und Tochter will ich meiner brennenden Rache opfern. (II:608)

> [Justice shall lend its arm to my rage. I will have terrible satisfaction for this insult. This kind of riff-raff should be able to ruin my plans and set father and son against one another?—Cursed ones! I will slake my hatred on your demise. I will sacrifice the whole brood, father, mother, and daughter to my burning vengeance.]

The substitution of a single will for the general will indicates another perversion of penal law and its enforcement under absolutism. The undepicted Herzog has spawned lesser versions of himself, who imitate or co-opt his abuse of power. The ranking of crime in this play is not as important as the agent that authorizes and facilitates this crime.

A discussion of the evaluation and measurement of the seriousness of crime, in Schiller's work must contain some reference to Christian Wolf, the *Verbrecher aus verlorener Ehre* [Criminal Out of Lost Honor], who is the subject of a later segment of this study. *Verbrecher* is a prose narrative, something for the contemplative readers Schiller describes above, and the hero is indeed more prosaic than dramatic, and appropriately free of greatness. Wolf is a thief who becomes a murderer but he does so without experiencing the aesthetic promotion Schiller described in "Gedanken über den Gebrauch des Gemeinen und Niedrigen in der Kunst". Though he enjoys an enhanced reputation among locals, the transition to murderer results in greater degradation for Wolf, both aesthetically and personally. Relevant to the foregoing discussion is that Wolf's crimes are also evaluated, not for the purpose of establishing a level of greatness—though some were quite daring—but rather for the sake of comparing them to the punishment received, specifically incarceration.

Schiller's narrator and Wolf himself in first-person narrative segments make it clear that punishment *causes* crime, by tracing Wolf's career from the level of a smitten poacher to that of a cold-blooded murderer. Poaching is thievery of a special kind, since it involves hunting animals on land owned by the nobility. These animals were to be preserved for the lords' hunting parties or their hunters, but they often devastated the local farmers' fields and their removal was a welcome relief in many cases. To the relative harmlessness of the crime, Schiller adds the factor of understandable motivation: Wolf loved a young woman and could compete with her suitors only by bringing her presents. Wolf becomes the victim of stricter laws passed to control poaching, loses all his money on the first offense, poaches again in order to feed himself, goes to prison on the second offense, and can find no work when he emerges as an ex-convict. Once again he is caught poaching and punished very harshly:

> Die Richter sahen in das Buch der Gesetze, aber nicht einer in die Gemütsverfassung des Beklagten. Das Mandat gegen die Wilddiebe bedurfte einer solennen und exemplarischen Genugtuung, und Wolf ward verurteilt, das Zeichen des Galgens auf den Rücken gebrannt, drei Jahre auf der Festung zu arbeiten. (VII:568)[10]

> [The judges looked at the law books, but not one looked at the defendant's state of mind. The law against poaching required a solemn and exemplary satisfaction and Wolf was sentenced, with the sign of the gallows burned onto his back, to three years hard labor at the fortress.]

In his new carceral circumstances, Wolf lives with murderers and other hardened criminals, who then educate him to their depravity. The causal relay of punishment and crime serves as early criticism of the prison system, such as it was, and its effect on those who pass through it. The relative mildness of the crime underscores the depravity of the *system* that is structured so that it isolates its victims permanently from society and non-criminal lives.

From the depiction and non-depiction of executions, to the evaluation of individual categories of crime and criminal, to the realistic rehearsal of the formation of the criminal by incarceration and its aftereffects, Schiller's works, so deeply invested in crime, tell a twisted story of punishment and its discontents and its failures. The next chapter will discuss the ways in which Schiller once again engaged incarceration, this time as isolation.

4
Schiller and the Prison in and around *Spiel des Schicksals*

FOUCAULT'S IDENTIFICATION OF A LATE EIGHTEENTH-CENTURY SHIFT in penal tactics, from technologies of the body to technologies of the soul, remains fundamental for most contemporary discussions of penal confinement. The transition from torture and dire corporal punishment, "the art of unbearable sensations," to confinement, "the economy of suspended rights" (Foucault, 11) had apparent affinities with the progress of the Enlightenment, and thus sits well with established accounts of the European history of ideas. The transformation of the prison from a short-term storage facility for bodies awaiting punishment to an organized reformatory thus emerges as a standard item of "knowledge" that in Schiller's case admits of deviations. In considering Schiller's historical and literary dealings with the prison, and specifically with the deep, dark isolation cell (the hole), we will encounter some ambivalence toward the Foucauldian standard of attempted or successful carceral reform. As a historical subject, Schiller witnessed the chilling success of the carceral project on Christian Friedrich Daniel Schubart, but, as a writer, he largely resisted depicting such unequivocal "reform." Schiller muddies the carceral in his treatments of confinement, blurring or explicitly denying reform, and opting instead for an indictment of incarceration that has its roots in his very serious devotion to beauty. Furthermore, where Foucault explores theories of the well-planned prison in his study of Bentham and other penal reformers, Schiller returns repeatedly to a more barbaric and less schematic condition that falls outside—or lags behind—that discussion, namely the condition of punitive isolation in the hole.

John Bender, also working with Bentham, describes the transformative operation of penal forces in terms of literary narrative.

For Bender reading Bentham, "the individual self . . . is a product of a detailed array of circumstances that can be described in exact narrative terms" (Bender, 39). The self is then subject to "renarration" (Bender, 39) or successful penal reform, an insidious instance of *Wirkung* applied to a genuinely captive audience. Building on Bender's observation, in light of the absolutist politics of Schiller's time, if we regard the self in correctional terms as a narrative or role that can be rewritten, we position the sovereign punisher as "author" of the reformed, socialized character. In the case of isolated confinement, Bender notes and it follows that: "Isolation divests the criminal of narrative resources and designates a 'character' to be formulated" (Bender, 292). Isolation, which is most literally "self" deprivation, may be regarded as the penal mode of the tyrant, who seeks to inscribe his own intentions where once there was individual character. At this point, a brief reminder of Schiller's troubled reception of tyranny and its penal habits is in order.

Schiller is today remembered as one of the eighteenth century's strongest advocates of freedom and his abhorrence of punishment, especially penal confinement, is palpable in almost everything he wrote. Even the bifurcating logic of the essays can be read as a series of "escapes" from the dead end of a conclusion and the dramas often strive to subvert prison and punishment, even at the obvious expense of historical accuracy. Joan of Arc, as we will see, does not do time in Schiller's *Jungfrau von Orleans*, where she ultimately dies a glorious death in battle. Only the most depraved government official would even think of locking up Schiller's legendary Wilhelm Tell for the murder he commits, and *Die Räuber* ends—most deliberately—before Karl Moor can pay his debt to society. Indeed Karl seems poised to remain autonomous by orchestrating (that is, willing) his own capture.

To review the collected works of Schiller, and point out all the ways in which he engages punishment by erasing, postponing, or transforming it, would exceed the limits of this discussion, but, based on the instances above and those to come, I want to assert Schiller's disturbed literary relationship to penal restrictions as the dark side of his famous preoccupation with freedom. Furthermore, since *successful* penal confinement—as opposed to an interval in which the body is restricted but the spirit soars freely—is the opposite or other side of freedom, its product is necessarily divorced from beauty and the aesthetic inasmuch as Schiller regarded beauty and freedom as united phenomena. As we will see, artificial restriction of the human spirit through incarceration registers on the body as ugliness.

It is first in the "Kallias" letters to Körner (1793) that Schiller arrives at his frequently cited definition of beauty as "Freiheit in der Erscheinung," or freedom in the realm of appearances. In this correspondence, Schiller proposes to locate objective standards of beauty, a task that involved casting off some of his Kantian fetters, since Kant had declared this to be impossible. Undaunted, Schiller attempts to get rid of the empirical component of *Geschmack* or taste in aesthetic judgment and to find an objective principle that holds (ideally) "ohne das Zeugnis der Erfahrung" [without the confirmation of experience] (VIII:277).[1] In pursuit of these principles, he comes up with the notion of beauty as visible freedom and thus raises the fundamental question, "what is freedom?" As Körner cautions him: "Dein Prinzip der Schönheit ist bloß subjektiv; es beruht auf der Autonomie, welche zu der gegebenen Erscheinung *hinzugedacht* wird" [Your principle of beauty is purely subjective; it rests on the autonomy which is *thought into* a given appearance] (VIII:287). Schiller does not respond easily to this objection and in fact, he defines freedom, that which we should recognize in beauty, most laboriously:

> Frei sein und durch sich selbst bestimmt sein, von innen heraus bestimmt sein ist eins. Jede Bestimmung geschieht entweder von außen oder nicht von außen (von innen), was also nicht von außen bestimmt erscheint, muß als von innen bestimmt vorgestellt werden. *Sobald also das Bestimmtsein gedacht wird,* so ist das Nichtvonaußenbestimmtsein indirecte zugleich die Vorstellung des Voninnenbestimmtseins oder der Freiheit. (VIII:298, Schiller's emphasis)

> [To be free and determined through oneself and to be determined from within are one and the same. Each determination occurs either from without or not from without (from within). Therefore what does not appear to be externally determined, must be thought of as being internally determined. *As soon as the state of being determined becomes the object of thought,* the not-externally-determinedness becomes indirectly the idea of internally-determinedness or freedom.]

It is not possible to determine what Schiller meant specifically, especially as he returned to this concept and modified it in various essays, and most especially because Schiller's philosophical arguments usually do not reduce to specifics. However, the concepts of freedom and beauty remain mutually dependent and we can say roughly—"roughly" in deference to the host of qualifications that follow in the "Kallias" correspondence and in *Anmut und Würde*—that beauty is the appearance of the inner autonomy that Schiller describes, that aspect of freedom that meets the eye.

This chapter is concerned with the *dis*appearance from human society, that constitutes penal confinement, the (physical) unfreedom that is, by fortuitous analogy to Schiller's (abstract) aesthetics, also the very obvious opposite of beauty and the aesthetic. Imprisonment is ugly and limiting and in the historical and literary examples I will reference below, the unaesthetic product of incarceration becomes the object of a very literal sovereign gaze that assesses the "punished" subject seeking confirmation of its formative penal intentions. This is a ritual that is enacted several times in and around Schiller's work and it merits attention for its presentation of the visible results of the revocation of physical freedom (*Unfreiheit in der Erscheinung*), and, further, for its effects or reflections on the author's position as an intellectual in the absolutist state. In the penal process under discussion, the monarch, through his or her minions prepares a program of reform and submission, which proceeds while the subject is out of sight, thus giving birth to the new, reformed individual, refashioned by the application of force, isolation, and usually religion. The inspection is a moment where the sovereign author of the reformed individual seeks empirical evidence of himself/herself and his/her intentions engraved in the sufferer's altered features and demeanor. This is thus a creative, reproductive moment—complete with expectations of "family resemblance"—but, assuming the project has been successful, the product is not autonomous beauty, but rather the ugliness of a broken and submissive *externally determined* individual. That to which the despot has applied transformative force can only present itself as reformed and compliant or as a failed penal project in need of renewed applications. To put it plainly, for Schiller, penal reform, an insidious technology of body and soul, conflicts fundamentally with personal freedom. Within this extreme mode of didacticism and *Wirkung*, the sovereign inspector, enforcer of external determination, creates a physical ugliness that reflects the loss of freedom, rather than reform or improvement.

A corollary detail of this discussion concerns gender relations in punishment, namely who is doing it to whom? The rule in Schiller's works seems to be same-sex punishment as we will see. Though he dwells mostly on the affairs of men—which would make the same-sexness an obvious result—instances in which women suffer punishment are usually engineered by other women. For example, Elizabeth of England holds Maria Stuart prisoner, and Elisabeth of Valois has Princess Eboli locked up. In *Jungfrau*, only Queen Isabeau is able to (very briefly) put Johanna in chains and threaten her life. Indeed, there is not much more for Isabeau to do as a figure in the drama—beyond her being referred to—and it may be that she owes her actual participation in the action to this function. Whether deliberate or automatic, the rule of same-sex relations in the penal transaction holds in most cases.

Of all social institutions, it is the prison that most aptly illustrates the idea of physical freedom, by enacting its absence and creating a space for the freedom or unfreedom of the human spirit to assert itself. In the case of *Maria Stuart*, we encounter a woman who spent nineteen years in penal confinement before her execution. Mary Stuart's ordeal predated Foucault's shift in penal practices, but Schiller's play was written just after this optimistic period and the heroine's experience—just this once—appears to be textbook carceral.[2] The long confinement of the body under the diligent surveillance of jailers like Sir Amias Paulet resulted in spiritual improvement, specifically freedom from the petty concerns and murderous intentions of her earlier life. Yet, this improvement is compromised because it is nowhere in evidence when Elizabeth, the monarch who ordered the incarceration, appears to assess its effects.

Previous to Elizabeth's arrival, the unsuspecting Maria is allowed out of the castle and into a walled park, where she experiences the illusion of freedom: "Bin ich dem finsteren Gefängnis entstiegen / Hält sie mich nicht mehr, die traurige Gruft" [Have I climbed out of the dark prison / Does the sad vault no longer hold me] (V:77). Her giddy dialogue moves toward reestablishing her as a free woman, but when her eye meets Elizabeth's in a scene where eye contact, and the queen's coldly inspecting gaze ("Eisesblick" [icy gaze] V:84) are repeatedly stressed, she begins to fear for her life. Elizabeth inspects and complains:

> Wer war es denn, der eine Tiefgebeugte
> Mir angekündigt? Eine Stolze finde ich,
> Vom Unglück keineswegs geschmeidigt.
>
> (V:83)

> [Who was it who led me to expect
> A supplicant? I see only a proud women
> In no way reduced by sorrow.]

Maria, realizing that she is about to fail the inspection, strategically reassures her that the carceral project has succeeded, making extravagant claims of reform:

> Ach meines Geistes Schwingen sind gelähmt,
> Nicht Größe lockt mich mehr—Ihr habt's erreicht,
> Ich bin nur noch der Schatten der Maria.
> Gebrochen ist in langer Kerkerschmach
> Der edle Mut—Ihr habt das Äußerste an mir
> Getan, habt mich zerstört in meiner Blüte!
>
> (V:87)

> [The flights of my spirit are lamed
> It is not greatness that lures me now—you have succeeded,
> I am only the shadow of Maria
> My noble courage was broken
> In my long languishing in prison.
> You have done all you could to me.
> You have destroyed me in my prime.]

Maria acknowledges both spiritual and corporeal mutilation, her inner and outer re-formation by the prison, but her later outburst and humiliation of Elizabeth, who tries in vain to control the scene with her gaze ("*schießt wütende Blicke*" [shoots angry looks] V:89) indicate rather dramatically that this reform does not apply in confrontation with Elizabeth. Maria is even able to appropriate and reverse the sovereign gaze as she tells Elizabeth "ich bin euer König" [I am your king] (V:89).

Elizabeth's sovereign gaze would fall on a successful penal project if she were truly gazing as a sovereign, but in the case of these two women, crass female rivalry results in a mixed purpose. Elizabeth has come seeking physical ugliness—the byproduct of submissive reform—having been promised by Leicester that Maria is "vor der Zeit gealtert" [prematurely aged] (V:74) by her sufferings in prison. Her perception of "eine Stolze" indicates that Maria's enduring beauty reflects some measure of inner autonomy. Maria has learned humility, but not toward her punisher, and the gender factor is crucial in this mixed exchange. The same-sex act of imprisonment has not yielded the promised results, namely a broken spirit and diminished beauty, and the latter is clearly the more important failure as two jealous women confront each other before Leicester, the man they both love. The Maria-Elizabeth face-off is an example of the incarcerated subject being inspected by the sovereign who enforces the confinement, but in this case, two sovereigns end up vying for the role of inspector. Maria's behavior indicates a measure of freedom ("Vom Unglück keineswegs geschmeidigt"), but Schiller's obedience to conventions of female rivalry or common jealousy complicates this "freedom" since Maria is still subject to a stereotypical intolerance of the other woman.

For the sake of adducing the significant moments, literary and historical, of Schiller's dialogue with the penal system and the *idea* of incarceration, we now return to the Karlsschule, young Schiller's own prison, to Württemberg and his jailer, Herzog Karl Eugen, and to life under small-time absolutism. Karl Eugen's experiment in education for boys isolated them from their families, and subjected them to the educational program and coerced fatherhood of *Landesvater* Karl (Schiller addressed him in letters as "father" and "father of my parents"), a transgressive conflation of the personal and the political. Having aspired to the clergy, Schiller was compelled to study medicine—a significant attempt at re-narration—his stay at school was prolonged by his superiors, and he had to write three dissertations before he could get out. The Karlsschule represented excellent educational opportunities, but, as noted above, it was a place of educational confinement and coercion.

While enduring the rigid discipline and unfreedom of the Karlsschule, Schiller was forced to undergo frequent ocular inspections by the duke, who regularly reviewed the cadets collectively and individually and assessed the progress of his educational project. Thus Schiller himself had been required to submit his externally prescribed *Bildung* to the sovereign gaze for approval. In fact, he was experienced at being inspected by a particularly controlling prince, and this youthful ordeal repeats itself in the many scenes of penal inspection Schiller included in his fiction and dramas.

Now, I would like to take a brief look at another of Karl Eugen's educational projects. In the Age of Enlightenment, the Duke of Württemberg was still capable of a modified tyranny as we have seen, and a good description of his practices can be found in a notorious satirical poem of 1775, which was attributed to Christian Friedrich Daniel Schubart:

> Als Dionys von Syrakus
> Aufhören mußt, Tyrann zu sein
> Da ward er ein Schulmeisterlein.³
>
> [When Dionysus of Syracuse
> Had to stop being a tyrant.
> He became a little schoolmaster.]

Largely inspired by this very poem, but also motivated by years of critical journalism, Karl Eugen sought to reform and educate *Schubart* in a more ostentatiously penal way, having him arrested and imprisoned at the fort Hohenasperg in the bottom of a dark and unheated tower, "in einem grauen düstern Felsenloche" [in a gray and dark hole in a cliff] as Schubart described it in his memoirs.⁴ Here Schubart spent 377 days literally in the hole, in complete isolation with no books, and no pen or paper. He was finally moved to more reasonable accommodations and held for another nine years, but it is his isolation that interests us. Bender notes that penal protocols—such as Schubart's—are narratives of reform, imposed on prisoners, especially through isolation. These narratives can be "read" in the reformed character they produce by the sovereign author of the criminal's imprisonment (or his representative). Schubart's separation from his own "narrative resources" in the hole and his subjection to re-narration did indeed have the effect of reformulating his character. Letters and other documents from his imprisonment show how brutal conditions caused him to embrace Karl Eugen's program of docile subjection to one's monarch. After four years of imprisonment, he was finally allowed to correspond with his wife and in his first letter to her, he wrote:

O wie selig bin ich, daß mich Gott noch hier zu dieser *Selbsterkenntnis* gebracht hat! Wie küß ich den Kerkerboden, der meine Bußtränen eingeschluckt hat! (my emphasis)⁵

[O how happy I am that God has now brought me to this self-recognition! How I kiss the prison floor that has swallowed my tears of penitence.]

A new Schubart was born as he came to recognize *as himself* (*Selbsterkenntnis*) the docile subject Karl Eugen had created, and though his sovereign did not come to observe his progress, he was regularly inspected by Karl Eugen's representative and co-author, Phillip Friedrich Rieger, the commander of Hohenasperg.

Schubart also embraced Pietism during his incarceration, at Rieger's ungentle urging. Rieger had found Pietism to be a great comfort during his own imprisonment, years earlier, also at Hohenasperg (before his transfer to Hohentwiel), also in isolation in the hole, and also at Karl Eugen's instigation—on a trumped-up charge of treason (Myers, 218, 254). He was held for four years, banished for five, and then reinstated. Rieger had been a high state official and Karl Eugen's enforcer in matters of selling soldiers into English service, and his fall had been sudden and unexpected. When absolutist caprice so weakens the boundaries between warden and prisoner that one might merely precede or succeed the other, the carceral project appears to have little value, but as Schubart's letter and Rieger's later faithful service show, the deficiencies of caprice are repaired by power in the interest of the state. We might also ask whether the same-sex oppression of Rieger was not more petty than that perpetrated by Elizabeth and answered by Maria in Schiller's play. Jealous men—Rieger was set up by a rival and accused of a correspondence with two of Karl Eugen's critics—can also inject emotion into the (real) affairs of state.

Meanwhile, back at the Karlsschule, Schiller was released in 1780, or rather *paroled*, since he went into the duke's service and remained in Württemberg under the eye of Karl. A few months later, in 1781, Schiller visited Schubart in Rieger's Hohenasperg under most unusual circumstances. As noted, Rieger was Karl Eugen's coauthor or ghostwriter, collaborating on Schubart's reform and even Schiller's visit had a literary quality to it, inasmuch as it followed a scenario, carefully composed by

Rieger, who had wanted to meet the author of *Die Räuber*. Rieger instructed Schubart to write a review of *Räuber* and then summoned Schiller to the fort to meet one of his youthful heroes—Schubart was the author of the story, "Zur Geschichte des menschlichen Herzens" [On the History of the Human Heart], which was Schiller's inspiration for *Räuber*. The two had never met and Schiller was introduced to Schubart under an alias, Dr. Fischer. Rieger then directed Schubart to read aloud his review, which he concluded by expressing the wish to meet Schiller personally. Schiller's identity was then revealed and Schubart embraced him tearfully. As he later wrote to his wife, "Schiller ist ein großer Kerl—ich lieb ihn heiß" [Schiller is a great guy—I love him passionately] (summer 1782; Honolka, 220). Schiller was able to view Schubart's original cell, his hole in the cliff, and became familiar with the circumstances of Schubart's incarceration. He already knew something of Rieger's history and he learned even more when both he and Schubart were recruited to write commemorative poems on the occasion of Rieger's death in 1782. More on that death later.

To summarize, we have an odd chain of historical events, experiences, and encounters uniting an odd group of Württemberg characters: from the Hohe Karlsschule and its rigors, to Schubart's alleged accusations of pedagogical tyranny, to Karl Eugen's application of genuine political tyranny to Schubart, to the ministrations of Rieger, who was previously held prisoner in the same fort he commanded as Schubart's jailer, by the same duke who attempted to form Schiller and re-form Schubart. In addition, we have literary history turning in on itself as Schiller, the Schubart fan, meets Schubart, the Schiller fan, under the watchful eye of Rieger, the author of the scenario of mistaken identity resulting in embraces, tears, and love. Let us now fast-forward to 1788 when Schiller produces *Spiel des Schicksals*, one of his lesser-known fictional narratives, inspired by Rieger's reversals, Karl Eugen's fickle brutality, the hole, the inspection, and so much more.

Spiel concerns an instance of same-sex incarceration with roots in a passionate relationship between an unnamed prince and his favorite, Aloysius von G***. In an era when steamy declarations of same-sex love (like Schubart's for Schiller) often denoted or passed for conventional sentimental friendship, their association is specifically qualified as more than friendship, "ein

Verhältnis . . . das alle Stärke von der Freundschaft und von der leidenschaftlichen Liebe alles Feuer und Heftigkeit besaß" [a relationship that had all the strength of friendship and all the fire and intensity of a passionate love] (VII:726–27).[6] The prince is impressed by G***'s intellectual qualities, but these are secondary to the physical attraction: "War der Prinz von dem Geiste seines jungen Gesellschafters bezaubert, so riß [G***'s] verführerische Außenseite seine Sinnlichkeit unwiderstehlich hin" [The prince was enchanted by his young companion's mind, but his sensuality was irresistibly drawn to (G***'s) seductive appearance] (VII:725). G*** advances quickly.

Yet, he who rose rapidly comes down even more rapidly as the villain Martinengo enters the picture. G*** procures the charming Italian count for his prince's amusement, so that G*** may attend to the duties of state that increasingly claim his interest, while Martinengo covers his former recreational role of constant companion. Yet Martinengo proves to be an insidious intriguer whose success rests on his establishment of an exclusive and corrupting relationship with the prince:

> Da ihm sehr gut bewußt war, daß der Mensch nirgends mehr eines Führers und Gehülfen bedarf als auf dem Wege des Lasters und daß nichts zu kühneren Vertraulichkeiten berechtigt als eine Mitwissenschaft geheim gehaltener Blößen, so weckte er Leidenschaften bei dem Prinzen, die bis jetzt noch in ihm geschlummert hatten. . . . Er riß ihn zu solchen Ausschweifungen hin, die die wenigsten Zeugen und Mitwisser dulden; und dadurch gewöhnte er ihn unvermerkt, Geheimnisse bei ihm niederzulegen, wovon jeder dritte ausgeschlossen war. (VII:729)

> [Since he knew well that men are nowhere more in need of a leader and guide as on the path of vice, and that nothing justifies bold confidences so well as mutual knowledge of confidential transgressions, so he awakened passions in the prince that until now had been sleeping. . . . He brought him to commit those excesses that tolerate only the smallest number of witnesses and confidantes and thus accustomed him to share secrets with him from which all others were excluded.]

Here the description of political intimacy is laden with homoerotic suggestion. As Paul Derks has observed, what the prince merely felt toward G*** seems to have been acted on in Martinengo's case.[7] Derks makes this observation during a discussion of Schiller's unrealized plan for a drama depicting a deep love between two Maltese knights, which was to be "das völlige Surrogat der Weiberliebe" [a complete surrogate for the loving of women].[8] He concludes that Schiller never finished the drama because he was able to imagine a homosexual relationship only as a perfectly analogous substitute ("völliges Surrogat") for a heterosexual one and thus was unable to resolve the question of natural dominance (men over women) in a situation he had conceived as based on equality. This dilemma may also inhabit *Spiel des Schicksals* where the love motif does not assume prominence and the apparent equality deteriorates into the starkest of hierarchical relationships with one player on the throne and the other in the hole.

Spiel depicts an initial political inequality that was neutralized for a time by the attraction between the two men. The inequality is reinstated dramatically when the rival appears. In short order, Martinengo usurps his predecessor, takes control, and arranges for G***'s removal. He surprises G*** on the parade ground, breaks his sword in front of "zahlloser Zuschauer" [countless spectators] (VII:733), throws him into a wagon, and has him transported to a dark hole in a fort, yet another *Felsenloch*.

Now we have our third man in a hole (after Schubart and Rieger), and *Spiel des Schicksals* is obviously based on Rieger's ordeal, and, to a lesser extent, on Schubart's experience. G*** faints during the transport and wakes up in "einer scheußlichen Grube unter der Erde" [a dreadful pit under the ground] (VII:733), far from the prince's sight, with no knowledge of his offense, of the charges against him, or of his sentence. He sees no one, no one speaks to him and he remains there for 490 days, far more time than was needed to begin the retooling of Schubart. His physical suffering is intense, but his spiritual ordeal is exacerbated by the realization that he knows this cell. G*** had recently taken a penal interest in a competent and inoffensive officer, who had irked him for some unspecified reason. In pursuit of this interest, he had prepared the hole in which he now languishes with "erfinderischer Grausamkeit" [inventive cruelty] (VII:734). He had also recently traveled to the fort to inspect the cell he designed for the object of his punitive intentions. G*** had no particular carceral program or narrative in mind, and was "von einer niedrigen Rachgier getrieben" [driven by a base hunger for revenge] (VII:734). He intended pure punishment, a frightening and irrational languishing without purpose. Similarly, he himself might now be the object of a non-pedagogical, purely vindictive, penal intention. The actual reason why the prince ordered G***'s imprisonment, what it was that Martinengo accused him of, is not recuperable, even for the narrator, and this omission of reason/purpose/crime/cause contributes to a larger condemnation of imprisonment as an exercise in futility.

The motif of the oppressor trapped in his own means of oppression is familiar to twentieth-century readers, as there are legends of wardens and executioners who die in their own machines, and figures such as Kafka's officer in the penal colony, who submits to his own killing device. G*** will suffer the torments he has designed for another, the other having—incidentally and coincidentally—recently become commander of the fort where G*** is imprisoned, and therefore G***'s jailer. The title, *Spiel des Schicksals*, is repeatedly vindicated. G***, who through ambition and favor had once been the clever "Beherrscher seines Fürsten" [ruler of his prince] and de facto head of state, now feels the full extent of his prince's power over him and within this greater reversal of a power relation lies the secondary reversal represented by G***'s subjection to the officer he intended to imprison. In these intricate couplings and de-couplings, G*** has most literally ended up on the bottom.

Like Schubart, Rieger, and Maria Stuart, G*** eventually emerges from the more restricted enclosure to a wider penal space, where he spends another eight years. His release from the hole, his gradual ascension to visibility, is secured by a priest who descends to his prison and inspects him for signs of humanity. He finds:

> ein Grauen erweckendes Scheusal. . . . [e]in blasses totenähnliches Gerippe, alle Farbe des Lebens aus einem Angesicht verschwunden, in welches Gram und Verzweiflung tiefe Furchen gerissen hatten. (VII:736)

> [a frightening wretch. . . . a pale death-like skeleton from whose face all colors of life had disappeared, and in which misery and despair had cut deep furrows.]

In other words, G*** is not a pretty sight. The ugliness of his unfreedom so repels the inspecting priest that he prescribes an immediate transformation and petitions the prince to restore G***'s "resemblance to humanity" (VII:736), a partial restoration of his physical condition or physical description that has been revised or re-narrated in the hole. Still there is no inspection by the sovereign, who only hears reports, and when G*** is released from prison, he is banished from the state and from the prince's sight.

However, many years later, when the prince is old and somewhat wise, he feels a "Sehnsucht nach dem Lieblinge seiner Jugend" [longing for the love of his youth] (VII:737) and summons G*** to court, where he finally inspects his former prisoner:

> Der Fürst ruhte mit einem nachdenkenden Blick auf dem Gesichte, das ihm so wohlbekannt und doch wieder so fremd war; es war als zählte er die Furchen, die er selbst darein gegraben hatte. Forschend suchte er in des Greisen Gesicht die geliebten Züge des Jünglings wieder zusammen, *aber was er suchte, fand er nicht mehr.* (VII:737, my emphasis)

> [The prince let his reflective gaze rest on the face that was so familiar to him and yet so foreign; it was as if he were counting the furrows that he had dug into it. Searchingly, he scanned the old man's face for the beloved features of the youth, but what he sought he no longer found.]

The sovereign gaze reads and measures the effects of the carceral project, in this case the regrettable extinction of beauty, the ravaging of the beloved's features. The deep lines of applied tyranny mark G***'s brow and these are incompatible with love. That G***'s appearance has been externally determined is clear, but there is no sign of change or revision of character, and this is consistent with the inclarity, and therefore futility, of the penal program. Schiller's prince has re-formed only the part of G*** that he most loved, and made ugly a beautiful body, once the object of an emotion that was anything but disinterested pleasure. The inspection, a configuration based on a power asymmetry, does not become a reunion between relative equals because, as Schiller notes, "Ein Anblick, der ihm seine schwere Übereilung wieder in seine Seele rief, konnte dem Fürsten nicht wohltun" [A sight that recalled his grievous rashness to him, could not benefit the prince] (VII:738). The un-aesthetic experience of seeing his marked prisoner documents an abuse of power and

G*** is now a physical reminder of the prince's tyranny. As for conventional reform, what goes on in G***'s mind, the inner workings of isolation on the incarcerated subject, is inaccessible to the reader. The narrator says simply, and oddly, "ich beschreibe seine Empfindungen nicht" [I will not describe his feelings] (VII:736), and, as noted the only evidence of penal impact is physical. The absence of a reason for incarceration and a program for reform seem to leave character unchanged, as G*** resumes his state service and advances rapidly once again. As commander of a fortress where prisoners are committed to his care, he seems unconcerned about their suffering:

Man wird erwarten, daß er gegen diese eine Menschlichkeit geübt, deren Wert er an sich selbst hatte schätzen lernen müssen. Aber er behandelte sie hart und launisch, und eine Aufwallung des Zorns gegen einen derselben streckte ihn auf den Sarg in seinem achtzigsten Jahre. (VII:738)

[One would expect that he behaved toward them with humane concern, the value of which he had himself learned to appreciate. But he treated them harshly and capriciously and a fit of anger against one of them laid him in his coffin in his eightieth year.]

G*** remains G*** and the benefits of incarceration that Maria Stuart experienced—but did not show to Elizabeth—elude him. He incorporates some of the horror of Rieger's blind allegiance to a power that abused him without cause. G*** exhibits no spiritual improvement, only physical decline, and his physical decline and ugliness are entirely adequate indicators of external determination or unfreedom.

Spiel des Schicksals revives and expands upon a motif of same-sex confinement, the hole, indebted to Schubart's and Rieger's histories, that Schiller had already explored in *Die Räuber*. It was, of course, his authorship of this very play that got him into Hohenasperg (just visiting) and into the presence of this unusual pair. In *Räuber*, Franz Moor confines his father, reversing the paternal-filial power relation and claiming the sovereignty that would devolve on him—in the absence of his brother—upon the death of his father. An insecure Oedipus, Franz will only facilitate and not directly cause his father's death. He locks his father in the hole to starve, but since Hermann brings him food, Old Moor has survived three months in the hole when Karl finds him. It is actually Karl, robber sovereign, who inspects the result of this brutal incarceration, "*Ein Gerippe*" [a skeleton] (II:113), according to the stage directions, which Karl concludes is a ghost. Old Moor is a conceptually compromised figure, inasmuch as he is described by his sons and Amalia as strong and virile, but appears always helpless, incompetent, and barely continent, and it is therefore difficult to assess the changes confinement has wrought. He is frail and weak, but he possessed these qualities in abundance before his first *Scheintod*—he had lost consciousness after hearing lies about Karl and awakened in his coffin—and before his imprisonment commenced. Death was the punisher's intention and it seems to have been realized visibly since Old Moor appears dead or ghostly to his son. He dies shortly after his release, but as a result of Karl's patricidal revelation that he is the leader of the robber band.

Here is yet another man in a hole, one who appears to embody the penal intentions of his oppressor, but who technically has remained unchanged, at least as far as the weighty matter of living or dying is concerned because he is technically not dead. Old Moor's dead-ness is mere appearance, but his actual death is soon realized. Franz Moor's carceral project, that of transforming a living father into a dead one, does and does not bear fruit. Isolation/imprisonment, as the production of the physically marked—Old Moor has indeed deteriorated from his original level of weakness—but spiritually unchanged unfree, makes an early appearance in Schiller's breakthrough drama.

"Der Verbrecher aus verlorener Ehre" is far more explicit on the effects of the prison, and makes somewhat different use of the hole. Christian Wolf is marked as ugly to begin with and he deteriorates spiritually during his three years in prison: " 'Ich betrat die Festung,' sagte er, 'als ein Verirrter und verließ sie als ein Lotterbube' " ["I entered the fortress," he said, "as an errant man and left it as a criminal"] (VII:568). As Wolf tells it, it was precisely the lack of isolation that caused the re-narration and negative re-formation of his character. He was confined together with twenty-three hardened criminals including two murderers, and under the aggressive guidance of this community, he was transformed from confused youth to fellow criminal.

For Wolf, the "hole" appears as the symbolic entry to a life of serious crime and social alienation. After he has murdered his antagonist, Robert, he follows a sympathetic robber to a "Kluft" in the forest, an abyss that leads to a society of criminals who live in isolation at the bottom of a ravine:

> Ich sah in den Schlund hinab, der mich jetzt aufnehmen sollte, es erinnerte mich dunkel an den Abgrund der Hölle, woraus keine Erlösung mehr ist. (VII:578)

> [I looked into the abyss that was now to take me in, it reminded me of the abyss of hell from which there is no more redemption.]

Wolf hesitates, but he enters, the product of prison and circumstances.

Among the remaining instances of actual imprisonment in Schiller's drama is the confinement of Don Carlos behind bars ("eine eiserne Gittertüre" [a gate of iron bars], III:951) in the king's palace by his sovereign punishing father. This is a different kind of incarceration from G***'s, Schubart's, Rieger's, and Old Moor's because Don Carlos is not in isolation—he has guards and numerous visitors to occupy him—and he is informed that he was locked up "aus Versehen" [inadvertently] (III:954). Though his detention was certainly not an accident, Don Carlos's jailers did not originally plan to reform him, only to restrain and punish, and his case is interesting within the framework of this discussion.

Don Carlos's knowledge of his father is related to the latter's penal practices. He first glimpsed the king at age six, while he was signing death warrants, and Don Carlos's most prominent childhood memory is that of being beaten by his father for Posa's transgression—a punishment he volunteered for. When Alba comes to release him from custody, Don Carlos demands to be pardoned and released by the king himself—again asking for the punishing father. As the king arrives to inspect and release his prisoner, Don Carlos, like Maria Stuart, appropriates and reverses the gaze. He identifies the marks of Posa's murderer (branded brow, bloody fingers) on his father's body (III:961–62), while the king stares at the floor (III:964). Simultaneously, the sounds of rebellion in Madrid are heard and the king inspects his retinue in vain:

> *Um den König herum ist eine tiefe Stille. Seine Augen durchlaufen den ganzen Kreis, aber niemand begegnet seinen Blicken.*

König. Nun? Will niemand
Antworten?—Jeder Blick am Boden—jedes
Gesicht verhüllt!—Mein Urteil ist gesprochen.
In diesen stummen Mienen les' ich es
Verkündigt. Meine Untertanen haben mich
Gerichtet. (III:965)

[*Deep silence all around the king. His eyes scan the whole group, but no one meets his gaze.*
King. So? Will no one
Answer? Every gaze toward the floor. Every
Face covered! My sentence has been passed.
I read it in these silent faces.
My subjects have
Condemned me.]

The sovereign gazes at the prisoner he believes he has just rehabilitated and realizes that Don Carlos is the traitor he always suspected. Imprisonment, and the murder of Posa, cause this knowledge to emerge. Finally, the king will turn his son over to his own punishing father figure, the blind grand inquisitor, who is better able to evaluate human intentions because he is not distracted by vision. Don Carlos is fated to register the most extreme depths of unaesthetic unfreedom on his body as the object of the political and religious tyranny he failed to alter. His reformed remains will be available to the more accurate inspecting gaze of the blind inquisitor.

In the foregoing varied, though not exhaustive, investigation of penal confinement in and around Schiller's works, that is as depicted by Schiller or as experienced—immediately or vicariously—by him, several constants have emerged from which we might proceed to theorize the other side of freedom. Imprisonment in Schiller's works is repeatedly a same-sex act of confinement,[9] performed by a sovereign on a subject (though Franz Moor rushes things) under the assumption that change, typically better subject-ion, will occur. The isolation of the subject usually produces a physical alteration (that may pass for character reform) and the results present themselves to the sovereign gaze for inspection and verification. Those who spend time in the hole appear to lose their inner determination (*Voninnenbestimmtsein*) and conform to some extent to the personality program of those who locked them up (*Vonaußenbestimmtsein*), but where Schiller controls the narration of character, no unambiguous improvement results from incarceration. G*** remains himself, a self dedicated to the prince's service (Vonaußenbestimmtsein); Rieger's case is similar, but Schubart, of whom Schiller was painfully aware, but not in control, comes to a new *Selbsterkenntnis*.

In the tale, the plays, and in Hohenasperg, the display of the products of the carceral process are ugly or repulsive in some way. Like freedom, which achieves visible form as beauty, the absence of freedom, the state of being, becoming, or having been externally determined has its own characteristic appearance, involving not only the absence of beauty, but a kind of negative beauty. Thus I would like to suggest that the aggregate of events and episodes from history and literature that I have presented here, what Schiller wrote and experienced—inasmuch as the experience has so obviously informed the writing—of penal confinement comprises a negative "Kallias." This negative or inverse "Kallias," itself a theoretical construct that must be assembled from various pieces, is a cumulative indictment of the excesses of absolutism, a system that empowers the sovereign not only to tax and govern, but also to punish in a way that intends to violate human self-determination. An idea of freedom negated by confinement and power recurs in Schiller's writing where he addresses and where he erases punishment. Schiller will always be ambivalent about the best of penal institutions because he cannot reconcile them with the sanctity of inner determination and his resulting abhorrence of confinement. The aesthetic of beauty-freedom has its underside in the empirical repulsiveness of confinement and the confined, and the construction of aesthetic theories—as well as the anti-aesthetic of unfreedom—serves as a counterweight to (actual and fictional) subjection to a punishing absolutist monarch.

I would like to conclude this chapter with a note on each of those star-crossed penal partners, Rieger and Schubart, and their experiences as perpetrator and victim of absolutism. Of course Rieger was both perpetrator and victim, an insider who was cast out and then reabsorbed. Like Schiller's Aloysius von G***, who had seen the other side of the carceral fence and yet had not let this experience soften his penal severity, Rieger is said to have died in a fit of rage against one of his charges. Interestingly, this is supposed to have occurred during an inspection of the type we have been discussing. Kurt Honolka reports a widely circulated version of Rieger's death, wherein the sovereign duke's representative regards a recently punished subject:

> Ein auf Riegers Befehl halb tot geprügelter unbotmäßiger Soldat gemeinsten Ranges habe dem Kommandanten, als dieser ihn im Lazarett inspizierte, herausfordernd den nackten Hintern gezeigt und dazu den schwäbischen Gruß entboten. (Honolka, 221)

> [An insubordinate soldier of the lowest rank, who was, at Rieger's command, beaten nearly to death, is said to have showed his naked bottom to the commandant, as the latter was inspecting him in the infirmary, and to have offered him the Swabian greeting.]

In this account, the inspection brought on the death of the punisher. The punished soldier, so clearly unaffected by the penal measures taken, enraged the old man to the point where he suffered a heart attack and died. It is a quintessentially free man, "bloodied, but unbowed," who can thumb his nose—and other body parts—at his tormenter but, in this case, his gesture of freedom, appropriate as it may have been, does not partake of the beautiful. Somehow history falls short of its aesthetic transformation.

So much for Rieger. I will give poor Schubart the last word by quoting two stanzas from a poem he wrote in prison, but did not intend for circulation. Its discovery may have lengthened his sentence, but it is an eloquent statement of the transitoriness of absolutism, called "Die Fürstengruft" [The Tomb of Princes].

> Da liegen sie, die stolzen Fürstentrümmer
> Ehmals die Götzen ihrer Welt!
> Da liegen sie vom fürchterlichen Schimmer
> Des blassen Tags erhellt!
>
> Entsetzen packt den Wandrer hier beym Haare,
> Geußt Schauer über seine Haut,
> Wo Eitelkeit, gelehnt an eine Bahre,
> Aus hohlen Augen schaut.[10]
>
> [There they lie, the proud ruins of princes,
> Once the idols of their world!
> There they lie, illuminated
> By the terrible light of the pale day!

> Horror grips the wanderer by the hairs,
> And sends shivers through his body.
> As vanity, leaning on a bier,
> Gazes out of empty eyes.]

In Schubart's bold poem, the prince's eyes are empty and the inspecting gaze of the sovereign jailer and reformer has been appropriated and reversed as the speaker considers the piles of bones before him. Such strong verses almost seem to have been written by a "free" and defiant prisoner. However, Schubart apologized profusely when the poem was discovered. He claimed that it referred only to bad monarchs and not to his sovereign, Karl Eugen. Then he "freely" added four more stanzas to soften the impression of the original. Once again, history deviates from Schiller's ideal, though not from Foucault's carceral standard. The mind of Schubart yielded and the rebellious journalist ultimately validated the ducal brainwashing that Schiller looked away from in *Spiel des Schicksals*, *Die Räuber*, and *Don Carlos*. Schiller withholds any confirmation of penal reform in the texts mentioned above, stressing the futility of cruel incarceration. What really happened to Schubart in the hole is nowhere reflected in Schiller's works. Schiller preserves human freedom and dignity in literature, though both were subject to absolutist caprice in the world he inhabited.

5
Murderous Fathers: *Wilhelm Tell* and the Decriminalization of Murder

SCHUBART, THE POLITICAL PRISONER WHO HAD, AMONG OTHER things, strongly criticized Karl Eugen's selling of soldiers to the British, was punished without actually having broken the law since he pursued his political journalism from outside Württemberg. Wilhelm Tell, Schiller's dramatic representation of a legendary figure, *does* break the law, but he is never punished. It is this lapse, not understood as the failure to inflict the death penalty ("if he has murdered, then he must die"), but as the overwhelmingly positive valuation of a murder, that I want to investigate here because it appears that Schiller's theater seeks to establish its *Wirkung* by means of a demonstration of a *good* murder. In *Die Räuber* we have seen the conjunction of murder and greatness in its contrast to low-life thievery. *Wilhelm Tell* raises the stakes and attempts to promote the acceptability of murder by conjoining it with fatherhood in a context of nationalistic insularity.

When confronted with the rich variety of *Wilhelm Tell*, with its cast of hundreds and more than fifty speaking roles, one might reasonably ask, what is this piece *about*? The long thematic arm of Schiller's late play embraces a collection of issues, beginning with the struggle to parse authority and remain loyal to the Holy Roman Empire, while resisting the emperor's representatives and abhorring the Hapsburgs. It is also about the opposition of good and evil, good being personified in the numerous staunch and stouthearted native Swiss and evil in the undifferentiated bad guys from elsewhere who govern the cantons for the emperor. It is about nature, the mountains, lakes, and valleys that constitute the Swiss *Boden* or homeland, the natural and political ground that the men will make a stand for.

It is about the porous membrane that separates public and private spheres, the political and the personal—the major political violations that occur being intrusions into the private life of the family, beginning with Wolfenschiessen's assault on Baumgarten's wife, continuing with the blinding of Melchtal's father and culminating in Geßler's forcing Tell to aim an arrow at his own son's head.

The play is also about romance. Though Rudenz and Berta seem curiously superfluous to Schiller's busy plot program, they do love, struggle, and unite amid the din. It covers the later stages of romance, namely postmarital as we look in on the domestic matters of Tell's family and Stauffacher and his wife. Beyond this, there is singing, fishing, herding, storms, a dramatic oath at dawn, the construction of a fortress or prison, fighting, children, the elderly—all the diverse elements of broad monocultural pageantry.

The play is also concerned with Wilhelm Tell, who, as legend prescribes, shoots the apple from his son's head, saving both of their lives. It is, however, Tell's second shot, the one that kills Gessler, that provokes this chapter, in which I will contend that all of the extravagant pageantry and pre-national nationalism function as support and backdrop for the play's highly transgressive argument for a justifiable murder. I label the argument transgressive because, unlike numerous commentators who have found support for Tell's actions in established law, I believe that this murder transgresses legal codes, and that its justification or decriminalization resides in an appeal to extralegal experience.

Demonstrations of the "legality" of Tell's "justifiable homicide," which incurs no punishment, generally depend on either the concept of *Notwehr* [self-defense] or that of *Selbsthilfe* [self-help]. Critics invoke Roman law and its various Germanic descendants, which authorize an individual to take action to avoid an impending threat, where the ruling hierarchy has failed to protect life and property.[1] *Notwehr* or simple killing in self-defense is defined very clearly in the *Carolina* penal code as an individual's acting "zu rettung seines leibs und lebens" [to save his body and life] (para. 139).[2] However, in para. 142, it is specified that this exculpatory condition does not obtain in cases where the perpetrator has lain in wait and killed the offender in a moment when the latter was not a threat:

daß der entleibt, nach gethaner ersten benöttigung gewichen, dem der totschläger auß freihem willen vnd vngenötter ding nachgeuolgt, vnd jn allererst inn der nachuolg erschlagen het, Mer, so fürgewendt wird. ... darumb die entleibung durch den verklagten totschläger nit auß einer rechten entschuldigten notweer, sondern böslich geschehen wer, vnd darumb peinlich gestraft werden solt. (*Carolina*, 91)

[if the one who was killed, retreated after posing the original threat, and if the killer freely and unnecessarily pursued him, and killed him during this pursuit, we determine that . . . the killing by the accused killer did not occur through legally justifiable self-defense, but was performed with malice and is therefore punishable by law.]

Thus Tell's attack is specifically disqualified as defensible in the foundational legal document of the Holy Roman Empire. *Notwehr* does not apply.

Selbsthilfe is a much broader concept than *Notwehr*, and Schiller himself invoked it in his correspondence with Iffland, where he famously argued for the retention of the two most awkward sections of the play, the Tell monologue and the Parricida episode, because he felt that they explained the murder and anchored its justification. In support of Parricida as a contrastive instance that diminished the gravity of Tell's deed, Schiller wrote:

Neben dem ruchlosen Mord aus Impietät und Ehrsucht steht nunmehr Tells *nothgedrungene Tat*, sie erscheint *schuldlos* in der Zusammenstellung mit einem ihr so ganz unähnlichen Gegenstück und die Hauptidee des ganzen Stücks wird eben dadurch ausgesprochen, nehmlich: Das Nothwendige und Rechtliche der *Selbsthilfe* in einem streng bestimmten Fall.[3]

[Next to the merciless murder that was motivated by impiety and ambition, stands Tell's necessary deed; it appears to be innocent by contrast with such a dissimilar counterpart and the main idea of the play thus comes to light, namely the necessity and legality of self-help in a carefully defined case.]

Selbsthilfe is, as noted, less specifiable than *Notwehr* and it is generally understood as covering a variety of actions that involve "taking the law into one's own hands" where the state does not or cannot protect its citizens: "unter besonderen Voraussetzungen eigenmächtig also ohne Hilfe des Staats in die

Rechtssphäre eines anderen einzugreifen, um entweder ein bedrohtes Rechtsgut zu schützen oder ein verlorenes wieder zu erlangen" [To intervene in the legally protected sphere of another on one's own initiative, that is without the assistance of the state, either to protect a legally protected right that is threatened or to restore one that has been lost].[4] The dual purpose of protection and recovery of that which is one's own is especially applicable here since Tell claims that he is *protecting* himself and his family ("ich hab' mein teuerstes verteidigt" [I have defended that which is most precious to me.] V:501) and therein lies his claim to *Selbsthilfe*. However, I believe that Tell acts in an attempt to *restore* something that is irretrievably lost and that, despite Schiller's stated intention that his hero should be understood as a *Selbsthelfer*, his Wilhelm Tell murders as a traumatized subject and father and that the destruction—after the fact—of the source of the trauma is meant to be the redeeming or exculpatory factor.

To return to the theater and the dramatically satisfying justification of murder, the play—like the law codes—tells its audience, *Thou shalt kill* under certain conditions and Schiller goes to great lengths to create those conditions theatrically, while grounding Tell's particular procedure philosophically (and perhaps medically) in ways that do not immediately disrupt the spectacle. Whether this demonstration is successful on either level or convincing is not at issue here. The secondary literature offers an abundance of conflicting opinions[5] and the play has enjoyed a long life and been adapted to a wide variety of purposes.

While considering the extent of Schiller's efforts to provide an emotionally satisfying, yet intellectually legitimate murder, I must of necessity revisit the critical debate on the proper evaluation of Tell's deed in somewhat more detail. The fact that Geßler's demise is a murder and that Tell gets away with this murder, both in the civil and moral realms, has not gone unnoticed, and there is a fair amount of critical commentary on the criminal or noncriminal nature of Tell's action. Back in 1938 W. G. Moore complained that, with the notable exception of "Bismarck, Börne, and Hettner,"[6] critics had accepted and praised Tell's ambush of Geßler as both justified and appropriate. Moore himself declared Tell a murderer, "This idealist is an assassin" (Moore, 280), and saw in the combination of idealist and assassin the tragic dimension of the play. More recently, Frank Ryder went beyond Moore by identifying the murder of Geßler as personal vengeance, Tell's way of ridding himself of the "dreadful guilt" of having risked his son's life, by killing "the man who was the agent of his fall from humanity."[7] Jeffrey Sammons sees no resolution and pronounces the play "an intelligently and penetratingly organized context for meditation."[8] Most recently, Christoph Schweitzer has thoroughly summarized the critical discussion of this controversial murder and attempted to reinstate the very reading that Moore complained about. Schweitzer defends what he considers "a necessary and praiseworthy deed," arguing that "our emotional response to the killing of Geßler must be positive" (Schweitzer, 261).

Schweitzer is correct in observing that the play promotes a certain satisfaction by removing its villain and he cites the many elements of justification that are built into the play—mainly indications and assurances that the evil, vindictive Geßler would avenge himself on the fugitive Tell and on Tell's family. However, and here is the problem cited by Moore, developed by Ryder, and formulated by Sammons as non-resolution, beneath—but not far beneath—the level of these obvious theatrical indicators that Tell may need to take preemptive action are the problematizing elements that do not yield to that explanation and that fall outside the parameters of *Selbsthilfe*. These include the deliberate ambush, the deliberations before the ambush, the excessive nature of the justifications, and the awkward arrival of the abject parricida. Reading *Wilhelm Tell* for a statement on murder has always meant assigning relative weight to the theatrical indicators or to the structure of dissonant events and rhetoric that fails to support them.

This investigation straddles the terms of the debate as I have described it, because I believe that Tell's second shot was to be recognized as murder, and that, working from this certainty, Schiller conducted an experiment in mitigating the ultimate transgression as a special, excusable instance of murder, the "carefully defined case" that contrasts with parricide, but not in the ways critics have assumed.

This special instance of murder is also not merely tyrannicide, "the tradition of striking down illegitimate, capricious, or impious rulers on grounds of principle," which has "for at least two and a half millennia . . . constituted in the eyes of philosophers the only respectable link between ethics and political violence."⁹ This definition is obviously at odds with Tell's murder of Geßler, which is more privately motivated, more nuanced, and less likely to pass for political heroism. Schiller's oft-cited remark to Iffland regarding Tell, "seine Sache ist eine Privatsache, und bleibt es, bis sie am Schluß mit der öffentlichen Sache zusammengreift" [his cause is a private matter and remains such until the end when it merges with the public cause] (V:755) suggests that the publicly tyrannicidal aspect is almost accidental and this tends to neutralize the exculpatory potential of political heroics. Wilhelm Tell killed a man who happened to practice political tyranny on others beside himself.

Like Sammons, I regard *Wilhelm Tell* as a forum for meditation, here specifically as an opportunity to consider whether the most heinous of criminal actions can be rewritten as "good" or worthy or necessary. Schiller has a history of removing the onus and the legal consequences of crime by considering the motives and the background of the perpetrators and *Tell* may be a refinement of *Die Räuber* and several other earlier pieces, a final attempt to demonstrate that the motives for crime are not undifferentiated, but actually admixtures of good and evil or benevolent and criminal.

A look at the theatrical surface of an enormously popular play indicates that Schiller creates an obvious good guy–bad guy polarity resembling that of the contemporary B-movie or action film in which a strong and righteous hero endures repeated injuries from the villainous opposition, and finally enacts his just and highly enjoyable revenge after some ultimate insult, often involving a wife or child. Like the authors of these films, Schiller carefully establishes the license to kill and encases the enjoyable deed itself within the famous exculpatory passages of the "Tell Monolog" (preceding) and Parricida scene (following). Schiller has lavished such care and consistency on the depiction and evaluation of Geßler's murder that it seems highly plausible that he was working on the question of whether there can be a "good," that is, ethically or morally necessary, murder.[10]

But beyond the theatrics that support the goodness of murder, the unambiguous staging of the good-versus-evil conflicts, Schiller has created a compelling web of value-laden activity and reflection that tends to secure cherished ideals of freedom in the face of overwhelming tyranny, by authorizing means other than sublime transcendence. Whereas the Schillerian sublime, which must will the inevitable, tends to promote reactions of the "if you can't beat 'em, then join 'em" variety, the attitude toward Geßler's tyranny in *Wilhelm Tell* is cautiously eliminationist—if you can't beat 'em, or reason with 'em, or appeal to their human compassion, then wait, think about it, ambush 'em and kill 'em. Tell himself travels from an attitude of stubborn optimism ("Die Schlange sticht nicht ungereizt" [the snake does not bite without provocation] V:403) to one of murderous vengeance. Wilhelm Tell, action hero, develops from docile subject to avenging angel and this transformation can be unproblematic for an action audience, dazzled by the pageantry and anticipating a kind of *quid pro quo* symmetry in the plot. However, on a deeper level, in the realm of meditation, reflection, and scrutiny where murder remains murder, we must look for additional explanatory structures for killing the bad guy.

Geßler is indeed a tyrant and his murder seems to benefit the public, but this tyrant is also a torturer and the text-internal authorization to abandon gentler means of processing the horrors of tyranny may be located or grounded in torture and the revision of reality that accompanies it. I rely here on Elaine Scarry's important work on pain and the infliction of pain, *The Body in Pain*,[11] and assume a reasonable homology between the understanding of torment in *Wilhelm Tell* and Scarry's meticulous research on torture, which drew on interviews with survivors of these practices. I will return to this presently, but for now, I want to explore, as a prelude to torture and its effects, the motif of the paternal in *Wilhelm Tell*, since it is precisely fatherhood that falls victim to torture.

The value-laden activity and circumstances mentioned above can be almost entirely subsumed under the idea of fatherhood. *Wilhelm Tell* is a pageant of the paternal and its Other, not only in terms of deep textual structures that might open up to psychoanalytic inquiry, but also in terms of surface-level phenomena. There is more actual paternal "matter" here than symbolic intimation of it and the play "names" the father frequently and obviously. Repeated references to various figures' status as progenitors are most common ("Mein Haus entbehrt des Vaters" [My home is now lacking its father] V:402); "Ihr selbst seid Väter" [You are yourselves fathers] V:453) and the appellation "Vater," which applies to all of the founding figures of Swiss democracy, is, in *Wilhelm Tell*, the name of the game. Fatherhood is an attribute of freedom-loving Swiss men, and the occasional sons (Melchtal, Walther Tell) who have as yet no children, are obviously appended to fathers. Stauffacher appears to have no children, but Tell labels him "Ein Vater der Bedrängten" [a father of the oppressed] (V:400), almost as if it were necessary to establish paternal credentials for him. All Swiss men are brought into conformity with fatherhood and the events of *Wilhelm Tell* are firmly grounded in the realm of the *Väter*. That Tell does not appear to have a father himself—his father is never mentioned and his sons are named after him and his wife's father—makes him an originary type, *the* father whose paternity is not adulterated by son status. As such he will act as representative father and his actions will have paternal repercussions beyond the *Privatsache*.

Gessler, the evil foreign governor, forms a curious exception to this community of fathers and even to the subcommunity of sons. As Gertrud explains, after invoking her father to establish her authority to speak ("Des edlen Ibergs Tochter ruehm ich mich" [I am proud to call myself the daughter of noble Iberg] V:396), Gessler is a younger son and thus has no property of his own. Already the victim of primogeniture, Gessler is also politically propertyless since he merely tends to the possessions of the emperor and acts as a bureaucratically remote representative of the current owner and ruler. Thus doubly disenfranchised, Gessler has, furthermore, failed to reproduce, a fact that sets him far apart from the emperor's Swiss subjects. Tell informs him, "Herr, ihr habet keine Kinder—wisset nicht, / Was sich bewegt in eines Vaters Herzen [Sir, you habe no children—you do not know / What lives in the heart of a father] (V:454). Well-positioned for spectatorial contempt, Geßler is the non-father who represents the Landesvater in this world of Swiss fathers. He performs his mediating function with a cold authoritarian harshness that most of the Swiss view as misrepresentation. Geßler is the quintessential foreigner, an alien agent of indirect rule, whose sterility and cowardice—he trembled when he encountered Tell alone—will be compensated in the apple-shot scene, where he uses Tell as his agent or intermediary in an attempt to de-father Tell by taking his son from him.

The emphasis on paternity and its corollary categories, husband and son, is neatly reproduced in the trinity of offenses perpetrated by the emperor's governors. The assault of bad foreign government on native familial relations begins, as noted, with Wolfenschiessen's attempt to rape Baumgarten's wife in their home, an act that, if it had been successful, might have planted the alien seed in the native Swiss ground. This narrowly averted act of miscegenation or "unauthorized reproduction"[12] gives added dimension to a line from the idyllic opening song,

> Wir fahren zu Berge, wir kommen wieder,
> Wenn der Kuckuck ruft, wenn erwachen die Lieder.
> (V:388)
> [We go to the mountains, and we return,
> When the cuckoo calls, when the songs awaken.]

The call of the cuckoo, so early in the play, indicates a foundational disquietude about fatherhood that is then enacted in Baumgarten's rather strong reaction to a rape that did not occur and in his compatriots' horror at hearing of Wolfenschiessen's attack. The inaugural event of *Wilhelm Tell*, reported and not staged, stands as a kind of primal trauma, an assault on the sanctity of the home, the "race," and fatherhood. Baumgarten, who smashed the Burgvogt's skull with an ax, tells his tale as he flees the governor's horsemen. His swift and righteous response to the attempted violation of his *Hausrecht* [domestic dominion] had made him the object of persecution and Tell risks his life to save this murderous husband, whose deed is never subjected to question or reflection. As Baumgarten puts it, "Daß er sein bös Gelüsten nicht vollbracht, / Hat Gott und meine gute Axt verhütet" [God and my good ax has [sic] seen to it that he was not able to enact his vile lust] (V:391). The nonagreement of subjects and verb may even indicate an identity of subjects. To put it plainly, Baumgarten did the right thing.

The Baumgarten episode also foreshadows the frightening conflation of the play's most significant terms, *Vater* and *Mörder*. The Swiss, while lamenting Baumgarten's predicament and justifying the risk involved in saving him, identify him as a father (V:441). But when the governor's horsemen arrive, they demand the murderer (V:394), and it is at this point that the play's argument for justifiable homicide takes shape, in the figure of the father as murderer. This figure has a simple, straightforward aspect, that of the enraged father who murders to protect those he loves, and there is no ethical reflection on

Baumgarten's deed. Yet, Tell, who also might have fit this description, is qualified and complicated in ways that distance him from Baumgarten's righteous display. The murder of Geßler could have been merely an intensification of Wolfenschiessen's murder inasmuch as the parallels are obvious: Swiss man kills foreign agent who threatens his family. But instead of working it into the prefabricated framework, Schiller offers Geßler's murder as a problem to be considered and ultimately allows Tell to rationalize it by confronting it with Parricida's viler deed.

Where Baumgarten was offended directly as husband, Melchtal is stricken as a son, when his father is tortured and blinded as a result of Melchtal's having struck one of the governor's servants. He will ultimately show mercy and end the cycle of vengeance because his father, the one who actually suffered the punishment, decrees it. Finally, Tell is put into the position of having to save his own son's life by shooting at him. The apparently hierarchical progression of offenses (against husband/wife, son/father, father/son) and reactions culminates in the terrible scene where Gessler literally tortures Tell with the mandate that he shoot at his son. The evocation of a father's grief in this segment is so vivid that it forms a glaring exception to the wooden declamatory style that dominates the play. Tell pleads with Geßler:

> Herr—Welches Ungeheuer sinnet ihr
> Mir an—Ich soll vom Haupte meines Kindes—
> —Nein, nein doch, lieber Herr, das kömmt euch nicht
> Zu Sinn—Verhüts der gnädge Gott—das könnt ihr
> Im Ernst von einem Vater nicht begehren. (V:453)

> [Sir, what monstrous capacity do you
> Attribute to me—I should from the head of my child—
> —No, no really, dear Sir, that cannot be your wish
> Merciful God forbid—You can't
> Seriously ask that of a father.]

Tell's lines, the stage directions, and the observations of bystanders record his physical deterioration, his trembling and loss of sight, and his final collapse after he has somehow managed the successful shot. As the stage notation before the shot indicates:

Tell steht in fürchterlichen Kampf, mit den Händen zuckend, und die rollenden Augen bald auf den Landvogt, bald zum Himmel gerichtet. (V:457)

[*Tell stands there in a frightful struggle with himself, with twitching hands, and rolling eyes, fixed alternately on the governor and on Heaven above.*]

And after the shot:

Tell stand mit vorgebogenem Leib, als wollt' er dem Pfeil folgen—die Armbrust entsinkt seiner Hand—wie er den Knaben kommen sieht, eilt er ihm mit ausgebreiteten Armen entgegen, und hebt ihn mit heftiger Inbrunst zu seinem Herzen hinauf, in dieser Stellung sinkt er kraftlos zusammen. Alle stehen gerührt. (V:459)

[*Tell stood bent forward as if he wanted to follow the arrow—the bow sinks from his hand. As he sees the boy coming, he runs to him with open arms, and lifts him with intense fervor to his heart, in this position he collapses, powerless. All those attending are moved.*]

As Tell struggles to overcome his human reactions and paternal grief to concentrate on marksmanship, while aiming at his son, Geßler remains composed and resolute. He appears to insist on the shot, "Ich will dein Leben nicht, ich will den Schuß" [I don't want your life, I want the shot] (V:457), but his reaction to it, "Er hat geschossen? Wie? Der Rasende?" [He shot? How? The madman!] (V:458), makes it very clear that Geßler was not trying to force a display of marksmanship, but rather to *torment* Tell. Had murder been Geßler's intention, he could have taken Tell's life at any time, such as when Tell offered it to him above, but instead he chose to torture his victim by perverting his paternal love. The shot itself is concealed on the surface or hidden in clear sight as an argument between Rudenz and Geßler distracts the spectators, but the preparation and aftermath, Geßler's taunting and torturing of Tell, and Tell's murder of Geßler, indicate that in that process of preparing to shoot, Father Tell was transformed in ways interestingly accounted for by Scarry's study.

Scarry has written eloquently on the structure of torture, its purposes and the torturer-prisoner configuration, noting that this experience of pain "un-makes" the prisoner's world, as all else is overwhelmed and superseded by the pain and the torturer's questions. Her insights into this form of scripted political cruelty are also enlightening for the confrontation of Tell and Geßler in Altdorf. Working from the accounts of political prisoners, Scarry concluded that torture has a consistent structure involving 1) the infliction of pain; 2) the objectification of the subjective attributes of pain, a process by which the sufferer's pain is made visible to others present; and 3) the translation of those attributes into the insignia of the regime (Scarry, 19, 51–59), "the conversion of an enlarged map of human suffering into an emblem of the regime's strength" (Scarry, 56). The Tell-Geßler encounter of the first shot begins with a perceived dismissal of the insignia of the regime as Tell fails to pay homage to an object that he does not recognize as symbolically charged, "Was kuemmert uns der Hut?" [What do we care about the hat?] (V:450). Geßler has placed his hat on a pike to be revered as a sign of his own borrowed and transitory power and that of the emperor and Tell's misreading or non-reading of the hat—in a play that represses and degrades symbols—is his entry into the realm of the political prisoner, whose deviance elicits the torture and concomitant "unmaking of the world" in the experience of pain. Scarry writes primarily of physical pain, but Tell's paternal suffering is of equal or greater severity—he even volunteers for physical pain and death, as noted above ("Erlasset mir den Schuß. Hier ist mein Herz," [Spare me the shot. Here is my heart] V:456), to avoid the horrible shot.

Scarry's third phase or moment of the torturer-prisoner transaction is the conversion of the attributes of pain into the insignia of the regime, a process that is intended to give substance to the fiction of power (torture being practiced overwhelmingly by unstable or threatened regimes). As Scarry writes:

> The physical pain is so incontestably real that it seems to confer its quality of "incontestable reality" on that power that has brought it into being. It is, of course, precisely because the reality of that power is so highly contestable, the regime so unstable, that torture is being used. (Scarry, 27)

Geßler, younger son, non-father, and stand-in for the emperor, has already threatened the propertied, such as Stauffacher, and vowed to make them propertyless like him. Now he undertakes to transform Tell into a non-father like himself, by forcing him to practice the opposite of paternal love in order to save his son—that is, to be a father by not being one, a fiendish unmaking of paternity, the very ground of all values in the play. As Hedwig remarks, "O Hätt er eines Vaters Herz, eh er's / Getan, er wäre tausendmal gestorben" [If he had a father's heart, he would have died a thousand times before he did it] (V:469). In fact, part of Tell did die under Geßler's tormenting order. Scarry writes of the torturer's habit of perverting domestic objects that signal nurture and using them as weapons. Similarly, Geßler has transformed the apple and, as Tell himself acknowledges in his monologue, the hunter's bow, but more important is his manipulation and perversion of fatherhood, that will reach fruition when Tell ambushes him.

Geßler fails to make Tell into a non-father—the shot is successful and Walter lives—but while appropriating the "incontestable reality" of a father's pain to legitimize the symbol of his power, Geßler redefines fatherhood. Geßler has, as Tell acknowledges, made him both father and murderer or, to put it another way, made murder into a loving paternal gesture. As noted, there is already some intimation of this collapsing of roles in the Baumgarten scene where the Swiss describe him as a father and the governor's men identify the same man as a murderer. As the play proceeds, a resemblance between the two terms is gradually established until Tell unites or merges them by killing Geßler. The two functions are then finally recombined in the *Vatermörder*, Parricida, who, true to his function as scapegoat, absorbs all the guilt and leaves the scene.

As Tell waits in ambush for Geßler, he describes the murder he plans as one resulting from paternal love—speaking of himself in the third person,

—Und doch an euch denkt er, lieben Kinder,
Auch jetzt—Euch zu verteidigen, eure holde Unschuld
Zu schützen vor der Rache des Tyrannen
Will er *zum Morde* jetzt den Bogen spannen! (V:480, my emphasis)

[And yet he thinks of you, dear children.
At this moment to defend and to protect
Your innocence from the vengeance of the tyrant
He draws his bow *for murder*.]

Tell names the deed as murder several times in his monologue, though he will abandon this nomenclature in the fifth act with Parricida.

Having unmade Tell's world and made him tremble and act in an unfatherly way, Geßler equalizes the inequality that emerged in their encounter in the pass. Tell's world has dissolved with the perversion of fatherhood and this is perhaps the compelling, and perhaps for Schiller irrefutable, justification of murder. Kant, for example, saw no murder where civil society had dissolved, as in the case of the unwed infanticide referenced earlier, whose act could be exempted from the category of murder because as a mother without a husband she was unconnected to civil society. As disenfranchised father, whose world of order and authority had been unmade, Tell is in a similar position. Victim Geßler has—following this logic—created his own murderer by dismantling the structures of family and civil society. Expectations of his vengeance are a factor and they are justified by a long record of his cruel and vindictive behavior—and thus they lead to a reasonably good foundation for Tell's killing him. But Geßler's death is still referred to as *Mord* by the bystanders and by the murderer himself. The retention of this word, which denotes a profoundly evil action, for the ambush that Tell describes as self-defense and father-love indicates that this killing is not being disqualified as murder, but rather considered as a subspecies of murder that is quite possibly useful and good *in the post-apple-shot world of compromised father(murderer)hood*.

Then Parricida shows up (what are the chances?). With this improbable and awkward final segment, Schiller avoids the impression of endorsing tyrannicide. He did not, after all, live in a free society and his play needed to be read and performed in absolutist states. Despots were easily offended and tyranny was often a matter of interpretation. Furthermore, in terms of comparative criminality, the fifth act gives Tell the opportunity to underscore most ostentatiously the virtuous nature of his murdering Geßler as opposed to the vile deed of the abject parricida. Tell killed *as* father—and it was a despised non-father whom he killed—but Parricida killed *a* father, his blood relative and everyone's *Landesvater*. Tell strongly supports the abjection of Parricida:

> Euren Ohm
> erschlagen, euern Kaiser! Und euch trägt
> Die Erde noch! Euch leuchtet noch die Sonne! (V:501)
>
> [You killed your uncle, your emperor
> And yet the earth carries you still!
> The sun still shines on you!]

He draws a clear line between their respective deeds, providing an ethical summary of a different kind of murder for the audience:

> Darfst du der Ehrsucht blutge Schuld vermengen
> Mit der gerechten Notwehr eines Vaters?
> Hast du der Kinder liebes Haupt verteidigt?
> Des Herdes Heiligtum beschützt? Das Schrecklichste,
> Das Letzte von den deinen abgewehrt?
> —Zum Himmel heb' ich meine reinen Hände,
> Verfluche dich und deine Tat—Gerächt
> Hab ich die heilige Natur, die du
> Geschändet—Nichts teil' ich mit dir—Gemordet
> Hast du, ich hab mein teuerstes verteidigt. (V:501)
>
> [Do you dare compare the bloody guilt of ambition
> With the righteous self-defense of a father?
> Did you defend your children's dear heads?
> Or protect the holy hearth? Repel
> A terrible threat from your loved ones?
> I raise my unsullied hands to heaven,
> And curse you and your deed. I avenged
> The holy nature that you
> Disgraced—I have nothing in common with you.
> You murdered and I defended my most precious goods.]

The easy certainty of Tell's reproach barely corresponds to what has gone before and this has not gone unnoticed in the critical literature. Hammer objects that Parricida is "clearly a double for Tell himself" and that "the difference between a national hero and a murderous demagogue seems uncomfortably fragile in this scene" (Hammer, 18–19). Tell ultimately casts off the label, murder, recasting his deed as *non-murderous* defense of home and family, his "most precious goods" being the fatherhood that Geßler conjoined with criminality.

What does the dramatic stage actually *do* in *Wilhelm Tell*? What it does is somewhat insidious. Schiller marshals all the pageantry of a *Volksstück* to expand the Swiss national legend of the apple shot to a carefully considered defense of murder as a viable and even ethical choice. In so doing he places values such as homeland, family, and domestic sovereignty (Baumgarten's *Hausrecht*) above human life, or, more precisely, above *certain* human lives. This is the very dark side of Schiller's stage where "we" and "they" become irreconcilably polarized, without a third term to relieve the opposition. All men will not become brothers as in "An die Freude," because some men are good and others are bad. The call of the cuckoo with its threat of hybridity drowns out the song of joy and the final operatic scene rings hollow even as Rudenz invokes greater equality by freeing those workers bound to him in servitude.

AN EARLIER MURDER: *DER VERBRECHER AUS VERLORENER EHRE* (1786)

Schiller's dark literary reflections on murder, responsibility, and reprehensibility culminated and concluded ambiguously in *Wilhelm Tell*, but they are funded by earlier works, including an excruciatingly precise examination of murder and motivation based on an actual case. Wilhelm Tell murders as a cultural agent attempting to recover or restore a prelapsarian fatherhood (publicly) and he also murders as a traumatized subject (privately) who has experienced a perversion of core values in the unmaking of his world in the apple-shot scene. In both types of agency, Tell has an interesting ancestor in another of Schiller's murderers, Christian Wolf.

Wolf, the *Verbrecher aus Infamie* and *verlorener Ehre* is not generally discussed in connection with Tell; he is more commonly associated with one of the Moor brothers. He leads a robber band, while never completely losing his sense of decency (Karl), and he functions as unsavory physiognomic specimen, a man led to do evil because of (society's reaction to) his considerable physical ugliness (Franz). In fact, as critics have remarked,[13] Franz Moor and Christian Wolf suffer from very similar cases of ugliness, a handicap that seems to consist of adulterated or mixed racial features, that evoke a history of hybridity or unauthorized reproduction. Franz is quite explicit in his description of his multiracial appearance:

> Warum gerade mir die Lappländers Nase? Gerade mir diese Mohrenmaul? Diese Hottentotten Augen? Wirklich ich glaube [die Natur] hat von allen Menschensorten das Scheußliche auf einen Haufen geworfen, und mich daraus gebacken. (II:28)

> [Why was I given this Laplander's nose? This Moor's mouth? These Hottentot eyes? Really, I believe [nature] took from all races the most hideous features, threw them in a pile, and baked me.]

In *Verbrecher*, the narrator's description of Wolf repeats some of these un-Caucasianisms:

> Die Natur hatte seinen Körper verabsäumt. Eine kleine unscheinbare Figur, krauses Haar von einer unangenehmen Schwärze, eine plattgedrückte Nase und eine geschwollene Oberlippe, welche noch überdies durch den Schlag eines Pferdes aus ihrer Richtung gewichen war, gab seinem Anblick eine Widrigkeit, welche alle Weiber von ihm zurückscheuchte und dem Witz seiner Kameraden eine reichliche Nahrung darbot. (VII:565–66)

> [Nature had neglected his body. He had a small, unremarkable figure, kinky hair of an unpleasant black color, a flattened nose, and a swollen upper lip, which on top of everything, was turned in another direction by a horse's kick, and this gave his appearance a disgusting aspect that frightened all the women away and offered much fodder for his friends' jokes.]

It is obvious that the range of Schiller's later subtly differentiated analysis of beauty far exceeds his (here) unanalyzed and untheorized grasp of ugliness as irregularity and non-European features. A radically different, and in racial terms, non-harmonious appearance marks each of these men as an outcast from his society and excludes him from the economy of love. For this and other reasons, each commits crimes and suffers the consequences. Franz's crimes are more enormous, it appears, but Franz never kills anyone except himself.

There are numerous other associations for Christian Wolf beyond Franz Moor, including the biblical tale of the prodigal son,[14] and, by way of the *verlorene Ehre* in Schiller's title, Heinrich Böll's murderess, Katharina Blum, but I would like to pursue the affinities with Tell in order to read their respective murders and the network of accusatory and exculpatory factors in which they are embedded.

In a recent investigation of the narration of actual murders, Sara L. Knox focuses on retellings, reenactments, and re-authorings of accounts of murder in the service of the "interestedness of [American] culture in the murderousness it ethically deplores."[15] Knox addresses the mutability of empirical detail in these re-narrations and the engineering of successive accounts toward romantic, titillating, or didactic ends. Schiller himself "received" the story of the bandit Fridrich Schwan from his teacher, Jacob Friedrich Abel, whose father had arrested Schwan. Abel later wrote an account based on his father's explanations of the affair and on his own conversations with Schwan, who for the most part shaped his story into a cautionary tale— appropriately, since he was narrating while awaiting execution. The facts of the matter were, for Abel, Schiller, and perhaps for Schwan himself, subordinate to the "mystery" of Schwan's development, of a reasonable man's choice of crime and murder. The transmission from Schwan to Abel to Schiller was largely oral, though Abel may have already had a manuscript to show to his pupil. "Eine wahre Geschichte" [A True Story] as the piece is subtitled, must, we assume, have appealed to a "higher truth" behind the human capacity for homicide. Basic details of Schwan's career and person are not preserved and one significant departure from the source involves the criminal's appearance: Abel, who knew Schwan, describes him as "schön" [good-looking] and a wanted poster makes reference to his "glatte Haare" [straight hair][16] both of which features or qualities are directly inverted in Schiller's tale (see descriptions of Wolf above). The introduction of ugliness into the re-authored version facilitates the identification of a cause for Wolf's radical human misbehavior and Schiller will emphasize appearance and its effects as contributory factors.

Narrator Schiller's purpose in retelling Schwan's tale as Wolf's is that of psychic explorer of those movements of mind and development that result in crime. His ambition is to transmit to the reader an understanding in the deepest sense of Wolf's character and how it was shaped by external environmental factors. He will suggest that the seeds of misdeeds are inherent in the species but that these threatening factors can be subdued and controlled by understanding and human kindness. As Knox notes, while speaking of the true crime genre, a contemporary form that Schiller's "wahre" "Verbrecher" story prefigures: "It is not the identification of the killer that provides *jouissance* in the true crime tale (as it does in detective fiction) but the ascription of an intelligible motive for the crime." (Knox, 110–11). To make murder intelligible, that is to explain and perhaps justify the human reasons behind it, is to re-humanize the perpetrator and to rescue humanity which has been degraded by association. This rescue can also be accomplished by abjecting the specimen and thus canceling the association. Schiller seems to employ both methods in *Tell*, explaining in the monologue and abjecting in the Parricida scene, but *Verbrecher* illustrates the dangers of abjecting in its descriptions of Wolf's subsequent life of crime. The tale itself concentrates on explanation and intelligibility:

Der Held muß kalt werden wie der Leser, oder, was hier ebensoviel sagt, wir müssen mit ihm bekannt werden, *eh'* er handelt; wir müssen ihn seine Handlung nicht bloß *vollbringen* sondern auch wollen sehen. An seinen Gedanken liegt uns unendlich mehr als an seinen Taten, und noch mehr an den Quellen seiner Gedanken als an den Folgen jener Taten. (VII:564)

[The hero must become cold like the reader or, in other words, we must get to know him before he acts; we should not just see him commit his crime, we should also be curious to see it. His thoughts are far more important to us than his actions and the sources of his thoughts are even more important than the consequences of his actions.]

Where the explanation for Wilhelm Tell's murder of Geßler is muddled by Tell's contradictory declarations and sedimented by almost two centuries of contentious critical commentary, the murder committed by Christian Wolf is mired in explanation and manufactured clarity. *Wilhelm Tell* is *about* many things whereas *Verbrecher* concentrates on the background and criminal career of one man, but there are strong similarities of detail between them. Both men are hunters who are oppressed by government officials and each endures repeated offenses before killing the enemy. Both kill to restore something that has been lost, rather than for gain as hunters do, and both murder as traumatized men, who have been detached from the moral fabric of their particular societies—in each case, the values of their culture no longer work for them.

Wolf is immediately established as a *specimen* of criminal humanity, a test case for a particular set of environmental factors and the result that these factors yields is a reasonable, intelligent man "gone bad." Wolf's father died when he was young—another Schiller-izing of the material since, in Schwan's case, it was his mother who died and Schwan actually identified his father as the *cause* of his crimes. By refusing to allow his marriage, Father Schwan prevented Fridrich from leading an honest life and provoked him to lead a dishonest one (Abel, 66), but it is the absence of Wolf's father that contributes to his felonious development.[17]

Wolf's widowed mother spoils him, and since the family inn (poorly managed by the mother?) does not draw many customers, the boy has excessive amounts of time unoccupied by work or productive activity ("müßige Stunden," VII:565). He furthermore has to contend with his unpleasant appearance and its repellent effects. Fatherless and ugly, Christian Wolf is both ethically and aesthetically disenfranchised and the narrative follows the stations of his descent into serious crime, encompassing several arrests, loss of his fortune, imprisonment in a moderate and then a severe penal institution, the corrupting influence of his confinement and, finally, murder. In a tale still familiar to contemporary penal studies, Wolf, who takes over the narrative, relates how imprisonment robbed him of his dignity and brought him under the influence of hardened criminals:

> Ich betrat die Festung . . . als ein Verirrter und verließ sie als ein Lotterbube. . . . Wie ich auf die Festung gebracht war, sperrte man mich zu dreiundzwanzig Gefangenen ein, unter denen zwei Mörder und die übrigen alle berüchtigte Diebe und Vagabunden waren. Man verhöhnte mich, wenn ich von Gott sprach, und setzte mir zu schändliche Lästerungen gegen den Erlöser zu sagen. . . . Anfangs floh ich dieses Volk und verkroch mich vor ihren Gesprächen, so gut mir's möglich war; aber ich brauchte ein Geschöpf, und die Barbarei meiner Wächter hatte mir auch meinen Hund abgeschlagen. . . . So gewöhnte ich mich endlich an das Abscheulichste, und im letzten Vierteljahr hatte ich meine Lehrmeister übertroffen. (VII:568)

> [I entered the fortress . . . as an errant man and left it as a criminal. . . . When I was brought there, I was locked up with

twenty-three prisoners, among whom two were murderers and the others notorious thieves and vagabonds. They mocked me when I spoke of God, and got me to utter terrible blasphemies against the redeemer. . . . In the beginning, I avoided these people and retreated from their conversations as much as I could, but I needed company and the barbaric guards had even taken away my dog. So I accustomed myself to the most abominable things and by the last quarter year I had outpaced my teachers.]

As a mere poacher, Wolf was not in a class with his cellmates. He had furthermore committed his crimes out of (imagined) love for a young woman, Hanne, for whom Wolf had to provide gifts in order to compete with her better-looking suitors. An enlightened segregation of criminals would presumably have prevented the transformation Wolf describes, and he does his part for penal reform by attesting to the effects of the indiscriminate grouping of all manner of offenders in the same cell.[18] Ugliness isolates, bad companions educate, and Wolf/Schiller seems to be piling up the unfortunate external circumstances that will make murder intelligible. These are the factors that distinguish Wolf from the similarly concupiscent, "dessen Laster in einer engen bürgerlichen Sphäre und in der schmalen Umzäunung der Gesetze jetzt ersticken muß" [whose vices must suffocate in narrow bourgeois society and the restricting pen of the law] (VII:563). Schiller insists on the elements of chance and environment, combined with a certain personal susceptibility, as formative causes of criminality. There are many others who could have committed the same crimes had it not been for the "smothering" influence of their bourgeois surroundings, and Wolf's affinity with so many others should inspire empathy and understanding.

The trigger that secures Wolf's exclusion from these bourgeois enclosures is his encounter with an attractive child who refuses a coin from him for no apparent reason other than his person: "Tränen, wie ich sie nie geweint hatte, liefen über meine Backen" [Tears, such as I had never shed, ran down my cheeks] (VII:570). Wolf realizes in retrospect that it was his appearance that had repelled the visually appealing child, particularly a beard he had grown in prison that "[seine] Gesichtszüge zum Gräßlichen entstellte" [distorted his facial features horribly] (VII:569). The beard appears to intensify Wolf's natural ugliness, but his expression of this intensification implicitly detaches the ugliness from his person and invests it in the (removable) beard, that *distorted* his features, making them ugly. Wolf then mimetically reproduces the wrong done to him—demonstrating a very clear and uncomplicated theory of crime or wrongdoing—with a repetition of the child's rejection directed toward a third party. Hanne comes along and greets him joyously, but he sees from her appearance that she has come down in the world and has contracted a venereal disease. Wolf rejects and insults Hanne because "ihr Anblick verkündigte die verworfenste Kreatur, zu der sie erniedrigt war" [her appearance heralded the depraved creature to which she had been reduced] (VII:570). *Sein und Schein*, reality and appearance, harmonize for Wolf in the abject Hanne, but the same social assumptions of a unity of essence and appearance are at the root of Wolf's criminality. He has absorbed society's mistreatment of him and redirected it toward society in much the same form. Offenses and reparations are repeatedly expressed as debits and credits in the economy of *Verbrecher* and Wolf who had been pre-punished, and thus had pre-paid his "debt to society" resolved to expend the credit he had built up: "Ich wollte mein Schicksal verdienen" [I wanted to earn my fate] (VII:571).

Wolf's victim is his chief persecutor, Robert a game official and previous rival for Hanne's affections who maliciously stalked him and arrested him three times for poaching. In the first case, Wolf lost his fortune in fines paid to avoid jail and Robert won Hanne. In the second, Wolf spent a year in the *Zuchthaus* or penitentiary and, finally, he was branded as a thief and sentenced to three years hard labor at the provincial fortress. As a previous offender, Wolf earned a stiffer penalty, but, as noted earlier, the narrator is highly critical of the sentencing procedure, complaining that the judges looked at the law books, but not at the defendant's state of mind. Robert's behavior was entirely legal, but nonetheless reprehensible because his motives were malicious and thus Robert emerges as the agent of a legal system that unjustly (or erroneously or unwisely) robbed Christian Wolf of the life opportunities he might otherwise have had (lost honor). Killing, for Wolf, is a counter-social act in the wake of a trauma that caused him to embrace lawlessness for its own sake, and at first he intends to kill anyone who tries to restrain him (VII:571). Killing *Robert* is an attempt to restore the balance

5: MURDEROUS FATHERS 115

that Robert upset with his aggressive and interested law enforcement, and thus to return to the prelapsarian or honorable stage of his life, that is, to recover his lost honor by avenging it. The attempt is unsuccessful and Wolf descends into criminal depravity.

The murders committed by Wolf and Tell diverge in many ways, chief among them the length of the period of premeditation and the ripeness of intention. Not only does Tell stake out a position in the narrow pass leading to Küßnacht, but he recalls in his monologue that he had vowed to kill Geßler if he missed the apple shot. Wolf tells of various bad intentions he formed in the wake of the child incident, but does not focus on a particular course of action other than generalized law-breaking and armed resistance to capture. His encounter with Robert in the forest is purely a matter of chance. Wolf is hunting and comes up behind Robert who is aiming at the same deer Wolf has been following, a recurrence of their rivalry, but also a detail from the source.[19] The ugly poacher reflects for only a moment before shooting him, though it is an extended moment:

> In diesem Augenblick dünkte mich's, als ob die ganze Welt in meinem Flintenschuß läge und der Haß meines ganzen Lebens in die einzige Fingerspitze sich zusammendrängte, womit ich den mörderische Druck tun sollte. Eine unsichtbare fürchterlich Hand schwebte über mir, der Stundenweiser meines Schicksals zeigte unwiderruflich auf diese schwarze Minute. Der Arm zitterte mir, da ich meiner Flinte die schreckliche Wahl erlaubte—meine Zähne schlugen zusammen wie im Fieberfrost, und der Odem sperrte sich erstickend in meiner Lunge. Eine Minute lang blieb der Lauf meiner Flinte ungewiß zwischen dem Menschen und dem Hirsch mitten inne schwanken—eine Minute—und noch eine—und wieder eine. Rache und Gewissen rangen hartnäckig und zweifelhaft, aber die Rache gewann's und der Jäger lag tot am Boden. (VII:572)

> [In this moment, it was as if the whole world lay in my rifle barrel and the hatred of my whole life was concentrated in that single finger tip, with which I was to murderously pull the trigger. A terrible invisible hand hovered above me and the clock hands of my fate pointed irrevocably toward this black minute. My arm trembled as I left the terrible choice to my gun—my teeth were clenched as in fever chills and my breath was trapped, suffocatingly in my lungs. For a minute, the barrel of my rifle oscillated, uncertain, between

the man and the animal—a minute and then another and then another. Vengeance and conscience struggled doggedly and yet in doubt, but vengeance won and the hunter lay dead on the ground]

In Wolf's account, as in Schiller's description of Egmont's execution, the killing is elided and there is furthermore an absence of integrated human agency. Guided by an invisible hand and by fate, the arm, the fingertip, the gun barrel, and finally vengeance conspire to effect the corpse on the ground. Wilhelm Tell disperses guilt, citing Geßler's provocations and chastising Parricida, but there is no question of agency—*Tell* did it, whatever it was. Wolf diffuses agency in his description and he elides the killing, but, unlike Tell, he accepts responsibility for the deed, calling himself a murderer. He then flashes back on the execution of a child-murderess he had witnessed as a youth, dreading punishment. It is an interesting comment on the efficacy/*Wirkung* of capital punishment as a deterrent that he recalls the execution *after* the deed and not before.

In the aftermath of their murders Tell and Wolf each experience a mirroring episode in which they encounter a doppelgänger figure, another murderer who seeks their company and reflects their civil and moral status. Murderer Tell meets murderer Parricida and hears him speak of their resemblance: "Auch ich / habe einen Feind erschlagen, der mir Recht / Versagte" [I too have killed an enemy who denied me my rights] (3152–54). This assertion of similarity sets the stage for Tell's vigorous rebuttal and an even stronger denial of guilt, as he dramatically raises his "unsullied" hands to heaven and so forth. Tell eventually relents somewhat and acknowledges a resemblance in their common humanity ("Ihr seid ein Mensch—Ich bin es auch—" [You are a human being—I am one too] V:503), but his bland appeal to this most general and ultimately insignificant type of resemblance does not effectively undermine the particulars cited by Parricida. They are obviously humans, but that they both have murdered is an important point of both similarity and difference. Tell does not contemplate his reflection in Parricida, the mirroring figure, but rather sends him away, and his refusal to look into the mirror of the murderer is an act of repression and denial that complicates and corrupts the joyous conclusion of the piece. The bondsmen may be free, but Wilhelm Tell has somehow slipped back into the "narrow bourgeois sphere," where murderous urges are smothered, as if he had never left it. This "unmaking" of Geßler's murder in the confrontation with Parricida remains profoundly disturbing.

Wolf, who feels degraded by the murder, which effects an intensification rather than a restoration of lost honor, is entirely willing to see himself in the wild man with the club whom he meets in the forest. He identifies himself to him as "Deinesgleichen" [one of your kind] (VII:575) and "ein Mörder wie du" [a murderer like you] (VII:576). In terms of physical resemblance—appearance being a major element of "fate," the man, like Wolf, has mixed racial features, and these are aggressively brought forth in the narrative which gives his skin color as being "von einer gelben Mulattenschwärze" [of a yellowish mulatto blackness] (VII:575). Rather than send him away, Wolf follows him into the deep caves where his band of robbers lives, and joins the group. The wild man is able to claim Wolf for his depraved society, whereas Parricida cannot persuade Tell that they have anything significant in common.

Verbrecher illustrates that early on Schiller had considered the act of murder and the question of what leads a human being to commit it in terms other than those invoked in *Die Räuber*, where the act appears more abstract and sublime on the melodramatic stage.[20] He had also worked out ways of "staging" this act and its problematic, which included the appearance of a second murder for purposes of contrast. For Wolf, there is no question of *Notwehr* or *Selbsthilfe* and in *Tell* we have only the appearance of these exculpatory conditions. In both cases, Schiller devises a murder that must be seen as just that *and then* explained via psychology and the effects of trauma. Tell emerges unpunished and righteous, but, as we learn from brief references in subordinate clauses, Wolf was tortured and executed for Robert's murder and a string of notorious crimes that followed it. Schiller stops the narrative at the point where Wolf is arrested and does not write of the punishment. In fact, he writes against it. *Verbrecher* pleads for understanding, not punishment, much as Wolf and Schwan pleaded for pardon from their dukes in exchange for service. As Thomas Nutz notes, Schiller is arguing for something that is still a matter of debate in twentieth-century penal circles:

> Schiller zeigte, daß der Staat mit Hilfe seiner Strafpraktiken, statt Verbrechen zu verhüten, seine Verbrecher eher selbst züchtet, indem

er sie immer tiefer in die Delinquenz hineintreibt, sie zu Verbrechen als Rachereaktionen auf die übermäßigen Strafen anstachelt.[21]

[Schiller demonstrated that with the help of its penal practices, the state, instead of preventing crime, actually cultivates its own criminals, by driving them ever more deeply into delinquency, and goading them into committing crimes as vengeance for excessive punishments.]

Wolf's memory of the execution of the child murderess has exactly this effect. Rather than occurring while he contemplated shooting Robert, it comes to him afterward and facilitates his entry into the wild man's robber band. Once again he will earn his fate, but this time in anticipation of the punishment that awaits him, a punishment that, like those cited by Nutz, may cause crime. Schiller's insertion of this detail—three years after *Geheimrat* Goethe voted to retain the death penalty for child-murderesses[22]—is intriguing because *Verbrecher* is a treatise on punishment and even the title can be read as a statement on penal practices. Both *Infamie* and *verlorene Ehre* result from a penal system that marks and excludes its criminals, leaving them no choice but to pursue a livelihood by illegal means.

Verbrecher is focused squarely on the injustices of a penal system that does not account for human background and motivation, whereas *Tell* finds its injustices in the excesses of foreign rule. Indeed the texts are very different, one being a narrative written early in Schiller's career and presented as a true story and the other being a late drama that elaborates on legend. But they are also very similar in that each piece examines the act of murder, its motivation, and its potential justification, without concern for retributive punishment. Thus the pairing marks an early and a late station in Schiller's lifelong engagement with those actions that subvert the law, and if we choose to identify a development in this engagement, it is the movement from the attempt to understand a murder by listing exculpatory factors to the sovereign dismissal of culpability (before the law) and an actual celebration of murder committed under the right circumstances.

6

Schiller's Heart, Joan's Crimes, and Johanna's Glory: Rescuing the Feminine From History

> Ein *starker* Geist in einem *zarten* Leib
> Ein Zwitter zwischen Mann und Weib
> —"Die berühmte Frau" (I:269)
>
> Jetzt ist eine schwere Zeit,
> Wo auch das Weib sich in den Panzer steckt![1]
> —*Die Jungfrau von Orleans* (V:259)

JOAN OF ARC WAS YET ANOTHER ADDITION TO SCHILLER'S GALLERY OF admirable aberrants and miscreants, though his processing of this material formed a curious exception to the rule as we have seen it. In practice, Schiller treated crime as a fascinating intervention into social symmetry that was not to be diminished by a rebalancing punishment. The fiction and the drama resist the restoration of (bourgeois) equilibrium, and tend to establish the exceptional disruption as a manifestation of the courage, strategic intelligence, or "greatness" that humans are capable of. Rarely does Schiller work from or share the perspective of law enforcement and this is where his engagement with punishment becomes so interesting. There is in bourgeois society and in the absolutist state an institution that purports to deter and to avenge crime and it is this institution, the penal industry, that Schiller repeatedly represses in his work, while glorifying or at the very least contextualizing the evils it attempts to counter. As we know, Joan of Arc's spectacular punishment disappears under Schiller's pen. However it is not only her punishment that is effaced, but—significantly in this one case—also her crimes. Though Schiller so frequently thematized crime and aberration, he does not allow Joan's historical crimes to stand as such and this may have something to do with the fact that they were crimes of a very different order from those of Karl Moor, Fiesko, Christian Wolf, Mary Stuart, and Wilhelm Tell. Joan of Arc's most conspicuous crimes were transgressions against her contemporaries' understanding of gender and the codified manner of its representation and her (literarily intolerable?) gender crimes are deliberately canceled in *Die Jungfrau von Orleans*. Though it seems unwise to efface her execution inasmuch as audiences would have expected to see or hear of this historically recorded punishment, the otherwise baffling absence of this necessary piece of history makes sense in the absence of the historically recorded crimes.

The Maid of Orleans was a well-established and widely known criminal long before she was a saint. She led an army against the factions that eventually prosecuted her; she told church officials that she communicated with the saints and the Virgin Mary, while they insisted this claim was blasphemy and heresy; she furthermore violated a number of commandments and contributed to a fair amount of death and destruction, thus combining both religious crime with the worldly variety. But her real crimes, the ones for which she was ultimately burned at the stake had to do—at least officially—with what the judges deemed to be the misrepresentation of her gender. Though Joan never professed to be anything but a woman, her hair and clothing conflicted with her anatomy according to contemporary codes and thus put her outside the law.

The historical figure, who was born in 1412, started hearing voices when she was thirteen and these voices told her to go to the aid of Charles VII who was in the process of losing the Hundred Years War. After four years of prodding by the voices, Joan finally obeyed and presented herself to the Dauphin, who became convinced that she was sent from Heaven to save France and himself. However, after several spectacular military victories, Joan also began losing the war and she was captured on May 23, 1430, sold to the English, and tried for heresy. As Valerie Hotchkiss has noted, the interrogators' and prosecutors' interest in the question of her clothing and short hair was second only to the matter of the voices that formed the basis of the heresy accusations.[2] The matter of her disruptive self-presentation was also incorporated into the heresy charges by means of scripture, namely Deuteronomy 22:5, that dictated, "No woman shall wear an article of man's clothing, nor shall a man put on a woman's dress; for those who do these things are abominable to the Lord your God."[3] Her transgression of this prohibition was conspicuous and determining and the following accusation was included in the final list of charges against her:

> Likewise, you have said that you wore and still wear men's clothing at God's command and at his good pleasure, and because you had orders from God to wear this habit, you have put on a short tunic, doublet and boots tied up with many pointed laces. You even wear your hair cut round above the ears, not displaying anything about you that confirms or demonstrates sex, except what nature has given you.[4]

Joan's partial misrepresentation of her gender or the failure to display its markers was an offense against nature because she did not allow nature/anatomy to extend to her clothing and this failure of representation was deemed to be criminal. The catalogue of gender crimes (tunic, doublet, boots, hair) is extensive and explicit and part of her heresy is the assertion that the deity actually authorized this abandonment of the appropriate gender signifiers for the disturbing mixture of the anatomical female and the sartorial masculine that was the historical Joan of Arc. Her punishment and the events leading up to it dramatized and reinforced the primacy of anatomy that her judges thought she had challenged. Under threat of execution, Joan abjured and was given a sentence of life in prison *in women's clothes*. She obediently put on a dress and began her sentence in a secular prison—not in the ecclesiastical prison she would have preferred and from which she might more easily have escaped. This was a crucial misplacement for Joan and historians speculate[5] that her male guards—an affront that secular imprisonment carried with it—may have attempted or committed rape. Joan resumed wearing pants in order to protect herself from the crime or its repetition and it was this act, her defiance of the order that she wear a dress that led to her execution. As Françoise Meltzer puts it: "the crime by which the Church finally 'got' Joan was that of cross-dressing" (202).[6]

When word of her sartorial relapse reached her judges, Joan was once again interrogated and this procedure ran 28–30 May

1431. Under questioning she declared that she had not knowingly promised to cease wearing men's clothes and that the voices of Sts. Margaret and Catherine had warned her to retract her abjuration for the good of her soul. At this point, the scribe who kept protocol wrote "responsio mortifera" in the margin of the transcript, indicating that this response led or would lead to her death sentence.[7] Thus the resumption of cross-dressing and the claim that the saints had advised her to defy the church, an instance of religious heresy and an enactment of gender heresy—linked in the trial and verdict—caused the court to abandon its earlier sentence of life imprisonment on bread and water and to burn Joan at the stake.

The execution followed immediately and it unfolded in two stages. First, the fire was lit and Joan died of smoke inhalation, as was usual for victims of execution by fire. Her clothes were also burned off. At this point, the fire was extinguished and her naked body was displayed to all observers as apparent confirmation of her status as a female, thus effecting a display of "what nature gave her" unconfounded by contradictory sartorial signals.[8] The fire was then relit and the dead woman was burned like her dress before her and the remains were thrown into the river.

Schiller had these records before him as he planned and executed his own dramatic version of the Joan of Arc story. He certainly considered the burning and he sought information from Körner on witch trials and executions (V:620), but as he wrote to Goethe, he had not only used history, but also "overcome" it: "Das historische ist überwunden, und doch soviel ich urtheilen kann, in seinem möglichsten Umfang benutzt" [I have overcome the historical and yet, in my judgment, I have used it to the greatest extent possible] (24 December 1800; V:626). This is a highly intriguing contention, namely that Schiller struggled with history and prevailed, and a subsequent letter to Göschen (10 February 1802) may have some explanatory value. In it, Schiller writes: "Dieses Stück ist *aus dem Herzen* geschrieben und *zu dem Herzen* sollte es auch sprechen" [This play was written *from the heart* and it should also speak *to the heart*] (V:634, italics Schiller's). Schiller had already told Körner during the writing process that the composition of *Jungfrau* was a matter of the heart:

6: SCHILLER'S HEART, JOAN'S CRIMES, AND JOHANNA'S GLORY

Schon der Stoff erhält mich warm, ich bin mit dem ganzen Herzen dabei und es fließt auch mehr aus dem Herzen, als die vorigen Stücke, wo der Verstand mit dem Stoff kämpfen mußte. (5 January 1801; V:626)

[The material itself keeps me warm; I am wholeheartedly involved with it and it flows much more from the heart than earlier plays, where my understanding had to struggle with the material.]

This emphasis on the heart as the source and target of his play is somewhat unusual for Schiller's historical drama, as he himself indicates. He may have beautified Mary Stuart and significantly reduced her age, but she still speaks like a lawyer while exploring the complexity of her predicament. Johanna also does not speak tenderly and one often hears the harsh voice of the historical trial transcripts as she responds to other figures or declaims her mission. But in Johanna's case, her harsh dialogue will be effectively undercut by events and by intriguing modifications of her appearance.

The heart-to-heart communication Schiller sought with his audience and the report of his struggle with history refer, I believe, to Schiller's need not only to humanize and romanticize, but also to feminize Johanna. *Jungfrau* subordinates history to heart and the gender crimes of the historical figure are here neutralized, if not completely reversed, as Schiller saddles up a revised figure who is far more feminine and also innocent of the crimes that led to Joan of Arc's execution—the event that is famously missing from the play. If Hölderlin's definition of crime is authoritative and crimes are those actions that attract punishment, then Schiller has completely exonerated his heroine of the actual woman's gravest offenses and it is this play that has been cited as the catalyst to the massive rehabilitation of Joan of Arc that led to her canonization in 1920. Schiller's mediation of the criminal element and his heroic portrayal of the protagonist literally transformed a sinner into a saint and it is of interest for this investigation that he was able to accomplish this by effacing the masculine aspects of his model. Schiller's Johanna is an artificially and artistically feminized version of Joan. Indeed, she appears as a woman warrior, but as one who is most strongly and effectively characterized by her suddenly conceived love for a man whom she is about to kill. It is this love that Johanna designates as her crime, but it is this capacity for love—however awkwardly played out—that cancels or distracts from the other crimes, those of not being feminine. Schiller has set up his rendition of Isabeau of Bavaria as the real *Mannweib* [masculine woman] who takes the heat of unnatural behavior in the play. Isabeau also finds Lionel attractive, but she and the play are very blunt about the status of her attraction as wanton lust and not love. As for Johanna, Schiller seems to be betting that if loving Lionel is wrong, the audience won't want her to be right or, more directly, that for a "real" woman, loving Lionel cannot be wrong. As it turns out, Schiller rescues Johanna's femininity with an awkward and inappropriate addition to her palette of emotions, namely an improbable occasion for heterosexual love.

But love alone does not suffice to establish Johanna's femininity. Schiller has followed a very precise sartorial program that preserves some of the historical signs of Joan's military work, but that emphasizes the womanly or the feminine in the presence of the military attributes. Johanna does on a few occasions wear what one assumes is full armor—the stage direction to act 3, scene 4 prescribes that she be *"im Harnisch"* or in armor, for example—but with the exception of these scenes, she does not wear pants in this play, pants being the crucial token of defiance that ended Joan of Arc's life. Johanna is not a breeches role and Schiller has devised combinations of gender signifiers that foreground the woman while enabling her to play the warrior. Johanna also does not cut her hair short, thus canceling what was perhaps the historical woman's greatest affront to feminine self-presentation. Real women let their hair grow and Schiller's Johanna is no exception. It is more or less traditional for Johannic representations in the visual arts to feminize her, often making her long-haired and beautiful or depicting her in her peasant dress—stressing the fact that her amazing feats were those of a girl with representations that will be recognized immediately as those as a girl. But a drama can accomplish this kind of recognition with exposition and dialogue and Schiller's feminization of the figure and the canceling of the crimes is a deliberate insertion of "heart" into a historical record that reads very differently. Overcoming history here is tantamount to denying the pants and affirming the anatomy, much in the manner of Joan's executioners. But this affirmation of anatomy and the gender roles assigned to it—for the sake of a remission of the gender crimes on record—requires some closer specification and this specification begins with the question, what, for Schiller, is feminine?

Ralf Schmerberg's innovative film "Poem" (2002) offers varied and quirky scenic contextualizations of nineteen different German poems and it closes with a rendition of Schiller's "An die Freude" [Ode to Joy]. Schmerberg illustrates this particular piece with epic shots of two pseudo-primitive armies approaching each other on the side of a hill. One consists of dozens of naked women, carrying implements and smeared with pink paint and the other of dozens of naked men, banging on drums and smeared with blue paint. They approach and confront each other with gender-appropriate noises (the women shriek and the men snort), present and shake sexual and sexualized portions of anatomy at one another in a threatening manner, throw paint, and ultimately unite and embrace to the orchestral strains of Beethoven's Ninth. This tribal orgy of opposition and communion seems an odd presentation of a poem that thematizes a more refined type of joy and that, strictly speaking, depicts brotherhood. But it provides a very good introduction into Schiller's parsing of the sexes, his assignment of characteristics and tendencies, and his insistence on the stark divisions that precede harmony or unity. Schiller was a dualist, though not a separatist and Schmerberg's enactment of his poem on the field of gender combat does portray rather well the idea of difference and productive union that emerges from what I will reference as Schiller's commentary on gender difference.

This commentary consists largely of a body of remarks in letters, passages in essays, and whatever can be read out of the plays in which he himself does not speak—though this latter practice is precarious at best. Schiller's record as an editor and nurturer of female writers was very good for his time, though he adopted what today sounds like a condescending tone when describing the efforts of *Dichterinnen*. He recognized deep differences that affected thought and expression and essentially distinguished women's writing from that of men at the highest level. Such reflections can be found in his correspondence with Goethe, who also acknowledged a clear distinction.[9] Additionally, in the letters to Wilhelm von Humboldt and Körner, one can find references to gender-appropriate behavior and to the transgression of particular individuals, but nowhere in the correspondence does Schiller attempt definitive statements of sexual or gender difference and the behaviors common or proper to each side. His only overt and sustained accounts of sex or gender distinctions are to be found, interestingly, in the poetry and it is very likely that Schiller saw lyrical expression as the proper format for considering universals regarding men and women. In any case his poetry became the repository for what must stand as his theory of gender difference and this thinking, which is very consistent, emerges most clearly in "Die berühmte Frau" [The Famous Woman], "Die Geschlechter" [The Sexes], "Würde der Frauen" [The Dignity of Women], and "Das Lied von der Glocke" [The Song of the Bell].

The first of these poems, "Die berühmte Frau," (1788) takes a humorous approach to specifying the limits of a woman's sphere of activity and influence. The piece takes the form of a beleaguered husband's lament to another husband who has complained of his own wife's infidelity. The speaker attempts to convince his interlocutor that it is better to have an unfaithful wife than a famous one, since a famous woman belongs conspicuously to the world not just secretly to another man. The speaker lists the gender transgressions of a once-loving wife and mother, who through her devotion to writing has become an unfit mother and a useless upstager of her husband. The satiric thrust is not aimed at the pitiful husband but at the woman, who appears to be functioning quite well as a writer. The point is that this is an unnatural function for her. Rather than tending to her husband and children, she belongs to the world and the world intrudes on their domestic circle, most literally, as letter carriers and representatives of the publishing industry troop up the stairs and into the house. Women belong in the home and when they have dealings with the world, as does the famous woman, the world comes into the home. In this case, Schiller mocks the ambitious woman who abandons her domestic role and thus fails to realize herself as a spouse. The effect of his humor reinforces socially compelled domesticity in its reproach to the dissenter and perhaps also to the husband who allowed this dissent.

The 1796 poem, "Die Geschlechter," describes sexual difference in more elemental terms, envisioning an originary division of nature: "Und von der holden Scham trennet sich feurig die Kraft" [and from chaste reserve, strength makes its fiery break] (I:44). The two essences then develop in the respective feminine and masculine directions, ultimately to unite through love. The

6: SCHILLER'S HEART, JOAN'S CRIMES, AND JOHANNA'S GLORY

developmental paths are familiarly dualistic, being characterized either by passivity or activity, stasis or movement, by chaste modesty or wild courage. The famous longer poem, "Das Lied von der Glocke" (1799) makes these differences most explicit and prescriptive in terms of everyday life with its spatial oppositions or distinct realms: "Der Mann muß hinaus / In's feindliche Leben / Muß wirken und streben / Und pflanzen und schaffen" [The man must go out into the hostile world, must act effectively and strive and plant and create] (I:59). Meanwhile, "Und drinnen waltet / Die züchtige Hausfrau / Die Mutter der Kinder / Und herrscht weise / Im häuslichen Kreise" [And inside the modest housewife prevails and reigns wisely in her domestic realm] (I:59). The normative thrust of "Glocke," which attempts a review of human social and family life, indicates that there is a serious investment in the responsible and compliant occupation of the particular roles described. Lest "rohe Kräfte sinnlos walten" [crude forces senselessly prevail] (I:66), this kind of balance and division is necessary and it is, I believe, in the interest of banishing those crude forces that Schiller has revised his Johannic figure.

The 1795 piece, "Würde der Frauen," is yet another poetic statement on gender divisions and gender roles. Upon completion of this poem, Schiller sent the manuscript to the composer Johann Friedrich Reichardt to be set to music and he explained that the poem was "noch ganz warm, wie es aus der Feder und aus dem Herzen kommt"[10] [still warm, as it has issued from the pen and from the heart], using the same imagery he was to use in the letter to Körner. That which issued from Schiller's heart six years before the composition of *Jungfrau* has frequently been cited as his definitive statement on gender or sex difference.[11] The first two stanzas establish the terms of this difference:

> Ehret die Frauen! sie flechten und weben
> Himmlische Rosen ins irdische Leben,
> Flechten der Liebe beglückendes Band,
> Und in der Grazie züchtigem Schleier
> Nähren sie wachsam das ewige Feuer
> Schöner Gefühle mit heiliger Hand. (I:185)

> [Honor women! they plait and weave
> Heavenly roses into mundane life

> They plait the joyous band of love
> And in grace's virtuous veil
> They nourish the eternal flame
> Of beautiful feelings with a blessed hand.]

Women are collectively portrayed as those who arrange, organize, order (plait and weave) and import celestial beauty into mundane life by virtue of their patient efforts. They are fixed in space, stationed at the loom or the hearth, and they remain in place performing their small and exacting work. In so doing they engender stability and security. This is a necessary complement to the activities of men that are described in the alternating stanzas.

> Ewig aus der Wahrheit Schranken
> Schweift des Mannes wilde Kraft,
> Unstet treiben die Gedanken
> Auf dem Meer der Leidenschaft.
> Gierig greift er in die Ferne,
> Nimmer wird sein Herz gestillt,
> Rastlos durch entlegne Sterne
> Jagt er seines Traumes Bild. (I:185)
>
> [Eternally outward from the confines of truth
> Man's wild strength roams,
> His thoughts drive him restlessly
> Over the sea of passion
> Greedily he grasps into the distance
> Never is his heart satisfied
> Restlessly through distant stars
> He pursues the image of his dream.]

The male stanzas contrast with the cozy security of the female stanzas, emphasizing open spaces, movement, unchecked strength, thought, passion, dreams, and ambition. It is interesting that Schiller so closely connected masculinity with distance and movement through space, since he himself was more of a fixed point, confined by illness much of the time to his room and rarely able to take even short trips. Schiller's literary weaving of texts about women confined to small spaces, "freier in ihrem gebundenen Wirken" (I:186) [with greater freedom in their restricted activity], occurred in the shadow of his own incapacity to move "restlessly through distant stars." He, the famous man, partook, in a sense, of the dignity of women.

The reception of "Würde der Frauen" was as bipolar as its depiction of the sexes. Friedrich Schlegel found it offensive and recommended that it be read backwards[12] and his brother August Wilhelm, equally underwhelmed, wrote a parody called "Schillers Lob der Frauen" [Schiller's Praise of Women] with lines like, "Ehret die Frauen! Sie stricken die Struempfe, / Wollig und warm, zu durchwaten die Sümpfe" [Honor women! They knit the socks / Wooly and warm, for wading through the swamp][13] Even in 1795, and even for a relatively lighthearted poem, this seemed an oversimplification of gender destinies and destinations—especially for the Romantics. Körner, however, appreciated "Würde," as did Reichardt. Wilhelm von Humboldt praised it and recognized in it some of the productive oppositions he had been developing in his essays, "Über den Geschlechtsunterschied" [On Sexual Difference] and "Über die männliche und weibliche Form" [On Masculine and Feminine Form], both of which had appeared in Schiller's *Horen* in 1795. The general discussion of gender differences was occurring at a time when the older model of anatomical difference/similarity that held that there was one body at conception and that men extruded their genitals at some point during gestation and that women did not—thus retaining a vagina rather then an extruded penis—had been abandoned for one of more substantial difference and these anatomical revisions had social repercussions.[14] Though Humboldt did not posit an inevitable connection between anatomy and gender role, he did celebrate the notion of opposing forces, working together in dynamic symbiosis, something Schmerberg has apparently dramatized in "Poem."

Schiller, writing from the heart, had gone on record on several occasions with his understanding of male and female nature, and in "Würde" and "Glocke" he indicated in normative fashion how these natures were to be expressed in terms of social behavior. Both of these were widely read and commented and they constituted a recognizable statement on proper male and female oppositions and activities, one that Schiller tried to approximate with his poetic operations on the difficult and resistant history of Joan of Arc. Joan was a "famous woman" pursuing a traditionally male vocation and she furthermore fit the description of the restless, active men that was offered in the two later poems.

Schiller's heart overcame history to create a substantially feminized warrior who did not commit the gender crimes of the original Joan, though she did end up as a somewhat confusing figure as reviewers of the play have lamented.[15] Her typological hybridity disturbs not because of the simultaneity of a will to preserve virginity and a desire for Lionel—this is a rather familiar dramatic conflict—but because this simultaneity plays out as additive, cumulative, and not truly conflictual. Her feminizing transpires in the context of this kind of overload. Johanna is so many things simultaneously and the figure strives to be the warrior and the woman in ways that Joan of Arc may never have dreamed of.

Though Schiller's poetry focuses on feminine behavior, the emphasis in the play is on feminine appearance, which, of course, in drama can also suggest and enhance behavioral traits. Early on, even before the completion of *Jungfrau*, Schiller betrayed his intention to evoke a hybrid appearance when he directed his publisher Unger (28 November 1800; V:625) to commission an illustration of Minerva for the book version, thus signaling the combination of military and feminine dress that is tradition for representations of the helmeted goddess in her flowing gown. This image also corresponds well to the visual impression created in the prologue where Johanna in her shepherd dress puts on the mysterious warrior's helmet. This particular segment, a playlet in itself with a "threatened pastoral" theme, begins with father Thibaut's summary of the grim political situation that threatens their roots in the land and in tradition. As three shepherds stand before him, Thibaut describes the foreign threat to their land and cites the unnatural mother, Isabeau, whose transgressions of the maternal have created this national turmoil.

> Denn aller Orten läßt der Engelländer
> Sein sieghaft Banner fliegen, seine Rosse
> Zerstampfen Frankreichs blühende Gefilde
> . . . .
> Der Enkel unsrer Könige muß irren
> Enterbt und flüchtig durch sein eignes Reich,
> Und wider ihn im Heer der Feinde kämpft
> Sein nächster Vetter und sein erster Pair,
> Ja, seine Rabenmutter führt es an. (V:151)

[The Englishman has in all places set
His victorious banner flying, his horses
Trample France's blooming fields
. . . .
The grandson of our King must stray
Through his own kingdom, disinherited and a refugee
And against him with the enemy's army fight
His closest cousin and his first vassal
Aye, and his faithless mother is behind it all.]

Thibaut then betroths two of his three daughters to their respective shepherds that they might have male protectors: "Die treue Brust des braven Mannes allein / Ist ein sturmfestes Dach in diesen Zeiten" (V:152) [Only the faithful breast of a good man / Can provide shelter from the storm in these times]. With his critique of Isabeau and his endorsement of men and marriage, Thibaut is pre-countering the career his third daughter is about to embark on. Though she will fight against the forces that Isabeau supports, she will in many ways imitate the unnatural mother as an unnatural woman who rejects the maternal and pursues military goals.

A neighbor then enters upon the scene of betrothal and resistance with a mysterious military helmet that he has received from a witch-like woman who thrust it upon him and ultimately refused payment—rather awkwardly suspicious origins for the symbolic object that portends the rescue of France and the transformation of Johanna. Thibaut, who is already distressed by Johanna's refusal to marry Raimond, "eine schwere Irrung der Natur" (V:153) [a serious aberration of nature], becomes quite indignant when Johanna takes possession of the helmet: "Was fällt dem Mädchen ein?" [What is that girl thinking?] (V:157). She is again confounding "nature" as a girl in a helmet—such a deep transgression of culture that it is seen as a blow to nature—but Raimond, whose forbearance knows no bounds, steps forth to argue an anatomical justification of the battle gear: "Wohl ziemt ihr dieser kriegerische Schmuck, / Denn ihre Brust verschliesst ein männlich Herz" [This warlike adornment suits her well / Because her breast encloses a masculine heart] (V:157). He, who has been trying for three years to *marry* Johanna with the full support of her father, provides the argument that would qualify her appearance and subsequent military career as *natural* by adapting the anatomy argument. Such a hybrid being may not be in violation of the standards expressed in "Würde" and "Glocke." Johanna is a man within, where it counts and, as we have seen, the heart enjoys a special privilege in *Jungfrau*.

Thus the play begins with a celebration of betrothal in which Johanna ostentatiously chooses the warrior's helmet rather than the bridal *Kranz* and stands onstage in her dress and helmet like a Minerva figure. The real Joan was not known to have mixed media in this manner; she was first a shepherdess, then a soldier, then a prisoner in a dress, then a prisoner in men's clothing. But Schiller's mongrelized heroine lives according to mixed dress codes—at least in anatomical poetic figuration—as "Ein Zwitter zwischen Mann und Weib." She maintains a feminine appearance to which is added the occasional element of battle dress and her representational ancestor is Minerva. Agnes Sorel, the king's consort who inhabits the far feminine end of the gender continuum, finds even Minerva to be far too masculine and tells Johanna that she is unable to love her properly "So lange du der strengen Pallas gleichst" (V:241) [As long as you resemble stern Pallas], pleading:

> Entwaffne dich!
> Leg diese Rüstung ab, die Liebe fürchtet,
> Sich dieser stahlbedeckten Brust zu nahn.
> O sei ein Weib und du wirst Liebe fühlen! (V:241)
>
> [Drop your weapons!
> And remove your armor, love fears
> To draw near to your steel-covered breast
> O be a woman and you will feel love!]

For Sorel, any sartorial deviation (accompanied by appropriate behavior) is not hybridity but disqualification. Sorel's immediate concern is that Johanna is rejecting the marriage proposal of Dünois, as she also rejects that of LaHire. The two suitors and their oft-expressed interest serve to situate her as the feminine object of marital intentions, as does the occasional presence of Raimond. Though Joan of Arc's soldiers testified that they felt no desire in her presence or when they shared quarters with her, Johanna lights up the eyes of three separate suitors, all of whom propose marriage, even before she encounters Lionel. Schiller is most aggressively overcoming history for the sake of his feminized heroine.

The war-implement-and-dress ensemble derives not only from Minerva, but also from Johanna's first vision of the Virgin Mary whom she describes as "ein Schwert / Und Fahne tragend, aber sonst wie ich / Als Schäferin gekleidet" [carrying a sword / And banner, but otherwise, like me / Dressed as a shepherdess] (V:186). The mixture persists in varying combinations with Johanna, who in subsequent stage directions is most conspicuously clad in *partial* battle gear with emblems of femininity to balance the effect. The stage directions describe her appearance:

> Johanna mit der Fahne, im Helm und Brustharnisch, sonst aber weiblich gekleidet. (V:200)
>
> [Johanna with the banner, in helmet and upper body armor, but otherwise dressed in a feminine manner.]

or

> Johanna zu den Vorigen. Sie ist im Harnisch aber ohne Helm, und trägt einen Kranz in den Haaren. (V:219)
>
> [Johanna joins the previous grouping. She is in armor but without helmet and she wears a garland in her hair.]

The prescription that she be dressed in a feminine manner in the first and the addition of the garland, a direct counter to the helmet, further enhance what is by now the almost overdetermined reassurance that this brash and warlike figure is to her sartorial depths a woman.

As for hair style, Johanna also does not cut her hair and she is described in an early scene as charging into battle "mit behelmten Haupt / Wie eine Kriegsgöttin" [with the helmet on her head / Like a war goddess] and we are furthermore told, "um ihren Nacken / In goldnen Ringen fiel das Haar" (V:182) [and around her neck / Her hair fell in golden ringlets]. Like Joan's judges, Schiller seems to have had problems with the short brown hair, but unlike them he was able to transform it into a crown of golden ringlets. This certainly falls within the purview of a playwright and, as I have remarked, visual artists frequently restored and colored her hair. But in Schiller's case, there was specific intent to transform and repair the nature of the figure, an intent that can be read in the normative poetry and in the play itself. In the case of this particular female heroine, the writer who restored Mary Stuart's beauty and got her into a jealous spat with her sovereign, seems to join the tribunal that condemned Joan of Arc. Along with them he decrees that there will be no masculine dress and succeeds in erasing Joan's previous and subsequent defiance of those decrees. The horror of Isabeau the unnatural mother-in-armor or mother-in-arms is compensated by the feminine and appealing appearance of Johanna.

Where Schiller elicited admiration for criminals like Fiesko and Karl Moor, and understanding for Christian Wolf, he ultimately got Joan of Arc, heretic, defiant cross-dresser, prisoner of war, disobedient daughter, and suspected witch *canonized*. He appears to have accomplished this intervention into church history by making Joan more palatable in the figure of Johanna. There is nothing in Schiller's play that confirms her heavenly mission and much that suggests black magic and sorcery, but the very positive portrayal of the Maid of Orleans, written in part in chivalric response to Voltaire's disparaging poem, "La Pucelle,"[16] was a turning point also in the career of the much-distorted historical figure. It would appear that Schiller's heart, the organ that overcame history, also succeeded in making it.

7
Schillerian Intertextuality in the Twentieth Century: Lost Honor, Aesthetic Education, and Free Will

SCHILLER'S WORK WITH CRIMINALITY AND ITS SKEWED RELATIONSHIP to punishment has had some extraordinary echoes in the works of successive generations of writers, who have imported Schillerian ideals to their social and historical contexts and processed these ideals in relation to practices and institutions that have arisen since the eighteenth century. In this segment I want to identify Schillerian allusions and artifacts in three important "criminal" texts of the later twentieth century and to examine his presence in the conceptual apparatus of each piece that invokes him. In so doing, I follow the lead of Stephanie Hammer, whose *Schiller's Wound* entails a program of pairing and comparing Schiller's plays with twentieth-century texts because "this canonical author forms a crucial link to contemporary cultural practices and issues of cultural life" (Hammer, 9). I will begin with the lost honors and generic disgraces of Schiller's Christian Wolf and Heinrich Böll's Katharina Blum and then move to *A Clockwork Orange* of Anthony Burgess and that of Stanley Kubrick. In every case, a major Schillerian ideal—honor for *Blum* and the effects of aesthetic education for Burgess/Kubrick—emerges amid inhospitable surroundings and struggles for survival in the modern world.

THE LOST HONORS AND GENERIC DISGRACES OF SCHILLER'S WOLF AND BÖLL'S BLUM

Though Böll denied a connection between his *Die verlorene Ehre der Katharina Blum* and *Verbrecher aus verlorener Ehre*, as "vollkommen irrig" [completely wrong][1] critics have generally considered the echo in the title to be deliberate. "Lost honor" in Schiller's tale is easily understood as the stigma of punishment that isolates Christian Wolf from society, denies him an honest means of making a living, and thus forces him into a life of active and intentional crime. The punishment that follows on punishment is that of a near-universal social abjection. In Katharina Blum's case, "lost honor" seems at first an odd usage and has been unconvincingly associated with chastity, whereas a much broader conception of reputation appears to be indicated—though the occasional affronts to Blum's prudishness do have a special sting. *Ehre* is not often mentioned in the text, where a systematic character assassination occurs as a by-product of a tabloid's quotidian need for scandal. However, the titular emphasis on "lost honor" evokes that other dishonored individual, whose fate Schiller used as an example of the inadequacy of general law as a guide to specific transgressions, and it highlights Katharina's position as a similarly pre-punished individual whose subsequent behavior is conditioned by the stigma of punishment that she carries. Böll expands the range of punishing agencies and our understanding of what constitutes punishment, as he opens up the concept of *Gewalt* [violence] in the novella, which is subtitled, *Wie Gewalt entstehen und wohin sie führen kann* [How Violence Can Arise and What It Can Lead To]. In an afterword written ten years after the original publication of *Katharina Blum*, Böll stated:

> Über die Gewalt von SCHLAGZEILEN ist noch zu wenig bekannt, und wohin die Gewalt von Schlagzeilen führen kann, darüber wissen wir nur wenig. Es wäre eine Aufgabe der Kriminologie, das einmal zu erforschen: was ZEITUNGEN anrichten können in all ihrer bestialischen "Unschuld."[2]
>
> [Too little is known of the violence of headlines and what the power of headlines can lead to; we know very little about that. It would be a task for criminologists to finally research: what newspapers can cause in all their bestial "innocence."]

That state-ordered punishment can itself be a violent crime, a reprehensible use of force, has long been established and even accepted, but Böll examines this same kind of transgression as committed by the news media. The power to punish and to mark an individual as punished resided in the state in Schiller's time and *Katharina Blum* argues that in an age of mass communication this power has been extended to the press, whose representative DIE ZEITUNG has thoroughly pilloried Katharina long before the state's initial investigation has concluded. The success of this demonstration rests in part on the intertextual affinities between the dishonored two protagonists.

Both Blum and Wolf are murderers, and in each case a massive narrative effort is undertaken to court the reader's understanding for the ultimate crime. Each was goaded by an adversary and pushed to the breaking point. Robert stalked and repeatedly arrested Wolf in order to disable him as a rival for Hanne's affections and Tötges, the unscrupulous and unsavory tabloid reporter, published lurid fictions about Blum that no denials could effectively counter. In fact the novella also evokes Schiller's original title, *Verbrecher aus Infamie*, because Böll follows the development of Blum's public reputation for criminal collusion, her fifteen minutes of infamy, rather than dwelling exclusively on her lost honor—though she does kill to restore her honor (and cancel her infamy).

There are further technical and structural parallels. Both protagonists lose a father while still young and this deprivation is cited as being formative. Wolf is known as the *Sonnenwirt* [innkeeper or proprietor of "The Sun"] because his family owns an inn or *Wirtschaft* called *Zur Sonne*, and Blum is a *Wirtschafterin* or housekeeper; Wolf is a *Räuberhauptmann* [leader of a band of robbers] and Blum appears in the tabloid headlines as a *Räuberliebchen* [robber's girlfriend] (36). Each provides a first-person account of the murder that is reproduced for the reader by a third-person narrator. Very interesting and highly unusual is the shared endorsement of constabular courtesy as partial reparation for the theft of honor. Both Blum and Wolf ultimately confess to the "polite policeman," that is to an official who treats them honorably and in each case, the account of this confession ends the tale, thus defining these chronologically disparate tales as individual journeys through (amply motivated) crime to the embrace of an honorable and respectful representative of the police force. When captured, Wolf originally refuses to answer any questions from a judge who speaks to him in a harsh and brutal tone. The judge then reflects that "die befehlshaberische Sprache würde nichts über seinen [Wolf's] Starrsinn vermögen, es wäre vielleicht besser getan, ihm mit Anstand und Mässigung zu begegnen" [the authoritarian language would not prevail over his stubbornness; it would probably have been better to approach him with decency and restraint] (VII:586). On the next morning, the judge apologizes to Wolf and Wolf responds:

> Ihr gestriges Benehmen, Herr Oberamtmann, hätte mich nimmermehr zu einem Geständnis gebracht, *denn ich trotze der Gewalt*. Die Bescheidenheit, womit Sie mich heute behandeln, hat mir Vertrauen und Achtung gegen Sie gegeben. Ich glaube, daß Sie ein edler Mann sind. (VII:586–87)

> [Your behavior yesterday, Sir, would never have moved me to a confession, because I defy coercive force. But the modesty with which you are treating me today has made me trust and respect you. I believe that you are a decent man.]

Wolf then reveals his identity as that of the infamous robber who has been sought throughout the territory and the piece ends with this acknowledgment: "Ich bin der Sonnenwirt" (VII:587).[3]

Blum does much the same thing after shooting Tötges, seeking out the one policeman who had been kind to her during her previous interrogations and surrendering and confessing to him, "und dann bin ich zu diesem Moeding gefahren, der damals so nett zu mir war" [and then I drove to see that Moeding, who was so nice to me back then] (137). Her story and Böll's tale also end with these words. Thus each protagonist, after much maltreatment finds his or her way to an official who, though he will enforce the law and deliver the prescribed punishment, also acknowledges the suspect's human dignity with politeness—as if each had not lost honor. This politeness is not the innocuous exercise of good manners, but a respect that undermines the *Gewalt* Wolf opposes and that has so oppressed and tormented Blum. Böll's subtitle announces what we can certainly understand as his opposition to *Gewalt*, here portrayed as a network of lies and sloppy law enforcement that imposes the contours of a sensationally lurid tale of terrorist conspiracy on what was apparently an unusually intense romantic encounter. Lost honor is partially restored in these exchanges with enlightened representatives of the law because in each case the suspect is treated with dignity. The polite policeman is the (only available) inverse of *Gewalt*, admittedly not a universal solution, but nonetheless a moment of restoration and even hope in these two grim tales. If the dishonored protagonist can be treated with respect, then the reach of the agency that removed honor is diminished—particularly when that respect emanates from the realm of the law. Moeding and the *Oberamtmann* [local magistrate] accomplish the important separation of crime and punishment from dishonor. The crime remains on the record and the punishment will be inflicted, but the perpetrator retains a basic dignity.

Most importantly, Wolf and Blum resemble one another in that they both murder as pre-punished, traumatized subjects, dishonored individuals who have—to some extent—already paid for the crimes they have yet to commit and thus have some claim to the reader's understanding despite the magnitude of these crimes. Wolf is absolutely specific on this matter. He started poaching for love and was excessively punished for that transgression and put in a position where repeated offenses were his only access to food. Wolf's conscious decision to begin a life of crime was based on his impression that he had already been punished: "Meine Infamie war das niedergelegte Kapital, von dessen Zinsen ich noch lange Zeit schwelgen konnte" [My infamy was the invested capital, and I could live off the interest for a long time to come] (VII:571).

Blum's problems also began with love, namely the improbably sudden love she conceived for a *Bundeswehr* deserter with whom she danced at a Carneval party, and who escaped the police from her apartment. The mass-circulation tabloid DIE ZEITUNG, a thinly disguised version of *Bild*, makes a leap of logic and portrays her as a terrorist, and interviews friends and family, twisting their words to achieve a sensational distortion of events. Finally, Tötges invades the hospital room of Katharina's mother, so upsets her as to apparently cause her death, and then blames Katharina in his headlines. Katharina has also been more or less adequately pre-punished and certainly traumatized at the moment that Tötges appears at her door for an exclusive interview and proposes that they have sex. She shoots him and feels no remorse.

The *jouissance* that in Knox's account results from the ascription of an intelligible motive for crime/murder is abundantly present here as both tales of lost honor are rather heavy on the intelligibility of motive. However, even though a mere recitation of the "facts of the case" and of the delinquent's background might have sufficed, both narrators self-consciously announce a specific tactic they will use in order to make this motivation intelligible—tweaking the genre in order to make their cases. Like mechanics reporting to work, Schiller's and Böll's narrators each describe a narratological-rhetorical methodology that has been custom-crafted to get the job done right. In Schiller's case, it involves heating and cooling and in Böll's drainage.

It is difficult to evoke understanding for a criminal, Schiller's narrator explains, because of the vast gulf between the agitated state of the person whose actions are being described and the calm, composed situation of the reader:

> Es bleibt eine Lücke zwischen dem historischen Subjekt und dem Leser, die alle Möglichkeit einer Vergleichung oder Anwendung abschneidet und statt jenes heilsamen Schreckens, der die stolze Gesundheit warnt, ein Kopfschütteln der Befremdung erweckt. . . . und die Geschichte, anstatt eine Schule der Bildung zu sein, muß sich mit einem armseligen Verdienste um unsre Neugier begnügen. (VII:563–64)

> [There is a gap between the reader and the historical subject that cuts off all possibility of comparison or application and instead of evoking the therapeutic fear that warns complacent health, it engenders the head-shaking of alienation. . . . and history, instead of being a school for improvement, has to be satisfied with doing a miserable service to our curiosity.]

This therapeutic fear recalls the "heilsame Schauer" or therapeutic shudders of *Schaubühne* and summarizes the purpose of the crime story, that of forging a link between law-abiding reader and law-breaking criminal that, in this quiver of fearful recognition, will serve as the basis for an apprehension of the proximity or the possibility of a similar fate—a prose version of the plan for dramatic *Wirkung* in *Schaubühne*. Schiller concludes that in order to make the human connection between reader and protagonist plausible and profitable: "Entweder der Leser muß warm werden wie der Held, oder der Held wie der Leser erkalten" [Either the reader must become warm like the hero, or the hero cold like the reader] (VII:564).[4] This leveling of relative body temperature or emotional register for the sake of empathy and understanding moves in the direction of heating for imaginative literature and in the direction of cooling for historical works.

Schiller claims that *Verbrecher* is a historical study, and it does follow closely the career of Friedrich Schwan, the *Sonnenwirtle* and infamous bandit who was captured by the (polite policeman) father of Schiller's favorite teacher, Jacob Friedrich Abel. As indicated above, Abel had met Schwan, who, while awaiting execution, often described his exploits to visitors in the form of a cautionary tale—re-narrating his life of crime for the common good. In the case of historical writing, Schiller insists (as cited above):

> Der Held muß kalt werden, wie der Leser, oder, was hier ebensoviel sagt, wir müssen mit ihm bekannt werden, *eh'* er handelt. . . . An seinen Gedanken liegt uns unendlich mehr als an seinen Taten, und noch weit mehr an den Quellen seiner Gedanken als an den Folgen jener Taten.

In *Verbrecher*, the criminal becomes Foucault's delinquent, the complex figure who is not defined merely by the crime he or she has committed, but who also has a past: an entire life history that criminologists and penologists can mine for causes and explanations of the crime. The sober collection of data can rationalize the crime and rehumanize the criminal and this process has important consequences for the enlightened application of penal law.

So it is that one proceeds with historical subjects, but in *Verbrecher*, there is such abundance of poetic license and overt fictionalizing that its generic status cannot be the one so earnestly announced by the author/historian who makes an ugly duckling out of the good-looking Schwan, creating an entirely different exculpatory past for the hero. Furthermore, we know that Schwan's father was very much alive and that the struggle between father and son, in which Schwan Jr. triumphed spectacularly, was (in his account) the defining moment of his formation and it is interesting that Schiller recasts Schwan's problematic relationship with his living progenitor as the problematic absence of the father. Beyond this, the manner of renarration of the crime places it well beyond that murky borderline between history and fiction. Schiller may have agreed because in his tale, neither the hero nor the reader remains cold. *Verbrecher* is a hybrid of fiction and history and it has its hot spots and cool points. Its (narratologically) triumphant conclusion, "Ich bin der Sonnenwirt" implies that *Sonnenwirt* is now a thoroughly known quantity and that the reader, repeatedly heated up and cooled down, has both empathized with and understood the ways of the criminal and has recognized her own humanity in Christian Wolf. "*Wir sind der Sonnenwirt*" or, to invoke a familiar refrain, "*Alle Menschen werden Verbrecher,*" or at least potential criminals. The communal politics of *Schaubühne* also play into the effect Schiller aims for in *Verbrecher,* namely the reassertion of universal brotherhood where one individual had been abjected—an effect that is missing in *Tell* where such brotherhood/fatherhood depends on the abjection and ejection of a scapegoat or two.

Where Schiller's tale is narrated with attention to temperature and the exchange of heat, Böll deals in fluids. His narrator writes with a mock-journalistic matter-of-factness that he interrupts repeatedly to appeal—with apparent irony—to community sentiment. But these "warm" spots are embedded in an attempted report of the facts that is pitched to a cold reader. Böll's narrator is primarily concerned with shaping his report and he reflects frequently on sources, chronology and the nuts and bolts of narration. The explanation of Katharina Blum's crime does not "unfold," but comes about as various puddles of information are tapped and conducted together in a downward direction: Drainage. The narrative "flow" is repeatedly disqualified as such and the account proceeds in a jerky, clogging motion with frequent starts and stops—or so the narrator tells us. Indeed the narrator apologizes in advance for any segments that may seem to flow or offer distinct focalization—possibly because he is writing in opposition to the tabloid press that allows its reporting to flow too freely into the familiar storylines that lead away from objective and accurate reporting. Böll's narrator seems to indicate that hard facts, if presented in the proper arrangement, are (superficially) sufficient to effect an intellectual understanding of the proceedings and the result is sympathy and understanding for the otherwise opaque and impenetrable Katharina. Despite his protestations and efforts at fairness, he ultimately prohibits different perspectives and so thoroughly demonizes the figure of Tötges that his murder seems, at the very least, appropriate.

There is also an implicit criticism of the state and its police force in the draining procedure. The police "leak" to the ZEITUNG and thus become direct collaborators in Katharina's prepunishment and the creation of her motive for murder. When

Katharina notes that details of her interrogation are appearing in the press, she asks "ob der Staat nichts tun könne, um sie gegen diesen Schmutz zu schützen und ihre verlorene Ehre wiederherzustellen" [whether the government can't do something to protect her from this filth and to restore her lost honor] (60). With this, the only echo of the title within the tale, she attempts to accomplish legally what she will ultimately do criminally. The officials tell her that she is a "Person der Zeitgeschichte" [figure of current events, much like a public figure for the purposes of media coverage] and essentially fair game, but the state is implicated directly in Blum's "verlorene Ehre."

Böll's improbable and also impenetrable narrative strategy of "Dränage" or "Trockenlegung" [drying] seems to be a response to press and critics' characterization of him as a terrorist sympathizer, part of a "Sympathisantensumpf" [swamp of sympathizers].[5] While draining that other swamp of the tabloid press's daily misrepresentations, Böll lets much of his initial methodological work go down the drain as he both neglects and belabors a difficult and demanding metaphor. Schiller could not sustain his cooling techniques or keep his cool and Böll loses his in confrontation with the object of his satire—which can be recognizably satirized only with the greatest difficulty. The narrative restoration of lost honor—be it one's own or that of one's representative or protagonist—involves Böll in competing projects and leaves *Die verlorene Ehre der Katharina Blum* a puddle of unrealized potential, despite its sharp political thrust and deft nuancing of the concept of *Gewalt*.

Schiller's *Verbrecher* seeks to impose human understanding between law codes and individual delicts and to this end he gives the history of the delinquent, served hot and cold. Böll has more on his plate, both politically and narratologically and his attack on the violence (*Gewalt*) of headlines is an attempt to use the powerful force (*Gewalt/Wirkung*?) of literature to enlighten and resist. His violated protagonist becomes a murderer out of lost honor and manufactured infamy and, pre-punished, she kills to reclaim her loss.

Both Wolf and Blum end their disgraceful quests for honor in the clutches of the polite policeman, finding in this representative of the penal system, the honorable reception that eluded them. This leads to the most banal—yet appropriate—of conclusions: namely that, had this polite policeman and the hypothetical enlightened legal system he represents, prevailed at the beginning of Wolf's or Blum's encounters with the law, the irrational sentencing and inappropriate placement of the mild offender, or the wild suspicions and leaks to the ZEITUNG, that resulted in the subtraction of honor might never have occurred. Furthermore, several murders would not have been committed and crime would thus have been prevented and there would have been no need for punishment.

Narratological innovation and generic confusion aside, both Schiller and Böll offer a lesson in manners to their local constables that serves as a credible basis for enlightened penal practices. As the title of Schiller's tale so clearly indicates, punishment that cancels honor causes crime. Böll adds to this observation his biting critique of the boulevard press and the very important observation that the press has become an independent judiciary, with distinct penal powers. Katharina loses her honor in the press and she regains it with a criminal act, becoming the quintessential *Verbrecherin aus verlorener Ehre*.

Joy and Violence: Friedrich and Anthony and Stanley and Alex

The perceived failure of Foucault's penitentiary has, as critics have observed,[6] turned penal attention away from the soul and back to the body of the criminal. Despairing of rehabilitation, more jurisdictions are resorting to death sentences in extreme cases and for lesser offenses increased physical discomfort in stripped-down prison circumstances and work details, including chain gangs. Anthony Burgess's most famous novel, *A Clockwork Orange* (1962), features a rehabilitative assault on the body that raises questions of free will, freedom, and the nature of humanity. And much of this proceeds from Schiller.

I have already mentioned above, that young Schiller wrote frequently of the dramatist's special access to secret areas of the human mind and heart and the changes to be effected there. He even indicates in a passage already cited that "diese auf der Schaubühne aufgestellten Gemälde mit der Moral des gemeinen Manns endlich in eins zusammen fliessen, *und in einzelnen Fällen seine Empfindung bestimmen*" (my emphasis). A model of the mind or heart, that faculty or combination of faculties

7: SCHILLERIAN INTERTEXTUALITY IN THE TWENTIETH CENTURY 145

that reasons and feels, *as susceptible to theater* emerges from *Schaubühne* and other essays of the period, and Schiller makes a variety of practical statements as to how the dramatist might penetrate such a faculty and bring it to recognize its failings and correct them. Unlike the law, which merely prohibits (Thou shalt not . . .), the stage can impress the principle behind these prohibitions on the individual spectator and change minds and lives. In the optimistic segment already quoted above, Schiller announced the success of his dramatic project:

> Menschlichkeit und Duldung fangen an der herrschende Geist unsrer Zeit zu werden; ihre Strahlen sind bis in die Gerichtssäle, und noch weiter—in das Herz unsrer Fürsten gedrungen. Wie viel Anteil an diesem göttlichen Werk gehört unsern Bühnen? Sind *sie* es nicht, die den Menschen mit dem Menschen bekannt machten, *und das geheime Räderwerk aufdeckten, nach welchem er handelt*? (latter emphasis mine)

While Schiller seems to thank the dramatic stage for the Enlightenment, he offers another metaphor for the secret regions of the human mind/heart, namely "das geheime Räderwerk," the secret clockwork mechanisms that, once understood, can explain and perhaps determine human motivation and behavior. Clockwork or gearing metaphors—references to that which makes us "tick"—are neither infrequent nor entirely consistent from the eighteenth to the twentieth century, but in conceiving of natural man with his secret clockwork behavioral mechanisms as the object of the didactic dramatist's efforts, Schiller outlined in both general terms and specific imagery the problem that Anthony Burgess addressed in its extreme with *A Clockwork Orange* and that Stanley Kubrick developed in his extraordinary film adaptation of that novel (1971).

In an attempt to explain the human capacity for violence, the authorities in the novel and film consider a variety of causes, ranging from the writer and cultural critic F. Alexander's vague "the modern age" to demonic possession, as P. R. Deltoid, the probation officer, asks Alex:

> What gets into you all? We study the problem and we've been studying it for damn well near a century, yes, but we get no further with our studies. You've got a good home here, good loving parents,

you've got not too bad of a brain. Is it some devil that crawls inside you?[7]

Burgess's basic philosophical foundation is generally acknowledged to be the Pelagian-Augustinian dualism, where a model of humanity as capable of amelioration by exercise of free will is opposed to one that rests on man's innate inclination to evil (original sin) that requires God's grace for the sake of salvation. This translates into the opposition of a penal system that allows choice and punishes where necessary (the retributive warden and his minions) and one that seeks to control or abolish choice (the Ludovico doctors) in order to prevent crime. Both types of argument are reproduced in the film, which follows the novel very closely on this central issue.

As noted above, *Schaubühne* cautions against the notion of a planned human community, "Menschen zu drechseln" (VIII:198), which might result from the normative dramatist's efforts or those of the Augustinian absolutist schoolmaster, and it concludes in terms that look forward to the ecstatic communal embrace of humanity in "An die Freude":

> Welch ein Triumph für dich, Natur . . . wenn Menschen aus allen Kreisen und Zonen und Ständen, abgeworfen jede Fessel der Künstelei und der Mode, herausgerissen aus jedem Drange des Schicksals, durch *eine* allwebende Sympathie verbrüdert, in *Ein* Geschlecht wieder aufgelöst, ihrer selbst und der Welt vergessen, und ihrem himmlischen Ursprung sich nähern.

On beyond brainwashing, a method Schiller had seen demonstrated on Schubart, "Alle Menschen werden Brüder" in the joyous recognition of their humanity in the theater. They have been transformed for the better, but their humanity has also been enhanced.

Burgess's novel showcases the transformation of Alex DeLarge, from criminally violent thug to what we might call a disabled or incapacitated criminally violent thug and back (and back again if one reads the twenty-first chapter, which was excised in the early American editions). These transformations occur within a world where the question of what constitutes humanity or what makes it tick is repeatedly posed. Alex, the first-person narrator, describes a regime of drug-supported aversion therapy that brings him to the point where he feels mortally nauseated whenever his natural inclinations to violence manifest themselves. Thus his subsequent "good" behavior proceeds from drug-induced, behaviorally ingrained nausea. His so-called evil intentions impel him toward the good and he must meet aggression with manufactured or mechanical kindness. Alex is thus turned against himself and he stands as an overdetermined illustration of Schiller's conviction that penal reform conflicts fundamentally with personal freedom (and that theatrical *Wirkung* and aesthetic education constitute the road to harmony). Yet while relating the actions that his nature and his therapy determine, Alex communicates his own twisted but insistent humanity splendidly, thus compensating rather well for the state's mechanistic view of him as criminal.

Alex's punitive therapy, the Ludovico Technique, represents the ultimate intensification of young Schiller's didactic aspirations as well as the visceral perversion of Lessing's third stage in *Erziehung des Menschengeschlechts* [Education of the Human Race]: the day eventually comes when he feels ill without the drugs and just as Lessing's educated human race will do the good because it is good, Alex's educated human body ("Your body is learning it" [110]) will strive to do the good also because it is the good and thus relieves the nausea he feels from his inclinations to evil. "He will be your true Christian," announces one of the doctors, "ready to turn the other cheek, ready to be crucified rather than crucify, sick to the very heart at the thought even of killing a fly" (131). Beyond *Erziehung des Menschengeschlechts*, this method of human improvement also recalls Schillers letters on the aesthetic education of man, where aesthetic education is promoted as an internalized playfulness, a true humanity activated by the experience of beauty, the induced freedom discussed in chapter 1. But Schiller claims that aesthetic education and *Wirkung* follow the path of nature in inducing freedom and do not transgress human autonomy. The Ludovico treatment, on the other hand, bluntly opposes therapy to nature and in so doing parodies aesthetic education with its claims to non-hegemonic *Wirkung*. Art is misused and Alex is conditioned to feel nausea not only when he has violent urges, but whenever he hears symphonic music (novel) or Beethoven's Ninth Symphony (film).

Just as Schiller's theoretical statements, his nontraditional treatment of crime and his charismatic criminals look forward to *A Clockwork Orange,* novel and film, so do Burgess and Kubrick look back to Schiller as they incorporate his work and his thought in various ways. One example is the central presence in both works of "An die Freude," Schiller's most palpable cultural footprint. The reference originates in the novel when Alex rapes the two young girls from the record shop to the strains of Beethoven's Ninth: "and then the lovely blissful tune all about Joy being a glorious spark of heaven, and then I felt the old tigers leap in me and I leapt on these two young ptitsas" (46). This scene serves to illustrate Alex's earlier ruminations on the linking of ethics and aesthetics:

> I had to have a smeck, though, thinking of what I'd viddied once in one of these like articles on Modern Youth, about how Modern Youth would be better off if A Lively Appreciation of the Arts could be like encouraged. Great Music, it said, and Great Poetry would like quieten Modern Youth down and make Modern Youth more civilized. Civilized my syphilised yarbles. Music always sort of sharpened me up, O my brothers, and made me feel like old Bog himself, ready to make with the old donner and blitzen . . . (CO:41–42).

In essence, Schiller's poem, the "Great Poetry" that here accompanies "Great Music," is used to undermine an essential tenet of Schiller's classicist aesthetics, namely that art is good for you.[8] In Schiller's writing on art and its benefits, as we have seen, the contemplation of art leads to freedom and to a "playful" and balanced humanity, free of the hypertrophic extremism exhibited by the "savage" and his counterpart the "barbarian," the two types developed in the Aesthetic Letters. In Alex's universe, Art, Great Poetry, and Great Music incite or abet ultra-violence. While retaining the poetry and the music, Kubrick also added the element of the visual arts to this dangerous grouping, decorating his sets with painting and sculpture.[9] Whereas Burgess's Alex kills the cat lady with a small silver statue—still an indictment of art as "bad for you"—Kubrick's protagonist kills her with an oversized Pop-Art phallic sculpture that is actually identified by the cat lady as a "work of art."

"An die Freude," which includes the line, "Freude, Freude treibt die Räder in der grossen Weltenuhr" [Joy, joy drives the gears in the great clock of the world] (I:249) recurs throughout in

7: SCHILLERIAN INTERTEXTUALITY IN THE TWENTIETH CENTURY 149

Burgess's *A Clockwork Orange* as if it were the driving force behind the novel. It accompanies crime and also surfaces under punishment. In the very significant moment when Alex awakens in prison to find that his victim has died and he is now a murderer:

> ... and then I heard the Ninth, last movement, with the slovos all a bit mixed-up, like they knew themselves they had to be mixed up, this being a dream:
>
>> Boy, thou uproarious shark of heaven,
>>   Slaughter of Elysium
>> Hearts on fire, aroused, enraptured,
>>   We will tolchock you on the rot and kick
>>   Your grahzny vonny bum.
>
> (73)

The primary reference in this case is to Beethoven's music, but the words are Schiller's and Alex is actually rewriting Schiller on the occasion of his first murder, inverting the message of universal brotherhood, or perverting it as a violent fantasy, even as he repeatedly addresses the readership as "O my brothers." I will briefly examine the ways in which both Burgess and Kubrick "rewrite" Schiller in their considerations of crime and the mutability of human behavior not only to chronicle the afterlife of a classical author, but also to follow the "progress" of ideals over time. Each artist takes direct aim at Schillerian freedom, the *Nichtvonaussenbestimmtsein* of the *Kallias* letters, that is visible in the phenomenon of beauty; at the boundaries of didactic control; at the linking of ethics and aesthetics that underlies freedom; and at the dramatist's didactic efforts. In order to establish Schillerian intertextuality in two texts that have not generally been associated with him, I will reference several scenes from the novel that also appear in the film.

A pivotal scene in the written text is the droogs' return to the Korova Milk Bar, after an evening of closely chronicled violence. A woman at the next table suddenly bursts into song and Alex is transported:

> I felt all the little malenky hairs on my plott standing endwise and the shivers crawling up like slow malenky lizards and then down again. Because I knew what she sang. It was from an opera by Fried-

rich Gitterfenster called *Das Bettzeug*, and it was the bit where she's snuffing it with her throat cut and the slovos are "Better like this maybe." Anyway, I shivered. (25)

Alex's shivers represent his physical or visceral reaction to beauty, here rendered as an aria sung by a figure whose throat has been cut. This is itself a significantly visceral image, as well as a physical impossibility, but a good example of Alex's specialized, bloody aesthetic. His repeated references to the beauty of blood once it is released and flowing freely indicate a hermetic standard of aesthetic contemplation, ultimately inaccessible to empathy, but intelligible nonetheless, and fundamental to his encounters with art. The marriage of music and blood, expressed in pleasurable shivers mocks the Schillerian ideal of harmony in an aesthetic education as do the paraphrases of "An die Freude." In Kubrick's film, where the musical score often diverges from Burgess's narrative catalog, the words of the fictional Friedrich Gitterfenster are replaced by the words of another Friedrich, as the woman in the Korova Milkbar breaks into "An die Freude" and Alex's reaction is reproduced almost verbatim in the voice-over. Thus the bloody diva who sings as she dies of the possible benefit of her demise yields on film to "Freude, schöner Götterfunken, Tochter aus Elysium" or the sanctified, personified joy celebrated by Schiller. Kubrick will make somewhat more frequent use of the Ninth than Burgess, who was also able to augment existing music with invented composers and compositions. Joy and the things that engender it are more central to the film where the original German words are repeated throughout, rather than translated or paraphrased as in the book.

As for the record shop scene mentioned above and the subsequent rape of the two girls in his room at home, in both versions, Alex visits the shop to pick up a copy of Beethoven's Ninth, "the Choral Symphony, that is" (42), which he has on order. In the novel, he meets two very young girls, feeds them, brings them home, gets them drunk, undresses them and then injects himself with an unnamed drug. The full passage runs like this:

Then I pulled the lovely Ninth out of its sleeve, so that Ludwig van was now nagoy [naked] too, and I set the needle hissing on to the last movement, which was all bliss. There it was then, the bass strings like govoreeting away from under my bed at the rest of the orchestra,

7: SCHILLERIAN INTERTEXTUALITY IN THE TWENTIETH CENTURY 151

and then the male human goloss [voice] coming in and telling them all to be joyful, and then the lovely blissful tune all about Joy being a glorious spark of heaven, and then I felt the old tigers leap in me and then I leapt on these two young ptitsas. This time they thoughts nothing fun and stopped creeching with high mirth, and had to submit to the strange and weird desires of Alexander the Large which, what with the Ninth and the hypo jab were choodessny and zamechat and very demanding, O my brothers. (46)

Alex describes the truant girls' suffering as coerced education, "Well if they would not go on to school, they must still have their education," and tells how he fell asleep "with the old Joy Joy Joy Joy crashing and howling away" (47), as Schiller's text and Beethoven's music both initiate and conclude a satisfying afternoon for him. He credits the Ninth as well as the drugs for his vicious energy, once again implicating art in his criminal activity and attacking the thesis that an aesthetic education or exposure to great art leads to a humane sensibility. The educational aspect of this adventure is more of a demonstration of inhumane treatment and this demonstration is powered by art, specifically Schiller's poetry.

Kubrick's representation of the same scene begins as Alex approaches the store with the Ninth playing in the background and the tenor singing the chorus that follows Schiller's reference to clockwork, "die Räder in der grossen Weltenuhr":

> Froh, wie seine Sonnen fliegen,
> Durch des Himmels pracht'gen Plan,
> Laufet Brüder eure Bahn
> Freudig wie ein Held zum siegen. (I:249)

> [Glad as his suns fly
> Along Heaven's glorious course,
> Walk, brothers, your path
> Joyously like a hero to victory.]

Alex, dressed in dandy-like finery and not the school clothes of the novel version, walks proudly, perhaps heroically, through the shop as the camera leads and follows him around a circular path. He also buys the Ninth and takes the girls, who are somewhat older, home. Kubrick films the sexual assault in Alex's room as a more perfunctory exchange, speeding up the film as if they were racing and choosing for musical accompaniment, not the Ninth, but another composition that is directly associated with one of Schiller's texts, namely Rossini's Wilhelm Tell overture. Viewers hear the movement familiar from the Lone Ranger series and this is a standard accompaniment of fast frenzied action in film, television, and cartoons. Thus it is appropriate to the scene we are viewing, but it is also interesting that while replacing or displacing Schiller's text, Kubrick reinstates him with the Tell reference.

The next scene that concerns us involves the actual implementation of the Ludovico Technique. *Schaubühne* describes the experience of the spectator in the theater in ambivalent terms, indicating a respect for human freedom and choice, but also speaking quite frankly of control, a control that could supersede free will, though only in the spectator's best interests. The *Clockwork Oranges* seize on this tenet of theatrical didacticism and carry it to its grotesque extreme. Both film and novel follow the debate surrounding this new brand of anticrime aversion therapy, weighing the benefits of an end to an individual's criminal activity against the cost to humanity of a medical procedure that robs that same individual of the ability to choose and to act on choice. The chaplain worries that good and bad have no value where choice is not involved and Ludovico proponents, who are merely concerned with preventing crime, respond that choice is a subtlety that has no place in the evaluation of the new technique or its success. This debate both encapsulates and undermines much of Enlightenment reflection on rational and volitional freedom, including Schiller's theory of beauty as presented in *Kallias*, where beauty symbolizes moral self-determination, a concept that rests on the possibility of autonomous choice. It is important to note that Alex's morality was a negative morality but it did represent self-determination. He is, in many ways, an inversion of Schiller's Pelagian *schöne Seele*—a corrective to Kant's Augustinianism—in whom duty and inclination coincide. Alex's inclinations run in the direction of violence, but he merges his inclination to "evil" with a conviction that this is not wrong, but rather natural. His "evil" is both effortless and graceful—a quality underscored by his dancing in the film as he brutalizes the writer and violates his wife. His criticism of those who seek to analyze, reform, or contain him explains this conviction most eloquently:

7: SCHILLERIAN INTERTEXTUALITY IN THE TWENTIETH CENTURY

> But, brothers, this biting of their toe-nails over what is the *cause* of badness is what turns me into a fine laughing malchick. They don't go into the cause of *goodness*, so why the other shop? If lewdies are good, that's because they like it, and I wouldn't ever interfere with their pleasures, and so of the other shop. And I was patronizing the other shop. More, badness is of the self, the one, the you or me on our oddie knockies, and that self is made by old Bog or God and is his great pride and radosty. But the not-self cannot have the bad because they cannot allow the self. And is not our modern history, my brothers, the story of brave malenky selves fighting these big machines? I am serious with you, brothers, over this. But what I do I do because I like to do. (40)

Alex definitely escapes Schiller's definition(s) of the sublime, but the harmony of his actions and his inclinations does put him in the category of the (inverted) beautiful soul that ranks ever so slightly below the sublime figure and he obviously qualifies as a charismatic criminal. He could furthermore be said to have an aesthetic relation to violence, performing it not for money or other reward than that of seeing beautiful blood flow, something of a disinterested contemplation of what he recognizes as beautiful.

The "reeducation" or reprogramming that will impose duties on Alex that thwart his inclinations takes place in the *theater* and it could well have been based on the model of theater that Schiller develops in *Schaubühne,* where spectators see "Bilder" or images that will persuade them to become better people. After healthy meals and shots of a drug that will abet nausea, Alex is wheeled into the projection room, a theater where he is to be taught to recognize and abhor the evil he has done—in fact evil in general—and to turn to his only alternative, goodness. This new concept of duty positions Alex in the nether regions of Kantian moral choice inasmuch as all of his good actions will result from a self-overcoming aided by nausea—not a sublime choice, but a forced behavior. Once in this theater, Alex is transformed physically and made to appear machinelike by the leads connecting him to the devices that will measure his reaction to the spectacle and by the restraints that will compel his spectatorship:

> And then I had a cap stuck on my gulliver and I could viddy all wires running away from it, and they stuck a like suction pad on my belly

and one on the old tick-tocker, and I could just about viddy wires running away from those. (81)

As Alex ticks away, the sensors will record the movements of his "geheimes Räderwerk," mechanically monitoring his reactions to the "performance." Additionally, clips are placed on his forehead that prevent him from closing his eyes. Alex, strapped in a chair with his eyes forced open is the captive audience, brought to the theater to recognize himself in the violent films he will view and to learn *viscerally* from this recognition. The films reprise many of the incidents of violence he had described, with actors performing the deeds Alex has already committed. Thus recognition, the goal of Schiller's stage is strongly—if a bit more literally—in play as Alex develops an aversion to violence. The "heilsame Schauer" that Schiller the healer imputed to his ideal spectators are reprised in Alex's nausea, the physical reaction to evil or violence that will prescribe his future behavior for him. When thoughts of violence occur to the reprogrammed patient, he is impelled to substitute some good action in order to quell the nausea, a very extreme rendition of Schiller's quivers of recognition. As the doctor tells Alex, "Violence is a very horrible thing. That's what you are learning now. Your body is learning it" (85). The healing shudders have a medical basis inasmuch as the Lucovico staff is treating crime as an illness and Alex is further told, "You felt ill this afternoon . . . because you're getting better. When we're healthy we respond to the presence of the hateful with fear and nausea" (86). Like pity and fear in the Aristotelian theater, fear and nausea in the clinical theater of Burgess's therapists lead to the purging of Alex's capacity for violence. Young Schiller's medical training and his interest in the "Zusammenhang der tierischen Natur des Menschen mit seiner geistigen" [The Connections between Man's Animal and Spiritual Natures], the title of his final dissertation,[10] brought him to attempt to heal people within the theater and Burgess places his protagonist in a more contemporary *movie* theater to lose his vices and learn to practice virtue, a punishment that will heal the criminal.

A side effect of the therapy is that Alex also develops an aversion to art, namely to the music that accompanies the terrible films and it is this mortal aversion to all orchestral music that his former victim, F. Alexander, will eventually use against him to drive him to a suicide attempt. While in the theater of horrors, Alex protests that using Beethoven's Fifth to accompany gruesome German war films is a "sin" (115). One of the doctors who watch along with him, notably without any aversion at all to the frightening spectacle, remarks neutrally, "So you're keen on music. I know nothing about it myself. It's a useful emotional heightener, that's all I know" (115). This degradation of art to a means to an end, "useful" for achieving certain results, draws a line in terms of the capacity for aesthetic apprehension between Alex and his reformers. The Ludovico doctors actually change beauty and cause it to offend and sicken the listener and Alex invokes the moral category of sin in describing the evil they have done in ruining Beethoven and ultimately orchestral music for him.

Burgess's reformed patient is also presented to the community in the theater, in a very self-consciously theatrical manner as spotlights seek out actors and Alex, and the audience witnesses the staging of his inability to choose, his unfreedom. It emerges that Alex's internal restraints are indeed strong—stronger than any of the external ones encountered by G****, or Rieger, or Schubart, though the latter developed his own internal restraints. Spectators laugh as an actor/bully taunts and pokes Alex who is unable to defend himself and a doctor explains, clinically and impersonally, the substance of his reaction to the provocations. Thus dehumanized, Alex tries to reassert himself "Me, me, me. How about me? Am I like just some animal or dog? . . . Am I just to be like a clockwork orange?" (128–29), to no particular effect. The accomplishments of the Ludovico theater, where humans are mechanized and repaired, directly counter those of Schiller's stage, where, theoretically, humanity is enhanced and celebrated as vices are cured. Dr. Schiller's methods, even as they probe the heart and mind and seek out all the secret corners, do not intend to violate humanity, though the door is left open to a more defined control, here practiced in its most extreme form by Alex's doctors and punishers, who have precisely determined his reactions as they demonstrate with scripted theatrical stimuli. *Their* drama depicts the demise of free will and the defeat of natural man.

Kubrick's rendition of Alex's reprogramming in the theater is one of the most disturbing sequences in all of cinema. The visual impact of Malcolm MacDowell's Alex, restrained, wired to various machines through a crown-of-thorns headpiece, with his eyes held open by calipers as he screams in terror, is unforgettable and I need not describe this almost universally familiar image at greater length. Suffice it to say that it conveys the visual impact of the Ludovico films on Alex most dramatically. Kubrick's camera focuses mainly on the captive, martyred spectator and registers his horror at the spectacle, so that we view the viewer and reflect on the viewing in this self-referential scene of film within film. Kubrick's Alex also sees German war films, in particular some Leni Riefenstahl footage of soldiers and of Hitler, which is accompanied not by the Fifth, as in the novel, but by the Ninth. Hitler walks proudly forward and the singer intones the "Wie ein Held zum Siegen" verse we have already heard as Alex enters the record store. The horror escalates and Alex the spectator protests that it is a sin to use the Ninth in this way, using the same morally charged word as his novelistic counterpart, but in this case the aversion to music he develops is limited to this one particular piece. And it is the Ninth that F. Alexander and his associates use to try to induce Alex to attempt suicide. Whereas Burgess's Alex awakens to the fictional "Symphony Number Three of the Danish veck Otto Skadelig" (172), this Alex hears the Ninth, previously the embodiment of joy in art for him, and jumps out of the window. He is nearly killed by the combination of Schiller's words of jubilation and humanity and Beethoven's music. Schiller the killer? By means of an elaborate process, Schiller's poetry and Beethoven's music are actually positioned by Kubrick as the stimulus to suicide, making of this one (gesamt) work of art (that earlier stimulated violence) neither a useful enhancement of the emotions nor the gateway to an aesthetic education, but a deadly weapon that incites Alex to commit violence against himself.

The Ninth is, however, restored to its former exalted position in Alex's bloody aesthetic. In both novel and film, it is "cured" along with the protagonist as Alex survives the fall, enters the hospital, and loses the aversion. After the scandalous reports of Alex's therapy in the newspaper, it becomes politically expedient for the Minister of the Interior to abjure the now-reviled Ludovico "Reclamation Treatment" by befriending its victim, so the minister visits Alex in the hospital. In the film, as the minister is making small talk and feeding Alex, one of the indignities the latter subjects him to is the demand to know his first name.

7: SCHILLERIAN INTERTEXTUALITY IN THE TWENTIETH CENTURY

"My name is Frederick," responds the minister, who has no name in the novel. "Frederick" then brings "An die Freude" to the protagonist in the form of two huge speakers blasting out the choral segment of the Ninth. Photographers rush in to photograph the two, MacDowell intones the famous line, "I was cured, allright," and the film ends with a fantasy scene that features Alex cavorting on the ground with a naked woman, while a group of people in Victorian dress applaud him—accompanied by the final bars of "An die Freude."

Schiller literally has the last word(s) in Kubrick's film and the novel concludes in the American edition with Alex listening to the Ninth, anticipating Schiller's words:

> Oh, it was gorgeosity and yumyumyum. When it came to the Scherzo I could viddy myself very clear running and running on like very light and mysterious nogas, carving the whole litso of the creeching world with my cut-throat britva. And there was the slow movement and the lovely last singing movement still to come. I was cured all right. (184)

The healing or cure is the return to his natural state after having been de-natured. As noted, there is another chapter that follows in the British edition—also included in American editions since 1987—in which Alex grows up and loses interest in violence, blaming youth for this kind of mindset and the Victorian dress of the spectators in Kubrick's last scene may refer to this resocialization or to Burgess's somewhat prudish dampening of his novel.

However, the most widely circulated version of Burgess's novel closes in anticipation of Schiller and the film version of that novel, which enhances the presence of the Ninth, ends with Schiller's words playing in the background. The novel features a deliberate rewriting of one of Schiller's strophes that portends a revision of Schillerian ideals and the film plays and replays the choral segments of the Ninth Symphony, while inserting Wilhelm Tell into a scene where Burgess's Alex had played the Ninth. Finally, each piece introduces a Friedrich (Gitterfenster)/Frederick (Minister of the Interior) rather gratuitously and both end with references to Schiller. The accumulation of these citations and allusions would suggest that more than Schillerian Joy is at stake. The introduction of the amoral but cultured charismatic criminal[11] into a futuristic dystopia where science is authorized to "reclaim" and re-form the wrongdoers becomes a problem for the theater and for the purpose of the theater. "Was kann eine gute stehende Schaubühne eigentlich wirken?" In the Ludovico theater, that which makes Alex human, namely his capacity for choice and his appreciation of beauty are taken from him, a process directly opposite of that described in *Schaubühne*. The manipulations of novel and film with regard to music (and poetry), crediting it with inciting violence (pre-treatment) and suicide (post-treatment) attack the principles of an aesthetic education and an aesthetic state.

Schiller was not a systematic philosopher as many, more recently Lesley Sharpe, have noted. As Sharpe indicates in her volume on the essays and their reception, "Like many commentators before me, I believe that bringing Schiller's aesthetic essays together into a system obscures the restless dynamic of his thought. Rather they should be regarded as a sequence of struggles with a set of aesthetic problems."[12] Furthermore, beyond palpable differences between early Schiller and late Schiller, pre-Kantian and post-Kantian Schiller, there are numerous inconsistencies and obscurities within single essays. Yet despite this doubleness or "ideological incompleteness" (Sammons, 86), there exist a number of identifiable Schillerian ideals and concepts that have emerged from the essays, even if we do not, with de Man, credit Schiller with all of our unreflected thinking on the nature and value of art. *A Clockwork Orange* brings ideas such as the charismatic criminal, the beautiful soul, the aesthetic education and beauty-as-freedom to bear on its/their own investigation of humanity and the right to free will. It does not do so systematically or with philological rigor and doubtless the novel and film are funded by the work of other thinkers (Pelagius and Augustine, for example). Nonetheless, there is a palpable engagement in both versions with the German poet of freedom. The revision of Schiller's ideals that begins in a revision of Schiller's "An die Freude," demonstrates more than the reach of Schiller's intertextual influence. It also indicates the durability of these ideals. Indeed they do not survive into the dystopic present intact, but they prove to be dynamic and durable in that they provoke revision and reversal. Schiller's ideals live on in these reversals and the questions he posed about human nature and its susceptibility to art provide the basis for two extraordinary contemporary works of art.

Conclusion

The foregoing investigation of Schiller's aesthetic engagement with crime and punishment has addressed a variety of issues and I want to conclude with some brief synthesizing remarks. These begin with a fairly important passage from Schiller that I have not addressed above, from the *first* version of "An die Freude" (*Thalia*, 1786). The poem that we all know so well and the one that Beethoven set to music in the Ninth Symphony was the second, revised version from 1803.[13] Ultimately, the revisions were not numerous and there are not so many differences between the two versions. There were minor changes in the first verse, but the second, third, fourth, fifth, sixth, seventh, and eighth verses and choruses are for all intents and purposes identical. What really distinguishes the two poems from one another is an omission in the revision and this omission constitutes a substantial distinction for my purposes in this study. The final verse of the *Thalia* poem was dropped, never to be resuscitated, and this is most likely due to the very radical nature of the sentiments it expressed. The excised verse reads:

> Rettung von Tirannenketten,
>   Großmut auch dem Bösewicht
> Hoffnung auf den Sterbebetten,
>   Gnade auf dem Hochgericht!
> Auch die Toden sollen leben!
>   Brüder trinkt und stimmet ein,
> Allen Sündern soll vergeben,
>   und die Hölle nicht mehr sein.
>
> (I:413)

[Rescue from the chains of tyrants,
Magnanimity even toward villains
Hope on the deathbeds!
Mercy at the last judgment!
Even the dead shall live!
Brothers drink and assent,
All sinners shall be forgiven,
and Hell no longer be.]

Here, Schiller proclaims, among other things, that the dead shall live and that all criminals and sinners shall be pardoned. Though "An die Freude" is a particularly expansive and effusive tribute to (some sort of, or all sorts of) unity, this is a very bold conclusion. In his reverie of unity and brotherhood, Schiller erases *all* barriers to a true embrace of all humanity, past and present, giving rise to an almost undifferentiated congregation of living and dead, of benefactors and malefactors.[14] The forgiveness of sins is standard Christian dogma, but Schiller goes even further in this invocation as he gives the dead, the dying, and all sinners genuine hope by eliminating hell, the site of eternal punishment, and the archetype for all punishment, retributive, deterrent, and just. Shortly after writing *Schaubühne*, in which he usurps the state and the judiciary in favor of theatrical improvement of wayward spectators, Schiller proclaims the abolition of punishment! That he does so in a minor lyric poem that he later regarded as defective,[15] may undermine the oracular grandiosity of the proclamation, but I believe that the tenacity of the conviction behind it is borne out by the literary texts and aesthetic theory examined above. Schiller has, for reasons he never elaborated, countered the retributive urge of his historical moment and repeatedly illustrated alternative reactions to crime or, to a lesser extent, sin. He has questioned the value of the state's penal apparatus and undermined the logic of its implementation or thwarted it outright in his dramas and narratives. To be sure, Schiller erased the verse that contains the extreme expression of these sentiments from "An die Freude," but his literary practice previous and subsequent to the 1786 version of the poem can be productively examined in light of these ideas—and I hope that I have done this.

The early poetic maneuver of abolishing punishment by obliterating its source establishes the parameters for a lifetime of radical literary tolerance of crime and criminals. Although it does not address the nuances of crime or of the criminal urge, this gesture does emphatically affirm Schiller's suspicion of the penal system. To cause suffering to those who have caused suffering is a primitive reaction to what may have been an intellectually intricate, creative, and courageous expression of the human spirit. By annihilating hell, Schiller is able to embrace a whole class of aberrants whom he admires. Many have argued that the "Freude" Schiller celebrated in the poem is really

"Freiheit" or freedom,[16] and it is important to note that the removal of the "chains of tyrants" precipitates the demise of hell. Political freedom for Schiller overlaps to a great degree with freedom from confinement and retributive punishment.

I have argued above that Schiller subverts punishment and points to new and different ways of receiving and reacting to crime, and that he considers crime to be a complex phenomenon that cannot be "solved" by simple retributive or deterrent punishment. I have also tried to demonstrate that these activities and opinions are grounded in Schiller's theater, which he opposes to the absolutist state as a viable and preferable counter-regime. This new state is also possessed of a judiciary and, in *Schaubühne*, Schiller argues that the judicial arm of the dramatic stage is more effective than religion or conventional governments. Yet Schiller, the power behind the dramatic stage—and behind the prose texts that in their own way advance the agenda of the theatrical pieces—does not punish and even seems to cherish crime. He elides the execution of Maria Stuart in a most ostentatious manner, eliminating that particular hell and diverting attention to the heroic spiritual transformations of the imprisoned queen, who was previously accessory to murder. By keeping Maria Stuart's head precisely where it belongs, Schiller is able to focus on the potential of the human spirit for courage, composure, and acceptance of the inevitable, even as he allows Leicester to disintegrate, paralyzed by his cowardice. The latter's transgressions were failures of loyalty and love, rather than overt criminal acts and his fear and duplicity contrast most effectively with Maria's serene composure.

This contrast of the great (criminal) spirit and the petty dishonesty of lesser souls was established in Schiller's earliest dramatic work. In *Die Räuber* and *Fiesko*, young Schiller had already inscribed a highly specific scale of value for deviations from virtue and law. The explicit contrast between the crimes of Karl Moor, who breaks the law both publicly and spectacularly, and those of his brother Franz, who practices intrigue and subterfuge in the comfort and concealment of his home, is reprised and codified in *Fiesko*, where Muley Hassan lectures the protagonist on the full range of great to despicable law-breaking. Hassan, the bearer of this knowledge, leans toward the despicable and does suffer punishment, in the form of a fully depicted execution onstage. His fate is the exception that suggests the rule.

In his initial dramatic efforts, Schiller ruptures the crime-punishment link and obfuscates the matter of culpability. In the early prose narrative, *Spiel des Schicksals*, he turns his attention to penal confinement and depicts the physical deterioration and spiritual stasis of a man confined to prison. The futility of this particular punishment-without-crime, as well as the critique of absolutism it advances recall Schiller's school days and his own restrictions under an absolutist apparatus that included Rieger, the model for G***. The erotics of the tale, and the interplay of G***'s beauty with the ugliness engraved on him by punishment, forge connections with Schiller's aesthetics, as we encounter the inverse of Beauty-Freedom in the repulsive appearance of the imprisoned courtier.

In *Verbrecher aus verlorener Ehre*, Schiller reflects on the ultimate crime and attempts to make murder intelligible by examining the state's penal practices. Christian Wolf is cursed by nature with physical ugliness that, when combined with sensations of love, leads to crime. His progress as a psychological subject, responding to repeated mistreatment and humiliation, is the focus of the narrative that condemns the law and its application for having caused the severe aggravation of Wolf's disposition toward crime. This is indeed the kind of punishment that should be abolished, if only to prevent further crime.

If murder is intelligible in *Verbrecher*, it can actually be read as praiseworthy in *Wilhelm Tell*, where the protagonist, along with the minor figure Baumgarten, murders to great acclaim and general appreciation. The absence of punishment (or Baumgarten's escaping it) certainly relativizes the crime in this world of broken or unmade fatherhood. The deeply punitive nature of the apple shot that precedes Tell's crime has more mythic and tragic resonance than a civil penalty because it tortures Tell as father and fatherhood is the ground of all political and personal activity in the pageant. Of course the shot *is* a myth and this enactment fades in significance as the murder of Geßler unmakes imperial oppression. However, the happy conclusion of this play about fathers, murderers, fathers who are murderers and father murderers (Parricida) is enabled only by the willing suspension of our disbelief.

It would be difficult to find many greater criminals or sinners than the heretic, Joan of Arc, who defied so many conventions and laws of her society and who, as history records, was burned at the stake. Yet Schiller was able to save his Johanna by "overcoming history" and to contribute to Joan's canonization by writing a popular play that portrays her as both heroic *and* feminine. The importance of Schiller's femininization of Joan, who is given so many female attributes to flaunt on his stage, cannot be overestimated. While transforming a criminal in pants into a palatable heroine in a dress—that is, by canceling the crime for which she was executed—Schiller rehabilitated a questionable and potentially offensive figure, transforming a sinner into a saint.

As with Joan, Schiller managed in various ways to get most of his criminals off the hook by tampering with conventional value systems and understanding crime as something other than simple malefaction. Punishment does not follow on these crimes and the repetition of the gesture of undermining or negating the crime-punishment symmetry, as expressed in our example from Kant ("Hat er aber gemordet, so muss er sterben"), points to a long, sustained attempt to humanize the state's response to those who defy its laws.

This also involves a partial humanizing of crime. Schiller parses criminality. He elevates and admires "great" criminal deeds as signs of a great human spirit, reflecting the same energy and intelligence that support heroism. These are open, public actions as opposed to the dissembling and duplicity that belong to the realm of lesser transgressions, which he abhors. In either case, Schiller, the physician and dramatic theorist, appears to believe that these problems can be "treated" and "cured" in the theater with healing shudders of recognition—and this is where the resemblance to Burgess's and Kubrick's respective versions of *A Clockwork Orange* is so troubling. There is a dark side to the utility that Schiller celebrates. Josef Goebbels can cite Schiller in support of his fascist aspirations and Burgess and Kubrick can, with some measure of exaggeration, recast his theater of effect as the space of the Ludovico Treatment. This is possible, I believe, first of all because these ideas are common property and subject to varied reception, but also because Schiller's discourse is embedded in the language of absolutism, and in the iron discipline and dire coercion he experienced in his youth and early adulthood. His defiance of that supreme force and the violence that transgresses human will is nonetheless expressed in that language and his plans for a humanizing, freedom-inducing, aesthetic surrogate for punishment often appear to be the substitution of one mode of control for another. The idea of the dramatic stage or aesthetic education as a solution to man's (illegal) inhumanity to man is in many ways a seriously flawed concept, especially when it appropriates the coercive element of nonaesthetic responses to crime. But where the solution is weak, the evocations of the problem are both strong and valuable for any consideration of transgression and retribution (or preemption). Schiller's aesthetic reflections on and incorporation of punishment, his poetics of punishment, can potentially open new avenues for thought on political and legal matters because they expose the irrational bases of the retributive urge. This gesture itself is not unique, but the manner of exposure is a powerful contribution to our thinking on social coexistence. Schiller's creative disruption of aesthetic symmetries mimics the individual human spirit in conflict with its social surroundings and his consistent insistence on individual freedom and self-determination is, despite a wealth of contradiction, something *beautiful*.

Notes

Chapter 1. Admiration for Aberrants

1. Phoebe C. Ellsworth and Samuel R. Gross, "Hardening of the Attitudes: Americans' Views on the Death Penalty," in *The Death Penalty in America: Current Controversies*, ed. Hugo Adam Bedau (New York: Oxford University Press, 1997), 111.

2. See W. Daniel Wilson, *Das Goethe Tabu: Protest und Menschenrechte im klassischen Weimar* (Munich: Deutscher Taschenbuch Verlag, 1999), 7.

3. See especially John Bender, *Imagining the Penitentiary: Fiction and the Architecture of the Mind in Eighteenth-Century England* (Chicago: University of Chicago Press, 1987).

4. Richard Evans, *Rituals of Retribution: Capital Punishment in Germany 1600–1987* (New York: Oxford University Press, 1996), vii.

5. Bedau argues for "the essentially *symbolic* role of the death penalty at present" (Bedau, 86) and it seems that this observation can easily be extended to its role in the past. The matter of public execution as a deterrent to crime rather than a purely symbolic act comes up in "Verbrecher aus verlorener Ehre." See chapter 4.

6. In his magisterial study, *Angenehmes Grauen: Literaturhistorische Beiträge zur Ästhetik des Schrecklichen im achtzehnten Jahrhundert* (Hamburg: Felix Meinert, 1987), Zelle traces the gradual development of a counter-movement in eighteenth-century aesthetics, that he characterizes as "pleasurable terror" or "angenehmes Grauen." The receptivity to that which is pleasantly unpleasant is also anticipated in Schiller's dramatic practice, that seeks to evoke "therapeutic shudders."

7. Kant, *Metaphysische Anfangsgruende der Rechtslehre*, E I 333; "Vom Straf- und Begnadigungsrecht," *Werke*, IV (Darmstadt: Wissenschaftliche Buchgesellschaft, 1966), 452–59.

8. Including Theodor Adorno and Paul de Man. See chapter 2.

9. *Friedrich Schiller: Werke und Briefe in zwölf Bänden*, ed. Otto Dahn, et al. (Frankfurt am Main: Deutscher Klassiker Verlag, 1988–), II, 32. Further references to this edition will be cited within the text by volume and page numbers.

10. "Re-dressing History: Mother Nature, Mother Isabeau, the Virgin Mary, and Schiller's *Jungfrau*," in *Women in German Yearbook* 14 (1998): 91–108.

11. Michel Foucault, *Discipline and Punish: The Birth of the Prison*, trans. Alan Sheridan (New York: Vintage, 1979), 7–12.

12. Hölderlin, "Über den Begriff der Strafe," in *Sämtliche Werke und Briefe*, II (Berlin: Aufbau Verlag, 1970), 362.

13. Bernt von Heiseler, *Schiller* (Gütersloh: C. Bertelsmann, 1959), 22 and passim.

14. See Friedrich Kittler, "Carlos als Carlsschüler," in *Unser Commercium: Goethes und Schillers Literaturpolitik*, ed. Wilfried Barner, et al. (Stuttgart: J. G. Cotta'sche Buchhandlung Nachfolger, 1984), 241–73. And especially Susan Kassouf, *Writing Masculinities Around 1800*, (dissertation, Cornell, 1996).

15. Uhland, Robert, *Geschichte der Hohen Karlsschule in Stuttgart* (Stuttgart: Kohlhammer, 1953), 72.

16. Peter Lahnstein, *Schillers Leben* (Munich, 1981), 44. Subsequent references to this volume will be cited within the text with "Lahnstein" and page number.

17. Heinrich Laube's dramatization of Schiller's education, "Die Karlsschüler," actually depicts Philip Friedrich Rieger, whom we will encounter in chapter 3, coming down from the fort with the intention of arresting Schiller. In *Dramatische Werke*, VI (Leipzig: J. J. Weber, 1847).

Chapter 2: What Does the Dramatic Stage Actually Do?

1. It was furthermore the basis of a potential German nation, and Schiller echoed Lessing's famous statement in the *Hamburgische Dramaturgie* in his declaration, "wenn wir es erlebten eine Nationalbühne zu haben, so würden wir auch eine Nation" (VIII:199).

2. This is of course only one of Schiller's Schillerian "improvements" on Kant. He substitutes theoretical and practical sublime(s) for Kant's mathematical and dynamic sublime(s). See "Kant and Schiller" in de Man, *Aesthetic Ideology*, ed. Andrzej Warminski (Minneapolis: University of Minnesota Press, 1996), 129–62, here 140–41. Subsequent references to this volume will be cited within the text with AI and page numbers.

3. *The Rhetoric of Romanticism* (New York: Columbia University Press, 1984), 289. Subsequent references will be cited within the text with RR and page numbers.

4. *Minima Moralia: Reflexionen aus dem beschädigten Leben* (Frankfurt am Main: Suhrkamp, 1951), 97.

5. *The Ideology of the Aesthetic* (Oxford: Blackwell Publishers, 1990).

6. It should be noted that there is considerable opposition among Schiller scholars to de Man's portrayal of Schiller's aesthetics, both in RR and as recorded from lecture notes in AI. Lesley Sharpe represents this reaction with elegant tact: "Many will find de Man strong meat, and, even if one accepts his premises, the tone of accusation, the implied ideological interrogation, may seem misplaced." *Schiller's Aesthetic Essays: Two Centuries of Criticism* (Columbia, SC: Camden House, 1995), 84. See also Michael T. Jones, "Schiller Trouble," *Goethe Yearbook* 10 (2001), 222–45.

7. *Nostalgic Teleology: Friedrich Schiller and the Schemata of Aesthetic Humanism* (Berne: Peter Lang, 1995), 4.

8. "The statesman is an artist, too. The people are for him what stone is for the sculptor. . . . To transform a mass into a people and a people into a state—that has always been the deepest sense of a genuine political task." *On

the Aesthetic Education of Man, edited and translated by Elizabeth Wilkinson and L. A. Willoughby (Oxford: Clarendon Press, 1967), "Introduction," cxlii. Quoted in full by de Man in AI:154–55. Schiller has been appropriated for various ideological causes. See Kathy Saranpa, *Schiller's Wallenstein, Maria Stuart, and Die Jungfrau von Orleans* (Rochester, NY: Camden House, 2002), 89–134, for a partial account of the uses to which Schiller and his works were put in Nazi Germany and the German Democratic Republic. Currently, Schiller is at the center of the Lyndon LaRouche organization's cultural arm and the LaRouche "Schiller Institute" may be visited at www.schillerinstitute.org.

9. Both Lessing (*Hamburgische Dramaturgie*) and Mercier (*Du theatre ou nouvel essai sur l'art dramatique*) had also written of the stage as an alternative judiciary (VIII:1250). Carsten Zelle, in his definitive history of the use of fear and the frightening, also takes up the question of the stage as judiciary and of its dramaturgy of deterrence: *Angenehmes Grauen*, 56ff.

10. For a well-crafted account of theater as therapy, see Stephanie Hammer, *Schiller's Wound: The Theater of Trauma from Crisis to Commodity* (Detroit: Wayne State University Press, 2001). Working with psychological categories, Hammer establishes the traumatic character of a separation from home, both for Schiller and for his dramatic figures, and she sees this trauma addressed in a kind of melodrama that brings the audience back to its own "mental wounds": "Having effected this simulacrum of trauma, melodrama then offers audiences a therapeutic experience in which traumas are re-presented, brought into the symbolic order and then cured" (33).

11. Karl Guthke stresses this aspect of the *Schaubühne* essay, which he designates "recht verstanden als Schule der Menschenkenntnis." Guthke sees consistency over time in Schiller's purpose, "den Menschen mit dem Menschen bekannt zu machen." *Schillers Dramen:Idealismus und Skepsis* (Bern: Francke, 1994), 20–21, 35. My purpose here is to examine the ways in which this common humanity was intended to be transmitted and received.

12. In Reinhard Buchwald, *Der Junge Schiller*, I (Leipzig: Insel, 1937) 352; Alan Leidner, "'Fremde Menschen fielen einander in die Arme': *Die Räuber* and the Communal Response." *Goethe Yearbook* 3 (1986): 57.

13. See Zelle, 68–74, for a discussion of Beccaria and his impact on the eighteenth-century theater of deterrence.

14. See Gerd Sautermeister's "*Maria Stuart*: Ästhetik, Seelenkunde, historisch-gesellschaftlicher Ort," in *Schillers Dramen: Neue Interpretationen*, ed. Walter Hinderer (Stuttgart: Reclam, 1979), 174–216, for a very thorough discussion of the interpretive literature on *Maria Stuart*. In this compact and succinct essay, Sautermeister also pursues many of the main (non-penal) themes of the literature on Schiller's drama, including Maria's ambivalence, the question of Maria as beautiful soul, and the politics of female throne occupation in a patriarchal society. Dieter Borchmeyer sees the unfolding of *Maria Stuart* as mimicking a law court procedure, noting that most of the dialogue is remote from the personal and geared toward public (legal) rhetoric. *Tragödie und Öffentlichkeit: Schillers Dramaturgie in Zusammenhang mit seiner ästhetisch-politischen Theorie und die rhetorische Tradition* (Munich: Wilhelm Fink Verlag, 1973), 200–201.

15. Hanging, electrocution and lethal gas were all in their turn—though

there is considerable overlap—thought to effect death with minimal pain. The arguments for electricity and gas are more familiar to the modern reader. For an engaging account of hanging as a painless means of death, see James Berry, *My Experiences as an Executioner*, ed. H. Snowdon Ward (Detroit: Gale Research Co., 1972).

16. See "Auf dem Schafott: Verbrechen und Strafen," in Richard van Dülmen, *Theater des Schreckens: Gerichtspraxis und Strafrituale in der frühen Neuzeit* (Munich: Beck, 1988), 102–20.

17. Franz Kafka, *Sämtliche Erzählungen*, ed. Paul Raabe (Frankfurt am Main: Fischer, 1970), 137.

18. William Camden's *Annales rerum Anglicarum et Hibernicarum regnante Elizabetha* (1615, translated into English as *The History of the Most Renowned and Victorious Princess Elizabeth Late Queen of England*, ed. Wallace MacCaffrey [Chicago and London: University of Chicago Press, 1970]) and David Hume's *History of England* (German translation, 1762) were among Schiller's sources and they mention only "two Stroaks" (Camden, 288; Hume, echoing Camden, whom he cites [New York: Harper and Brothers, 1850], 238), whereas numerous other accounts make of the sawing a third stroke; see Wolf Middendorf, *Der Prozess gegen Maria Stuart* (Cologne and Hamburg: Verlag Dr. Otto Schmidt, 1972), 6.

19. Middendorf adds a quotation from Gerda Doublier, *Maria Stuart* (Graz/Cologne, 1959): "Auf dem Boden aber rollte das Haupt, dessen ehedem so schöne Züge sich bis zur Unkenntlichkeit verzerrt haben. Es ist das Antlitz einer uralten Frau, eingerahmt von eisgrauen Haaren" (284; Middendorf, 6). The passage appears to be a descendant of the eyewitness account of Robert Wyngfield, "An Account of the Execution of Mary Queen of Scots," *The Clarendon Historical Societies Reports*, series II, 2 vols. (Edinburgh, 1844–46): "Then her dressing of lawn fell from her head, which appeared as if she had been 70 years old, polled very short, her face being in a moment so much altered from its form when she was alive, as few could remember her by her dead face" (I:1). I am grateful to Jayne Lewis for the Wyngfield reference.

20. See Dorothea von Mücke's comments on the spiritual benefits of the carceral in *Maria Stuart* in *Virtue and the Veil of Illusion: Generic Innovation and the Pedagogical Project in Eighteenth-Century Literature* (Stanford: Stanford University Press, 1991), 221ff.

21. For a different view, one that contests findings of sublimity, see Andreas Mielke, "'Maria Stuart': Hermeneutical Problems of 'One' Tragedy with 'Two' Queens," in *Friedrich Schiller and the Drama of Human Existence*, ed. Alexej Ugrinsky (Westport, CT: Greenwood Press, 1988), 49–56.

22. Rolf-Peter Janz, "Die ästhetische Bewältigung des Schreckens: Zu Schillers Theorien des Erhabenen," in *Geschichte als Literatur: Formen und Grenzen der Repräsentation von Vergangenheit*, ed. Hartmut Eggert (Stuttgart: Metzler, 1990), 151–60.

23. Such as that of Louis XVI, who had, as Schiller wrote, recently met his own decapitation.

Chapter 3. "Die Schande nimmt ab mit der wachsenden Sünde"

1. This is not by any means a unique method of describing such an event. William Thackeray's "Going to See a Man Hanged: July 1840," in which

Thackeray attends the execution of Courvoisier and elides the actual deed is another prominent example of this kind of historiographical undepiction. *The Works of William Makepeace Thackeray*, III, ed. Anne Thackeray Ritchie (New York and London: Harper & Brothers Publishers, 1898), 635–49.

2. In both cases, truly high crimes transcend punishment, since he who successfully steals a crown immediately becomes the law and he who commits shocking crimes terrifies his victims and makes them incapable of retribution.

3. See Stephanie Hammer's excellent, "Schiller, Time and Again" *German Quarterly* 67, no. 2 (Spring 1994): 153–72, for a discussion of lack and repetition, and Walter Hinderer, *Von der Idee des Menschen:Über Friedrich Schiller* (Würzburg: Königshausen und Neumann, 1998), 185ff., for a very thorough review of critical commentary on Old Moor.

4. In *Schiller's Wound*, Hammer sees Schiller's dramatic output as a "form of traumatic compensation" (152), one that is mirrored in both Franz's and Karl's activities, seen as reactions to a staggering lack of paternal presence (27–49).

5. Bruce Beiderwell, *Power and Punishment in Scott's Novels* (Athens and London: University of Georgia Press, 1992), 3.

6. This is the conclusion that Leidner reaches in "'Fremde Menschen."

7. Rolf-Peter Janz, "Die Verschwörung des Fiesko zu Genoa," in *Schillers Dramen: Neue Interpretationen*, 37.

8. In his stunningly thorough two-volume biography of Schiller, Peter-Andre Alt notes that Dr. Schiller, the military physician, was excessively fond of prescribing emetics to his mostly elderly patients: "Derartige Vomitive solle er häufig, zumeist in hoher Dosierung, verordnet haben." *Schiller: Leben-Werk-Zeit* (Munich: C. H. Beck, 2000), I, 207. That Schiller makes the connection with aesthetics here recalls the very visceral *Wirkung* he advocates in the *Schaubühne* essay.

9. In a discussion of Schiller's morally neutral approach to power, Guthke quotes Thomas Mann's assessment of the difference between Goethe and Schiller from Mann's "Versuch über Schiller:"

> Goethe: Noi, noi, mein Bester, wo denken Sie hin, das ist ja greulich!
> Schiller: Aber ich schwöre Ihne, es wird grossen Effekt machen und dem Publico so recht in die Seele schneide'. (Guthke, 17)

10. The *Deutsche Klassiker* edition, which I am using in this study both for its reliability and for its accessibility uses the text of the original 1786 *Thalia* version that had the title, "Verbrecher aus Infamie." The 1792 version is almost identical to the earlier one and the major change is the transformation of the title to "Verbrecher aus verlorener Ehre." Since the latter title has established itself and the first now sounds quaint or philologically fastidious, I have elected to use the "verlorener Ehre" title. The passages quoted from the *Deutsche Klassiker* edition are identical in both versions.

Chapter 4. Schiller and the Prison

1. Schiller acknowledges his pessimism about overcoming the experiential requirement at the outset, but resolves to try.

2. See von Mücke: "The main key to her reformation can be found in her incarceration" (221).

3. Quoted in von Heiseler, 31. Kurt Honolka indicates that, though the poem is attributed to Schubart, and was doubtless thought by Karl Eugen to be his work, it may have been written by Leopold von Goeckingk, an early associate of Schubart's (*Schubart: Dichter und Musiker, Journalist und Rebell* [Stuttgart: Deutsche Verlags-Anstalt, 1985], 180–81).

4. Michael Myers, *Für den Bürger: The Role of Christian Schubart's "Deutsche Chronik" in the Development of a Political Public Sphere* (New York: Lang, 1990), 218, 254.

5. Quoted in Myers, 255.

6. Ulrike Rainer disagrees that there is homoerotic value in Schiller's language. She indicates, "Schiller bedient sich starker Ausdrücke, um ein Scheinglück darzustellen, dessen Urheber nicht von Vernunft und Staatsraison, sondern von einem irrationalen Gefühl regiert wird" (*Schillers Prosa: Poetologie und Praxis* [Berlin: Erich Schmidt Verlag, 1988], 111–12). Yet there is nothing to indicate that the "irrational feeling" is not libidinal.

7. Derks, *Die Schande der heiligen Päderastie: Homosexualität und Öffentlichkeit in der deutschen Literatur 1750–1850* (Berlin: Verlag rosa Winkel, 1990), 372.

8. Quoted in Derks, 374.

9. There is a glaring exception to the same-sex rule in the case of rape victim Bertha in *Fiesko*. In all versions, her father orders her isolation and imprisonment until such time as she is avenged. Therefore, her rehabilitation depends on whether outside actors can kill Giannetino and not on any inner acceptance of a penal program. She is also the victim and not the perpetrator. Nonetheless, it is interesting that this young woman, locked up by an enraged man, reappears in the first version dressed as a boy (II:428).

10. *Gedichte aus dem Kerker* (Wien: Preßburg, 1785), 199–200; Honolka, 215.

Chapter 5. Murderous Fathers

1. See Hans-Jörg Knobloch, "Wilhelm Tell," in *Schiller Handbuch*, 495.

2. *Die Peinliche Gerichtsordnung Kaiser Karls V. von 1532*, ed. Gustav Radbruch (Stuttgart: Reclam, 2000), 88. Cited in text as *Carolina*.

3. *Schiller Handbuch*, 500

4. Josef Sander, *Die Begründung der Notwehr in der Philosophie von Kant und Hegel* (Bleicherode am Harz: Verlag Carl Nieft, 1939), 7.

5. See Knobloch, 498–502, for the one of the most recent summaries of critics' opinions on the character, import, and justifiability of the murder. The most recent is Christoph E. Schweitzer's, "A Defense of Schiller's Wilhelm Tell" in *Goethe Yearbook 9* (Columbia, SC: Camden House, 1999): 253–63.

6. W. G. Moore, "A New Reading of 'Wilhelm Tell,'" in *German Studies: Presented to Professor H. G. Fiedler* (Oxford: Clarendon, 1938), 280.

7. Frank Ryder, "Schiller's Tell and the Cause of Freedom," *The German Quarterly* 48, no. 4 (1975): 499.

8. Jeffrey Sammons, "The Apple-Shot and the Politics of *Wilhelm Tell*," in *Friedrich Schiller and the Drama of Human Existence*, 86.

9. Franklin L. Ford, *Political Murder: From Tyrannicide to Terrorism* (Cambridge: Harvard University Press, 1985), 2.

10. Interestingly, when such questions come up as issues of popular ethics, Hitler is often the example cited, as in "would the murder of Hitler to prevent further deaths have been an ethical deed?" Georg Ruppelt indicates that in 1941, Hitler decreed through Martin Bormann that *Wilhelm Tell*, a play that was popular in Nazi Germany, no longer be performed or taught in schools. No reason was given, but Ruppelt argues compellingly that Hitler saw a possible connection between repeated attempts on his life by a Swiss theology student, Bavaud, and Schiller's supposed justification of tyrannicide. *Schiller im nationalsozialistischen Deutschland* (Stuttgart: Metzler, 1979), 40–45; Sammons, 86–87.

11. Elaine Scarry, *The Body in Pain: The Making and Unmaking of the World* (New York: Oxford University Press, 1985).

12. Unauthorized reproduction is Judith Roof's term in her *Reproductions of Reproduction: Imaging Symbolic Change* (New York: Routledge, 1996), where she develops the topic as it extends to space alien fictions and vampire stories.

13. See Koopmann's summary in *Schiller Handbuch*, 702–3.

14. Achim Auernhammer, "Engagiertes Erzählen: *Der Verbrecher aus verlorener Ehre*" in *Schiller und die höfische Welt*, ed. Auernhammer, et al. (Tübingen: Max Niemeyer Verlag , 1980), 254–70.

15. Sara L. Knox, *Murder: A Tale of Modern American Life* (Durham, NC: Duke University Press, 1998), 195. Knox focuses on late nineteenth- to mid-twentieth-century texts, but her conclusions are importable and relevant to Schiller's eighteenth-century crime story.

16. Jacob Friedrich Abel, "Lebensgeschichte Fridrich Schwans," in *Friedrich Schiller: "Der Verbrecher aus verlorener Ehre"* (Stuttgart: Ernst Klett Verlag, 1983), 31–71. The "Beschreibung des famosen Bößwichts Friderich Schwahnen, von Eberspach Göppinger Amts" that follows Abel's text portrays Schwan as being "eines starcken Kopfs, weissen saubern Angesichts, dicker rother Backen, braun oder vielmehr belblecther kurzer glatter Harren, schwarzbrauner Augen, breiter Schultern, und starcker Waaden" (83).

17. Auernhammer sees the absence of the father as being compounded by a fatherless society: "Denn der Sonnenwirt entbehrt eines Vaters nicht nur im familiären Sinn, sondern auch im Sozialverband der Vaterstadt und im staatspolitischen Verband mit dem Landesherrn an der Spitze. Die Vaterlosigkeit steht für die fehlende Gnadeninstanz, so daß . . . die Erzählung auch 'Der Verbrecher aus verlorenem Vater' heißen könnte" (270).

18. Beccaria, in a segment of *On Crimes and Punishments* criticizes the mixing of accused and convicted in the same cell and concludes: "still discernible are the barbaric impressions and savage notions of those people of the North who hunted down our forefathers." See Cesare Bonesana Beccaria, *On Crimes and Punishments*, trans. Henry Paolucci (New Jersey: Prentice Hall, 1963), 20).

19. Schwan also encountered his enemy in the forest while deer hunting.

Abel reports: "Die ganze Wuth seiner Seele überfiel ihn bey diesem Anblick; Er richtete die gegen das Thier gezückte Flinte gegen seinen Feind. Aber noch vermochte er nicht die furchtbare That zu begehen. Alle Greuel des Mords giengen dunkel und schnell, aber schreckend und furchtbar durch seine Seele. Er zog die Flinte zurück, um sie wieder gegen den Hirsch zu richten; aber sogleich übermannte ihn die Wuth aufs neue, er zielte wieder gegen seinen Feind, und zog wieder zurück, viermal zielte er also aufs neue, und viermal zog er wieder zurück. Endlich bemeisterte sich eine gänzliche Verwirrung seiner Sinne, Kampf und Wut und Schrecken umnebelten seinen Geist, die Wuth siegte, er schoß, und vollbracht war sein erster Mord (45)."

20. Hammer does a second reading of *Die Räuber* in relation to its status as melodrama and its themes of trauma and (the trauma of) departure in her *Schiller's Wound*. See especially the first chapter, "My Villain, My Self: Melodrama, Laughter, and Abjection in *The Robbers*," 27–49.

21. Thomas Nutz, "Vergeltung oder Versöhnung? Strafvollzug und Ehre in Schillers *Verbrecher aus Infamie*," *Jahrbuch der deutschen Schillergesellschaft* 42 (1998): 146–64, 155.

22. See Wilson, 7–8.

Chapter 6. Shiller's Heart, Joan's Crimes, and Johanna's Glory

1. A strong spirit in a fragile body / A mongrel out of man and woman; These are grave times / When women too are donning armor.

2. Hotchkiss, Valerie, *Clothes Make the Man: Female Cross-Dressing in Medieval Europe* (New York: Garland, 1996), 59.

3. Françoise Meltzer, *For Fear of the Fire: Joan of Arc and the Limits of Subjectivity* (Chicago: University of Chicago Press, 2001), 203, from the New English Bible; Thomas Aquinas also addressed the prohibition in *Summa Theologica*, indicating that women could wear men's clothes in certain situations if necessity dictated—for disguise and protection or if no other clothes are available (Hotchkiss, 55).

4. Quicherat, Jules, *Proces de condamnation et le rehabilitation de Jeanne d'Arc dite La Pucell* (Paris: Renouard, 1841–49), 1:432–33; quoted in Hotchkiss, 59.

5. See Meltzer, 189 n. 42.

6. Meltzer adds, "The deeper crime, the unacknowledged one, was that she could so easily succeed in the exploits that masculinity claims as its own, to the explicit exclusion of the other sex" (202).

7. Quicherat 1:456; Meltzter, 190.

8. I have also discussed the execution in an essay on the unnatural and the significance of cross-dressing in "Re-dressing History: Mother Nature, Mother Isabeau, the Virgin Mary and Schiller's *Jungfrau*."

9. In his letter to Goethe of 30 June 1797, Schiller wrote: "Ich muß mich doch wirklich drüber wundern, wie unsere Weiber jetzt, auf bloß dilettantischem Wege, eine gewisse Schreibgeschicklichkeit sich zu verschaffen wissen, die der Kunst nahekommt." This remark, with its acknowledgment of certain

talented women's writing as actually approaching (but not reaching) the status of art more or less summarizes the discussion in the Goethe-Schiller correspondence.

10. NA 28, 34; quoted in Helmut Brand, "Angriff auf den schwächsten Punkt: Friedrich Schlegels Kritik an Schillers *Würde der Frauen*," in *Aurora* 59 (1993): 110.

11. Hans Mayer, for example, notes: "[Schiller's] conception of women, a bourgeois one, with all its philistine aspects, is known from the poem "Würde der Frauen," in "The Scandal of Joan of Arc," in *Joan of Arc*, ed. Harold Bloom (New York: Chelsea House, 1992) 159. Mayer, an East German critic, uses "bourgeois" in its most pejorative sense, but he finds Schiller's opinion of women to be limited and locates this "conception" in "Würde der Frauen."

12. *Kritische Friedrich Schlegel Ausgabe*, ed. Ernst Behler, II, pt. 2 (Paderborn, 1967), 6; Brand, 112.

13. A. W. Schlegel, *Sämtliche Werke*, ed. Eduard Böcking, II, pt. 2. Theil, (Hildesheim and New York), 172, Brand, 114.

14. Dina El Zarka cites this anatomical model as elaborated by Thomas Laqueur as relevant to the discussion in "Liebe und Sexualität in der Geschlechtslehre Wilhelm von Humboldts: Humboldt zwischen Platon und Freud," *Kodikas* 23 (2002): 1–2. Karin Hausen's well-known essay, "Die Polarisierung der Geschlechtscharaktere" argues that a transition from one form of social organziation (household) to another (nuclear family) intensified the need to define and codify gender roles as inherent in human beings. In *Sozialgeschichte der Familie in der Neuzeit Europas*, ed. Werner Conze (Stuttgart: Klett, 1976), 363–93.

15. See Christian Otto's letter of 20 November 1801 to Jean Paul: "Daher ist seine Jungfrau bald eine Heidin, bald eine Christin, bald eine Griechin, bald katholisch abergläubig, bald eine Tochter des 19ten und bald ein Geschöpf des 15ten Jahrhundert" (V:650).

16. See Otto W. Johnston, "Schillers politische Welt," in *Schiller Handbuch*, 62–63.

Chapter 7. Schillerian Intertextuality in the Twentieth Century

1. Böll, *Werke. Interviews 1*, ed. Bernd Balzer, interviewed by Manfred Durzak, 327ff.

2. Heinrich Böll, *"Die verlorene Ehre der Katharina Blum oder: Wie Gewalt entstehen und wohin sie führen kann": Mit Materialien und einem Nachwort des Autors: Zehn Jahre Später* (Cologne: Kiepenheuer und Witsch, 1992), 266. Further references will be cited within the text by page number.

3. In a 1986 essay, "Friedrich Schiller's 'Der Verbrecher aus verlorene Ehre' or the Triumph of the Moral Will," (*Sprachkunst* 18, no. 1: 1–9), Steven Martinson defends the integrity of this representative of the police against Sharpe's questioning of his sincerity in "*Der Verbrecher aus verlorener Ehre*: An Early Exercise in Schillerien Psychology," (*German Life and Letters* 33 [1980]: 102–10). At stake is Wolf's perception of an honest man to whom he can connect as

a principled individual and honestly confess. Sharpe focuses on the narration of the magistrate's mental deliberations that lead to the conclusion that politeness will be more effective than imperiousness and makes the valid point that the magistrate alters his manner for reasons of advantage. I don't go into the deeper motives for either Möding's or the magistrate's behavior, but will optimistically assume their sincerity. The latter figure was modeled on Abel's father, but this information actually allows one to argue in either direction.

4. Gerd Sautermeister follows this personal appeal to the reader or the effort to induce a "there, but for the grace of God, go I" effect by means of close, sequential textual analysis in "Unverjährte Aufklärung," *Die Horen* 30, no. 4 (1985): 273–79.

5. See the "Materialien" section of *Die verlorene Ehre der Katharina Blum* for documents relating to the controversy (193–269).

6. See Beiderwell, x.

7. Anthony Burgess, *A Clockwork Orange* (London: Heinemann, 1962), 39. Further references to this volume will be cited within the text by page numbers.

8. Robert Hughes, in "The Decor of Tomorrow's Hell," (*Time*, 27 December 1971), his review of the film, identifies a critique of "the popular 19th-century idea, still held today, that Art is Good for You, that the purpose of the fine arts is to provide moral uplift"(59).

9. See Vivian C. Sobchak, "Decor as Theme: A Clockwork Orange," *Literature Film Quarterly* 9, no. 2 (1981): 95–96.

10. Schiller had his first two dissertations rejected and this *Probeschrift* was accepted in their place. It was his entry into the field of medicine.

11. Douglas Pearson, Jr. makes the comparison of Alex with the highly cultured and charismatic Dr. Hannibal Lecter of Thomas Harris's novels and the film version of *The Silence of the Lambs*, noting that "Lecter" is an approximation of "Lector" or reader and citing Gregory Aggeler's observation that "Alex" breakes down into "a-lex," suggesting "an absence of law and a lack of words." "Anthony Burgess's *A Clockwork Orange*" in *Censored Books: Critical Viewpoints*, ed. Nicholas J. Karolides, et al. (Metuchen, NJ: The Scarecrow Press, 1993) 185–90; here 186–87.

12. *Schiller's Aesthetic Essays: Two Centuries of Criticism*, 66.

13. Beethoven was aware of the first version and bits of it surface in his work before the Ninth: a line in *Fidelio* echoes the poem and there is a musical treatment of the poem in the *Schillerouvertüre* of 1812. According to Friedhelm Brusniak, Beethoven first became aware of the second version in 1823. "Schiller und die Musik," in *Schiller Handbuch*, 167–89.

14. There is the famous exception of that person who is unable "nur eine Seele / sein [zu] nenn[en] auf dem Erdenrund!" The invocation "Und wer's nicht gekonnt, der stehle / weinend sich aus diesem Bund" is a direct exclusion, but in the very next stanza, Schiller speaks once again of "alle Wesen" and "Alle Guten, alle Bösen" (I:410), reversing the previous exclusionary gesture.

15. In his letter to Körner of 21 October 1800, Schiller called it a "schlechtes Gedicht," modish, and a youthful effort (I:1039).

16. Leonard Bernstein's performance of the Ninth on 25 December 1989 in

the Berliner Schauspielhaus, in which he actually substituted "Freiheit" for "Freude" in order to celebrate the fall of the Berlin wall, is the example most accessible to recent memory. Brusniak, however, shows that this tradition begins in 1838 when Robert Wolfgang Griepenkerl's Novelle "Das Musikfest oder die Beethovener" established the opinion that joy meant freedom in the piece (Brusniak, 180).

Bibliography

Abel, Jacob Friedrich. *Lebensgeschichte Fridrich Schwans.* In *Friedrich Schiller: Der Verbrecher aus verlorener Ehre,* edited by Bernd Mahl. Stuttgart: Klett, 1983.

Adorno, Theodor. *Minima Moralia: Reflexionen aus dem beschädigten Leben.* Frankfurt am Main: Suhrkamp, 1981.

Alt, Peter-Andre. *Schiller: Leben-Werk-Zeit.* Munich: C. H. Beck, 2000.

Auernhammer, Achim. "Engagiertes Erzählen: *Der Verbrecher aus verlorener Ehre.*" In *Schiller und die höfische Welt,* edited by Auernhammer, et al. Tübingen: Max Niemeyer Verlag, 1980, 254–70.

Beccaria, Cesare Bonesana. *On Crimes and Punishments.* Translated by Henry Paolucci. New Jersey: Prentice Hall, 1963.

Behler, Constantin. *Nostalgic Teleology: Friedrich Schiller and the Schemata of Aesthetic Humanism.* Bern: Peter Lang, 1995.

Beiderwell, Bruce. *Power and Punishment in Scott's Novels.* Athens and London: University of Georgia Press, 1992.

Bender, John. *Imagining the Penitentiary: Fiction and the Architecture of the Mind in Eighteenth-Century England.* Chicago: University of Chicago Press, 1987.

Berry, James. *My Experiences as an Executioner.* Edited by H. Snowdon Ward. Detroit: Gale Research Company, 1972.

Böll, Heinrich. *Die verlorene Ehre der Katharina Blum oder: Wie Gewalt entstehen und wohin sie führen kann.* Cologne: Kiepenheuer und Witsch, 1992.

Borchmeyer, Dieter. *Macht und Melancholie: Schillers Wallenstein.* Frankfurt am Main: Athenäum, 1988.

———. *Tragödie und Öffentlichkeit: Schillers Dramaturgie im Zusammenhang seiner ästhetisch-politischen Theorie und die rhetorische Tradition.* Munich: Wilhelm Fink Verlag, 1973.

Brand, Helmut. "Angriff auf den schwächsten Punkt: Friedrich Schlegels Kritik an Schillers *Würde der Frauen.*" *Aurora* 59 (1993), 108–25.

Brosniak, Friedhelm. "Schiller und die Musik." In *Schiller Handbuch,* edited by Helmut Koopmann. Stuttgart: Alfred Kröner Verlag, 1998, 167–89.

Buchwald, Reinhard. *Der junge Schiller.* Leipzig: Insel, 1937.

Burgess, Anthony. *A Clockwork Orange.* London: Heinemann, 1962.

de Man, Paul. *Aesthetic Ideology.* Edited by Andrzej Warminski. Minneapolis: University of Minnesota Press, 1996.

―――. *The Rhetoric of Romanticism*. New York: Columbia University Press, 1984.

Derks, Paul. *Die Schande der heiligen Päderastie: Homosexualität und Öffentlichkeit in der deutschen Literatur 1750–1850*. Berlin: Verlag Rosa Winkel, 1990.

Eagleton, Terry. *The Ideology of the Aesthetic*. Oxford: Blackwell Publishers, 1990.

Ellsworth, Phoebe C., and Samuel R. Gross "Hardening of the Attitudes: Americans' Views on the Death Penalty." In *The Death Penalty in America: Current Controversies*, edited by Hugo Adam Bedau. New York: Oxford University Press, 1997, 90–126.

El Zarka, Dina. "Liebe und Sexualität in der Geschlechtslehre Wilhelm von Humboldts." *Kodikas* 23 (2002): 115–37.

Evans, Richard. *Rituals of Retribution: Capital Punishment in Germany 1600–1987*. New York: Oxford University Press, 1996.

Ford, Franklin. *Political Murder: From Tyrannicide to Terrorism*. Cambridge: Harvard University Press, 1985.

Foucault, Michel. *Discipline and Punish: The Birth of the Prison*. Translated by Alan Sheridan. New York: Vintage, 1979.

Guthke, Karl. *Schillers Dramen: Idealismus und Skepsis*. Bern: Francke, 1994.

Hammer, Stephanie. *Schiller's Wound: The Theater of Trauma from Crisis to Commodity*. Detroit: Wayne State University Press, 2001.

―――. "Schiller, Time and Again." *German Quarterly* (1994): 153–72.

Hart, Gail K. "Re-Dressing History: Mother Nature, Mother Isabeau, the Virgin Mary, and Schiller's *Jungfrau*." *Women in German Yearbook* 14 (1998) 91–108.

Hausen, Karin. "Die Polarisierung der Geschlechtscharaktere." In *Sozialgeschichte der Familie in der Neuzeit Europas*, edited by Werner Conze. Stuttgart: Klett, 1976, 363–93.

Hinderer, Walter. *Von der Idee des Menschen: Über Friedrich Schiller*. Würzburg: Königshausen und Neumann, 1998.

Hölderlin, Friedrich. "Über den Begriff der Strafe." In *Sämtliche Werke und Briefe*, volume 2. Berlin: Aufbau, 1970, 360–64.

Honolka, Kurt. *Schubart: Dichter und Musiker, Journalist und Rebell*. Stuttgart: Deutsche Verlags-Anstalt, 1985.

Hotchkiss, Valerie. *Clothes Make the Man: Female Cross-Dressing in Medieval Europe*. New York: Garland, 1996.

Hughes, Robert. "The Decor of Tomorrow's Hell." *Time*, 27 December 1971, 59.

Janz, Rolf-Peter. "Die ästhetische Bewältigung des Schreckens: Zu Schillers Theorien des Erhabenen." In *Geschichte als Literatur: Formen und Grenzen der Repräsentation von Vergangenheit*, edited by Hartmut Eggert. Stuttgart: Metzler, 1990.

―――. "Die Verschwörung des Fiesko zu Genoa." In *Schillers Dramen: Neue Interpretationen*, edited by Walter Hinderer. Stuttgart: Reclam, 1979.

Johnston, Otto. "Schillers politische Welt." In *Schiller Handbuch*, edited by Helmut Koopmann. Stuttgart: Alfred Kröner Verlag, 1998, 44–69.

Kafka, Franz. *Sämtliche Erzählungen*. Edited by Paul Raabe. Frankfurt am Main: Fischer, 1970.

Kant. *Metaphysische Anfangsgründe der Rechtslehre. Werke*, volume 4. Darmstadt: Wissenschaftliche Buchgesellschaft, 1966.

Kassouf, Susan. *Writing Masculinities Around 1800*. Dissertation, Cornell University, 1996.

Kittler, Friedrich. "Carlos als Carlsschüler." In *Unser Commercium: Goethes und Schillers Literaturpolitik*, edited by Wilfried Barner, et al. Stuttgart: J. G. Cotta'sche Buchhandlung Nachfolger, 1984, 241–73.

Knobloch, Hans-Jörg. "Wilhelm Tell." In *Schiller Handbuch*, edited by Helmut Koopmann. Stuttgart: Alfred Kröner Verlag, 1998, 486–512.

Knox, Sara L. *Murder: A Tale of Modern American Life*. Durham, NC: Duke University Press, 1998.

Lahnstein, Peter. *Schillers Leben*. Munich: List Verlag, 1981.

Laube, Heinrich. *Die Karlsschüler*. In *Dramatische Werke*, volume 6. Leipzig: J. J. Weber, 1847.

Leidner, Alan. " 'Fremde Menschen fielen einander in die Arme': *Die Räuber* and the Communal Response." *Goethe Yearbook* 3, 1986, 57–69.

Martinson, Steven D. "Friedrich Schiller's 'Der Verbrecher aus verlorener Ehre', or the Triumph of the Moral Will." *Sprachkunst* 18, no. 1 (1987) 1–9.

———, *Harmonious Tensions: The Writings of Friedrich Schiller*. Newark: University of Delaware Press, 1996

Mayer, Hans. "The Scandal of Joan of Arc." In *Joan of Arc*, edited by Harold Bloom. New York: Chelsea House, 1992.

Meltzer, Françoise. *For Fear of the Fire: Joan of Arc and the Limits of Subjectivity*. Chicago: University of Chicago Press, 2001.

Meyers, Michael. *Für den Bürger: The Role of Christian Schubart's **Deutsche Chronik** in the Development of a Political Public Sphere*. New York: Peter Lang, 1990.

Middendorf, Wolf. *Der Prozeß gegen Maria Stuart*. Cologne and Hamburg: Verlag Dr. Otto Schmidt, 1972.

Mielke, Andreas. " 'Maria Stuart': Hermeneutical Problems of 'One" Tragedy with 'Two' Queens." In *Friedrich Schiller and the Drama of Human Existence*, edited by Alexej Ugrinsky. Westport, CT: Greenwood Press, 1988.

Moore, W. G. "A New Reading of 'Wilhelm Tell.' " *German Studies: Presented to Professor H. G. Fiedler*. Oxford: Clarendon, 1938, 278–92.

Nutz, Thomas. "Vergeltung oder Versöhnung? Strafvollzug und Ehre in Schillers *Verbrecher aus Infamie*." *Jahrbuch der deutschen Schillergesellschaft* 42 (1998), 146–64.

Pearson, Douglas. "Anthony Burgess's *A Clockwork Orange*." In *Censored Books: Critical Viewpoints*, edited by Nicholas J. Karolides, et al. Metuchen, NJ: The Scarecrow Press, 1993, 185–90.

Die peinliche Gerichtsordnung Kaiser Karls V. von 1532. Edited by Gustav Radbruch. Stuttgart: Reclam, 2000.

Quicherat, Julea. *Proces de condamnation et le rehabilitation de Jeanne d'Arc dite La Pucell.* Paris: Renouard, 1841–1849.

Rainer, Ulrike. *Schillers Prosa: Poetologie und Praxis.* Berlin: Erich Schmidt Verlag, 1988.

Roof, Judith. *Reproductions of Reproduction: Imaging Symbolic Change.* New York: Routledge, 1996.

Ruppelt, Georg. *Schiller im nationalsozialistischen Deutschland.* Stuttgart: Metzler, 1979.

Ryder, Frank. "Schiller's *Tell* and the Cause of Freedom." *German Quarterly* 48, no. 4 (1975): 487–504.

Sammons, Jeffrey. "The Apple-Shot and the Politics of Wilhelm Tell." In *Friedrich Schiller and the Drama of Human Existence*, edited by Alexej Ugrinsky. Westport, CT: Greenwood Press, 1988.

Sander, Josef. *Die Begründung der Notwehr in der Philosophie von Kant und Hegel.* Bleicherode am Harz: Verlag Carl Nieft, 1939.

Saranpa, Kathy. " *Schiller's Wallenstein," "Maria Stuart," and "Die Jungfrau von Orleans" The Critical Legacy.* Rochester, NY: Camden House, 2002.

Sautermeister, Gerd. "*Maria Stuart*: Ästhetik, Seelenkunde, historisch-gesellschaftlicher Ort." In *Schillers Dramen: Neue Interpretationen*, edited by Walter Hinderer. Stuttgart: Reclam, 1979, 174–216.

Scarry, Elaine. *The Body in Pain: The Making and Unmaking of the World.* New York: Oxford University Press, 1985.

Schiller, Friedrich. *Werke und Briefe in zwölf Bänden.* Edited by Otto Dann, et al. Frankfurt am Main: Deutscher Klassiker Verlag, 1988–.

———. *On the Aesthetic Education of Man.* Translated and edited by Elizabeth Wilkinson and L. A. Willoughby. Oxford: Clarendon Press, 1967.

Schlegel, Friedrich. *Kritische Friedrich Schlegel Ausgabe.* Edited by Ernst Behler. Volume 2. Paderborn, 1967.

Schweitzer, Christoph. "A Defense of Schiller's Wilhelm Tell." *Goethe Yearbook* 9. Columbia, South Carolina: Camden House, 1999, 253–63.

Sharpe, Lesley. *Schiller's Aesthetics: Two Centuries of Criticism.* Columbia, SC: Camden House, 1995.

———. "*Der Verbrecher aus verlorener Ehre*: An Early Exercise in Schillerian Psychology." *German Life and Letters* 33 (1980), 102–10.

Sobchak, Vivian. "Decor as Theme: A Clockwork Orange." *Literature Film Quarterly* 9.2 (1981), 92–102.

Thackeray, William Makepeace. *The Works of William Makepeace Thackeray.* 13 vols. Edited by Anne Thackeray Ritchie. New York and London: Harper & Brothers Publishers, 1898.

Uhland, Robert. *Geschichte der Hohen Karlsschule in Stuttgart.* Stuttgart: Kohlhammer, 1953.

van Dülmen, Richard. *Theater des Schreckens: Gerichtspraxis und Strafrituale in der frühen Neuzeit.* Munich: Beck, 1988.

von Heiseler, Bernt. *Schiller*. Gütersloh: Bertelsmann, 1959

von Mücke, Dorothea. *Virtue and the Veil of Illusion: Generic Innovation and the Pedagogical Project in Eighteenth-Century Literature*. Stanford: Stanford University Press, 1991.

Wilson, W. Daniel. *Das Goethe Tabu: Protest und Menschenrechte im klassischen Weimar*. Munich: Deutscher Taschenbuch Verlag, 1999.

Wyngfield, Robert. "An Account of the Execution of Mary Queen of Scots." In *The Clarendon Historical Societies Reports*. Edinburgh, 1884–1886.

Zelle, Carsten. *Angenehmes Grauen: Literaturhistorische Beiträge zur Ästhetik des Schrecklichen im achtzehnten Jahrhundert*. Hamburg: Felix Meiner Verlag, 1987.

Index

Abel, Jacob Friedrich, 110, 112, 141, 171 n. 16, 171–72 n. 19
Adorno, Theodor, 29,
Aggeler, Gregory, 174 n. 11
Alt, Peter-Andre, 169 n. 8
Auernhammer, Achim, 171 n. 17

Beccaria, Cesare Bonesana, 15, 38, 171 n. 18
Bedau, Hugo Adam, 165 n. 5
Beethoven, Ludwig van, 125, 147–49, 155–56, 159, 174 n. 13
Behler, Constantine, 30–32
Bender, John, 72–73, 165 n. 3
Bentham, Jeremy, 19, 38, 72–73,
Bernstein, Leonard, 174–75 n. 16
Böll, Heinrich: *Die verlorene Ehre der Katharina Blum*, 22, 110, 135–40, 142–44
Borchmeyer, Dieter, 167 n. 14
Brusniak, Friedhelm, 174 n. 13
Burgess, Anthony: *A Clockwork Orange*, 22, 32, 135, 144–59, 163

Charles VII, 120

Damiens, Robert François, 36–37, 42
de Man, Paul, 27–30, 32, 48, 158, 166 n. 6
Derks, Paul, 82–83

Eagleton, Terry, 30
El Zarka, Dina, 173 n. 14
Evans, Richard, 12, 165 n. 4

Foucault, Michel, 16–18, 29, 32, 36–37, 42, 72, 76, 92, 141, 144, 165 n. 11
Frederick II, 17–18

Goebbels, Josef, 32, 163
Goethe, Johann Wolfgang von, 11, 27, 118, 122, 125, 169 n. 9, 172–73 n. 9
Guthke, Karl, 167 n. 11, 169 n. 10

Hammer, Stephanie, 7, 107, 135, 167 n. 10, 169 nn. 3–4, 172 n. 20
Hausen, Karin, 173 n. 14
Hinderer, Walter, 169 n. 3
Hölderlin, Johann Christian Friedrich, 17, 21, 38, 61, 67, 123, 165 n. 12
Hohenasperg (prison), 21, 79, 80, 86, 90
Honolka, Kurt, 81, 91, 170 n. 3
Horen, Die, 30, 129
Hotchkiss, Valerie, 120, 172 n. 2
Hughes, Robert, 174 n. 8

Iffland, August Wilhelm, 98

Joan of Arc, 16, 73, 119–24, 133–34, 161–62
Jones, Michael T., 166 n. 6

Kafka, Franz, 43, 67, 84
Kant, Immanuel, 13–15, 22, 27–28, 32, 45, 48, 74, 106, 152, 158, 163, 165 n. 7, 166 n. 2
Karl Eugen, 18–21, 25, 59, 78–81, 92, 93
Karlsschule, 17–21, 33, 36, 39, 78, 81
Kassouf, Susan, 166 n. 14
Kittler, Friedrich, 166 n. 14
Kluge, Gerhard, 59
Knobloch, Hans-Jörg, 170 n. 5
Knox, Sara L., 110–11, 139, 171 n. 15
Körner, Christian Gottfried, 74, 122, 125, 129, 174 n. 15

Kubrick, Stanley: *A Clockwork Orange*, 22, 135, 145–59, 163
Kurpfälzische Deutsche Gesellschaft, 24, 32

Lahnstein, Peter, 166 n. 16
Laube, Heinrich: *Die Karlsschüler*, 166 n. 17
Leidner, Alan, 64
Lessing, Gotthold Ephraim: *Erziehung des Menschengeschlechts*, 147; *Hamburgische Dramaturgie*, 166 n. 1; 167 n. 9

MacDowell, Malcolm, 155, 157
Mann, Thomas, 169 n. 9
Martinson, Steven, 173 n. 3
Mayer, Hans, 173 n. 11
Meltzer, Françoise, 121, 172 n. 6
Meyers, Michael, 80
Middendorf, Wolf, 168 n. 19
Mielke, Andreas, 168 n. 21
Moore, W. G., 96–97,

Nicolai, Friedrich, 18
Nietzsche, Friedrich, 61
Nutz, Thomas, 117–18

Otto, Christian, 173 n. 15

Pearson, Douglas, 174 n. 11

Rainer, Ulrike, 170 n. 6
Reichardt, Johann Friedrich, 127, 129
Rheinische Thalia, 24, 56, 159, 169 n. 10
Riefenstahl, Leni, 156
Rieger, Phillip Friedrich, 80–86, 88, 90–92, 155, 161
Roof, Judith, 170 n. 12
Rousseau, Jean-Jacques, 58
Ruppelt, Georg, 171 n. 10
Ryder, Frank, 96–97

Sammons, Jeffrey, 97–98, 158
Saranpa, Kathy, 167 n. 8
Sautermeister, Gerd, 167 n. 14, 174 n. 4
Scarry, Elaine, 99, 103–4

Schiller, Friedrich: *An die Freude*, 146, 148, 150–51, 157–61; *Die berühmte Frau*, 119, 126; *Don Carlos*, 76, 88–89, 92; *Fiesko* 22, 29, 54–59, 63, 67–68, 120, 134, 161; *Gedanken über den Gebrauch des Gemeinen und Niedrigen in der Kunst*, 64–65, 70; *Die Geschlechter*, 126; *Des Grafen Lamoral von Egmont Leben und Tod*, 56–57; *Die Jungfrau von Orleans*, 16, 22, 73, 76; *Kabale und Liebe*, 68–69; *Kallias*, 74–75, 90, 149, 152; *Das Lied von der Glocke*, 126–27, 129, 132; *Maria Stuart*, 38, 40–53, 55–57, 76, 80, 120, 123, 161; *Die Räuber*, 14, 16, 20, 22, 29, 35–37, 39, 53, 59–71, 73, 81, 86–87, 89, 92, 98, 109, 117, 120, 134, 161; *Spiel des Schicksals*, 22, 72, 81–92, 161; *Über Anmut und Würde*, 75; *Über das Erhabene*, 48; *Über das gegenwärtige Teutsche Theater*, 25–27; *Über die ästhetische Erziehung des Menschen in einer Reihe von Briefen*, 25; *Über das Pathetische*, 48, 64; *Über Matthisons Gedichte*, 31; *Verbrecher aus verlorener Ehre*, 15, 22, 69, 87–88, 108–18, 120, 134–39, 141–44, 161; *Was kann eine gute stehende Schaubühne eigentlich wirken?*, 21–23, 24–40, 140, 142, 144–46, 153–54, 158, 161–2; *Wilhelm Tell*, 16–17, 22, 73, 93–108, 111, 117, 120, 142, 157, 161; *Würde der Frauen*, 126–29, 132
Schiller, Johann Kaspar, 20
Schlegel, August Wilhelm, 129
Schlegel, Friedrich, 129
Schmerberg, Ralf, 125, 129
Schubart, Christian Friedrich Daniel, 21, 72, 79–86, 90–93, 155
Schwan, Fridrich, 110, 112, 141, 171 n. 16, 171–72 n. 19
Schweitzer, Christoph, 97
Sharpe, Lesley, 7, 158, 173–74 n. 3

Thackeray, William M., 168–69 n. 1

van Duelmen, Richard, 44
Voltaire, 15, 134
von Goeckingk, Leopold, 170 n. 3
von Humboldt, Wilhelm, 125, 129
von Heiseler, Bernd, 166 n. 13
von Mücke, Dorothea, 51, 168 n. 20, 170 n. 2

Wilkinson, Elizabeth, 32, 167 n. 8
Willoughby, L. A., 32, 167 n. 8
Wilson, W. Daniel, 165 n. 2

Zelle, Carsten, 13, 165 n. 6, 167 nn. 9 and 13